A Counsel[...] to the
Dissertation
Process

Where to Start & How to Finish

Brandé Flamez, A. Stephen Lenz, Richard S. Balkin, & Robert L. Smith

AMERICAN COUNSELING
ASSOCIATION
6101 Stevenson Avenue, Suite 600 | Alexandria, VA 22304
www.counseling.org

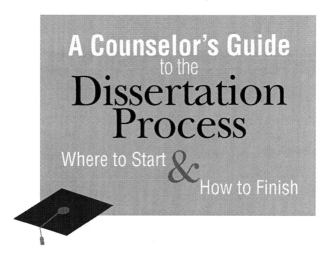

A Counselor's Guide
to the
Dissertation Process
Where to Start & How to Finish

American Counseling Association
6101 Stevenson Avenue, Suite 600 | Alexandria, VA 22304

Associate Publisher | Carolyn C. Baker

Digital and Print Development Editor | Nancy Driver

Senior Production Manager | Bonny E. Gaston

Production Coordinator | Karen Thompson

Copy Editor | Lindsey N. Phillips

Cover and text design by Bonny E. Gaston

Library of Congress Cataloging-in-Publication Data

Names: Flamez, Brandé, author. | Lenz, A. Stephen, author. | Balkin, Richard S., author.
Title: A counselor's guide to the dissertation process : where to start and how to finish / Brandé Flamez, Lamar University, A. Stephen Lenz, Texas A&M University Corpus Christi, Richard S. Balkin, University of Louisville, Robert L. Smith, Texas A&M University Corpus Christ.
Description: Alexandria, VA : American Counseling Association, [2017] | Includes bibliographical references and index.
Identifiers: LCCN 2017003945 | ISBN 9781556203596 (pbk. : alk. paper)
Subjects: LCSH: Counseling psychology. | Dissertations, Academic–Authorship. | Research–Methodology.
Classification: LCC BF636 .F553 2017 | DDC 158.3071/1—dc23 LC record available at https://lccn.loc.gov/2017003945

To my children, Evelyn and Braeden.
Your laughs, snuggles, and our evening dance parties
are some of the best things in life!
Always remember I love you more than
all the sand on the beach and the stars in the sky.

—Brandé

To Rachel and Hayes.

—Stephen

To Unk and Aunt Marilyn.

—Rick

To all of the professors who are mentoring doctoral students
during the journey of completing a dissertation.
And to the many doctoral students who have completed,
or are now completing this exciting journey!

—Robert

Table of Contents

Table of Contents

Preface

The journey to becoming a doctor of philosopy (PhD) is life changing. Although students spend countless hours working through the course work and acquiring knowledge along the way, up to 50% of doctoral students nationwide do not complete their dissertations and become "all but dissertation" (ABD). We have heard countless stories from colleagues who felt that they had not received proper support or guidance when it came time to write the dissertation. We have also found that many of our students often say, "I don't know where to start," "I am not sure I can do this," or "I just can't seem to sit down and write." Our motivation to write *A Counselor's Guide to the Dissertation Process: Where to Start and How to Finish* stems from our personal passion to help students plan, write, and defend a dissertation. Our aim is to provide step-by-step guidance, make the journey to becoming a PhD smoother, and create an experience that is both rewarding and exciting.

When we formulated our vision for this book, we decided we wanted it to be a resource that spoke to our readers. Although there are several useful and comprehensive books that help guide doctoral students, we found that many books did not account for the holistic wellness of students during the writing process; report practices that are consistent with American Psychological Association (APA) standards for conceptual, qualitative, or quantitative works; and include strategies for preparing the completed dissertation for subsequent submission to peer-reviewed journals. Our text includes these components through a lens that is specifically for counselors, counselor educators, and related professionals. Our style of writing is personal and conversational with its straight talk, and we offer practical advice much like a coach talking to someone one-on-one. To enhance learning, we have provided quotations from previous students, a realm of examples specific to the counseling profession, chapter exercises, and a checklist at the end of each chapter, along with additional resources. Our main hope is that this book will help students complete their dissertations.

Graduate faculty working with student research may also find the content beneficial. Regardless of the topic or discipline, the steps for writing a dissertation are much the same. We aim to address the questions that students routinely ask. Our checklist will help students stay on track and not rush to the next dissertation chapter without including major components.

Chapters 1–3 of the book are dedicated to introducing readers to the doctoral program, providing tips for staying well throughout the dissertation process, selecting committee members, and narrowing down the dissertation topic. In Chapters 4–9 of the book, our focus shifts, and we take the reader through all the major components for the dissertation. In addition, these chapters include tables and activities for writing problem statements and research questions, collecting and analyzing data, and presenting results that align with APA guidelines. The book comes to an end by preparing students for their dissertation defense and discussing how they can disseminate their findings and remain active in the profession.

Acknowledgments

Writing a book is a remarkable journey. This book is a true collaborative effort, and it could not have been accomplished without the support, encouragement, and assistance of many individuals.

Thank you to our families who loved and encouraged us during this process. We appreciate you graciously supporting us during our intense writing sessions. We are thankful for our friends and children for the humor and love they provided throughout this process.

We would like to thank those at the American Counseling Association who helped turn our vision into reality, especially Carolyn Baker, the associate publisher of the American Counseling Association. Your patience, guidance, encouragement, and support are invaluable, and this book would not have been possible without your involvement.

A special thank you to all our students who have been our greatest teachers. The contributions to this text reflect the practices and processes developed in collaboration with you, and they would never have been possible had we not met you. We are deeply grateful for your experiences and allowing us to share in your journey toward completing your dissertations.

Finally, we would like to acknowledge all the students who aspire to finish their dissertations. Your decision to pursue a graduate degree in counseling, counselor education, or some related profession is a gift to the many people who will benefit from your commitment, energy, and professional activities. There will be times when this journey seems impossible, but you can do this. The best way to finish your dissertation is to begin. This is your year; let's get started!

About the Authors

Brandé Flamez, PhD, LPC, NCC, is a licensed professional counselor and clinical professor in the Department of Counseling and Special Populations at Lamar University. Dr. Flamez is also the CEO and founder of the nonprofit SALTworld (Serving and Learning Together), which provides donations and volunteer services to developing countries. Her clinical background includes working with children, adolescents, and families in community-based and private counseling settings. In addition, she helped design an outpatient program for court-referred adolescents. Dr. Flamez is active in the counseling profession. She has served on the American Counseling Association (ACA) Governing Council for the International Association of Marriage and Family Counselors (IAMFC), ACA Finance Committee, and ACA Investment Committee, and she has chaired the ACA Publications Committee. She is also the past president of the Association for Humanistic Counselors (AHC) and currently serves as the president of IAMFC, cochairs the AHC Bylaws/Ethics Committee, and is the secretary for AHC.

Dr. Flamez is on the editorial board for *The Family Journal*. She has presented nationally and internationally and coauthored several book chapters and articles. Dr. Flamez is the coauthor of the assessment textbook *Counseling Assessment and Evaluation: Fundamentals of Applied Practice* and the coeditor for *Diagnosing Children and Adolescents: A Guide for Mental Health Practitioners* and the forthcoming book *Practical Approaches to Clinical Supervision Across Settings*. She is the recipient of numerous national awards, including ACA's 2012 Gilbert and Kathleen Wrenn Award for a Caring and Humanitarian Person, IAMFC's 2012 Distinguished Mentor Award, ACA's 2014 Kitty Cole Human Rights Award, ACA's 2015 Counselor Educator Advocacy Award, and ACA's 2017 Dr. Judy Lewis Counselors for Social Justice Award.

A. Stephen Lenz, PhD, LPC, is an associate professor and clinical mental health counseling program coordinator at Texas A&M University–Corpus Christi. His counseling background has been working with children, adolescents, and families in community-based, university, and private counseling settings. His research interests include community-based program evaluation, counseling outcome research, single-case research, instrument development, and holistic approaches to counseling, counselor education, and supervision.

Dr. Lenz is the past president of the Association for Assessment and Research in Counseling (AARC). He is also an associate editor for research with the *Journal of College Counseling*, and he served as the editor for the special issue Single-Case Research Design for the *Journal of Counseling & Development*. He currently serves as an editorial board member for *Counseling Outcome Research and Evaluation* and is a past editorial board member for the *Journal of Professional Counseling* and *Journal for Creativity in Mental Health*. Dr. Lenz has authored several peer-review publications and has served on dissertation committees for a number of counseling and counselor education students. He is a recipient of the AARC's 2013 Exemplary Practices Award and ACA's 2014 Best Practice Award for his program evaluation activities within community-based counseling settings.

Richard S. Balkin, PhD, LPC, is a professor and doctoral program coordinator in the Department of Counseling and Human Development at the University of Louisville and a fellow of the ACA. He is the editor for the *Journal of Counseling & Development*, ACA's flagship journal, and past president for the AARC. His primary research interests include counseling outcomes, research methods, counseling adolescents, and cultural differences in counseling. He is a past recipient of the Association for Counselor Education and Supervision's 2011 Counseling Vision and Innovation Award and ACA's 2012 Best Practices Research Award.

Dr. Balkin has published more than 70 peer-reviewed articles, books, and book chapters, with the majority being quantitative in nature. He is the author of *The Theory and Practice of Assessment in Counseling, Counseling Research: A Practitioner-Scholar Approach,* and *Relationships in Counseling and the Counselor's Life,* and has authored book chapters and articles on research methods.

Robert L. Smith, PhD, NCC, CFT, FPPR, is coordinator of the doctoral program in counselor education and supervision at Texas A&M University–Corpus Christi. He has chaired close to 100 doctoral dissertations at three universities. He is also the chair of the Department of Counseling and Educational Psychology at Texas A&M University–Corpus Christi. His scholarly record includes more than 100 refereed publications and eight textbooks.

Dr. Smith is an international leader who served as the 63rd president of ACA and past president of IAMFC and the National Career Development Association. He currently serves as executive director of IAMFC. For several years, he taught courses and supervised research in Venezuela and has presented internationally in Nicaragua, England, Ireland, Canada, Malesia, and Singapore. His research emphasis includes theory and practice of addictions counseling, achievement motivation measurement and training, predicting achievement, and an increasing interest in STEM studies. He lives on North Padre Island with his wife Susan and their rescues consisting of two dogs and four cats. They enjoy kayaking, jogging, and walking their four-legged family members.

Chapter 1

The Doctoral Dissertation

Pursuing an advanced degree is a major life decision. You are embarking on a journey full of learning and growth. Now it is time for you to demonstrate your plan to write and defend an original research study by completing a dissertation. You may be asking yourself, "Why did I sign up for this?" "What have I gotten myself into?" and "Am I smart enough?" (And the answer is yes!) I bet if we went back and looked at how you got here, your friends and family would say you embody the following characteristics: commitment, perseverance, courage, stamina, and a positive attitude.

We begin this chapter by discussing what makes a dissertation so difficult. We discuss how a doctor of philosophy (PhD) in counselor education and supervision (CES) is unique because it provides you with the opportunity to effect positive social change. The remaining part of chapter focuses on getting comfortable with the dissertation process. We break down the major components of a dissertation into 11 steps and provide you with the overall structure of the dissertation. We also discuss the roles and responsibilities to which both you and your committee will be expected to adhere. At the end of the chapter, we invite you to complete exercises, explore previous graduate accomplishments, and formulate dissertation guidelines to help you successfully complete this journey. Every chapter of the book ends with a checklist. We hope that you will work through each checklist so you are prepared to tackle subsequent chapters of this journey.

What Makes a Dissertation So Difficult?

You have probably heard stories by students just like you who have completed a PhD. Included within these stories are comments about the rigor of the process, demands to meet deadlines, and committee member personalities clashing. By design, a doctoral dissertation is challenging. Let's face it. You are trying to obtain the highest degree offered by a university and you may not have a reference point. After all, you have never been down this road before.

Intellectual and Emotional Challenges

Completing a dissertation not only tests your intellectual ability but also brings out emotional and behavioral issues. We call the first challenge the *intellectual challenge*. Students often ask, "Am I smart enough to complete the dissertation?" Well, the answer is "YES!" You have already proven your intellectual ability by arriving at this point. It is important to keep in mind that completing a dissertation is not a measure of intelligence but perhaps is more about endurance. At some point, you may find that parts of the dissertation process are particularly challenging. You may have to devote more time, ask for help, do additional reading, and learn more about a complex methodology to accomplish your goal. During these times, realize that this is a process and you have the internal and external resources to succeed. We invite you to see times when you may be challenged, questioned, or critiqued as opportunities for growth of knowledge and skills, rather than a sign of inadequacy.

In addition to the intellectual challenge, there are also personal challenges that you may face. The most common emotion we see among doctoral students is anxiety. Many students see the dissertation as a gigantic project and struggle to see how to break down the dissertation into smaller and more manageable parts. If you have unclear goals, it is easy to feel overwhelmed and struggle to figure out where to start. We often see anxiety manifested through procrastination and writer's block.

Writer's Block

Over the years, we have found that students experience writer's block, which is simply the inability to write despite one's desire and ability to do so. If you find that designated writing times are now filled with other activities (e.g., checking Facebook, cleaning, watching television) and you are not making deadlines, chances are you might be experiencing writer's block. We have found that students experience writer's block because of anxiety, fear, interpersonal problems, and institutional issues.

Students often ask us, "Should I write 15 minutes a day? In blocks of time?" The answer is do what works for you. Think about the places and times you are most productive in your writing and then establish a routine. What type of work space do you prefer? What is your writing time like? (What time of day? How long?) What methods do you use to begin your writing? Once you have reflected on what works for you and have established a routine, write regularly. Remember your writing does not have to be polished at this point. Just write and protect your writing time. Schedule your writing time in your planner just as you would a doctor's appointment or other important meetings. We also encourage you to meet with your dissertation chair and create a schedule of deadlines. Most important, remain positive and be your own best support system. We discuss this topic further in the upcoming chapters.

How is a PhD in CES Unique From Other PhD Degrees?

CES doctoral programs prepare you to work as a counselor educator, researcher, supervisor, and an advanced practitioner and clinician in academic and private practice settings. This doctoral program is designed to teach you how to evaluate theory and the practice of counseling through research and prepare you to be a leader and advocate for social change in the counseling profession. Most CES doctoral programs emphasize the five core areas of counseling, supervision, teaching, research and scholarship, and leadership and advocacy. In each of these core areas, you will gain fundamental knowledge that is required for you to graduate with a CES doctoral degree.

CES doctoral programs place a special emphasis on leadership and advocacy by focusing on social change theory and advocacy action planning, which is unique. Throughout the program, you can build your skills not only as a scholar-practitioner but also as a professional advocate who is capable of assuming leadership positions. The 2016 Council for Accreditation of Counseling and Related Educational Programs (CACREP) Standards (CACREP, 2015) highlight 12 competencies for leadership and advocacy under the heading of professional identity. Thus, many programs require that dissertations have implications for positive social change at the individual, community, or societal level. Some CACREP-accredited CES programs include social change as one of the key indicators in the proposal rubric. Students must satisfy the question, "Does your project have the potential to effect positive social change?" In Chapter 11, we discuss how you can positively influence social change by submitting your dissertation research findings to multiple outlets that are well suited to advocate for changes in social policy or practice.

Eleven Major Steps of the Dissertation Process

In the following sections, we provide brief descriptions of the steps to follow to complete a dissertation. These steps can vary from university to university, so you will want to check with your dissertation chair and be familiar with the dissertation procedures set forth by the university. Chapters 3–11 highlight each step in greater detail.

Step 1: Select a Topic

Many students have shared that deciding on a topic was one of their biggest challenges. The process of selecting a topic will depend on your professional experiences; the research background of your dissertation chair and members; and your knowledge of the literature, including gaps in the literature.

It is important that you consider if the topic is doable in the amount of time and with the budget you have available. Also, consider the following questions: "Does this topic have the potential to make an original and significant contribution to the current body of knowledge?" and "Can a study of this topic effect positive social change?" In Chapter 3, we discuss in detail how to narrow down your topic.

Step 2: Develop a Prospectus

A prospectus is a brief document that provides your potential dissertation chair and members with preliminary information about your dissertation. Essentially, it is a plan for developing your dissertation proposal. A prospectus might include title page, problem statement, purpose statement, significance of the study, background information, theoretical framework that will guide the study, research questions, nature of the study (e.g., quantitative, qualitative, mixed methods), sources of data, and references. Some universities may require you to submit the prospectus to faculty members before dissertation committee selection.

Step 3: Select a Dissertation Chair and Choose Your Committee Members

The selection of your committee is a process that involves assessing what you need and what you are looking for and then meeting with faculty members to learn their interests and expertise. Once you have selected your dissertation chair, you will select committee members. This is usually a joint decision between you and your chair. Also, some universities will appoint members to your committee. In Chapter 3, we walk you through the steps of selecting your dissertation chair and committee members.

Step 4: Complete and Defend the Dissertation Proposal

Now that you have a committee in place, you will continue working on your dissertation proposal. The dissertation proposal will closely resemble the first chapter, or possibly the first three chapters, of your dissertation. You will submit several drafts in response to the feedback received from your committee. After you have incorporated all suggestions from your committee members and your chair and they agree that your proposal is satisfactory, you schedule a formal dissertation proposal meeting. During this meeting, you defend your proposal. It is important during this stage to find out if your dissertation chair would like you to write in future or past tense. Some universities require you to write in future tense and then go back and edit the chapters to past tense after the study is completed.

Step 5: Obtain Institutional Review Board Approval

Your university's institutional review board (IRB) will determine if the benefits of your study outweigh the risks associated with your participants. Typically, you submit your IRB application after you have successfully defended your dissertation proposal. However, we encourage you to begin working on the IRB application while the faculty is reviewing the dissertation proposal. You will draft the IRB application and submit it to your chair before you submit it to the university's IRB.

Step 6: Conduct Your Study

After receiving IRB approval, you will conduct your study. In this phase, you will collect and analyze your data and report findings.

Step 7: Write the Remaining Chapters of the Dissertation

At this point, you most likely have completed the first three chapters, particularly if they were a requirement for your dissertation proposal. Now you must write the remaining two chapters. If you know writing is not a strong point, it is important for you to access university resources. Many universities have a writing center. You may also want to consider hiring an outside editor to review your dissertation. It is important to remember that your chair's role is not to serve as your editor.

Step 8: Schedule an Oral Defense

After you have revised several drafts of your dissertation, your dissertation chair will let you know when you are ready to defend. During the oral defense, you will present your full dissertation. In Chapter 10, we discuss in detail what an oral defense is and how you can prepare before, during, and after.

Step 9: Complete Final Steps Before Graduation

After you successfully defend your dissertation, you will need to complete all the necessary paperwork to prepare for graduation. Chapter 10 provides a more detailed discussion of the additional paperwork requirements.

Step 10: Graduate and Celebrate!

This is the step you have been waiting for. Now you can celebrate your accomplishments. In Chapter 10, we also discuss the importance of taking care of yourself after this long journey.

Step 11: Disseminate the Findings and Effect Positive Social Change

Now it's time to share your knowledge and research findings to effect social change. Chapter 11 provides various outlets of where you can disseminate your dissertation findings.

Structure and Components of a Dissertation

The structure of a dissertation can vary among academic programs. However, most counseling programs have similar formats with slight variations often based on the design of the study. Figure 1.1 illustrates the overall structure of a dissertation.

The components of a dissertation include the following:

1. Title Page
2. Committee Approval Page
3. Copyright
4. Abstract
5. Dedication (optional)
6. Acknowledgments (optional)
7. Table of Contents
8. List of Tables and Figures
9. Chapter 1: Introduction
10. Chapter 2: Literature Review
11. Chapter 3: Method
12. Chapter 4: Results
13. Chapter 5: Discussion
14. Reference List
15. Appendixes
16. Curriculum Vitae

We discuss each major component in more detail in the following paragraphs.

Title Page

The title page includes the dissertation title; author; previous degrees, including the university and year in which they were received; the degree

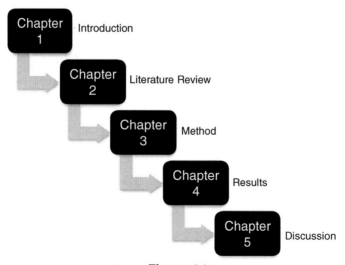

Figure 1.1
Dissertation Structure

requirements that the dissertation fulfills; and the graduation date (see Figure 1.2). The title should include key terms from your study and not exceed 15–20 words.

Committee Approval Page

The committee approval page includes the defense date and the original signatures from your committee members and the dean. This page indicates that you have met the university's standards for graduation and your dissertation has been approved.

Copyright

The copyright appears on the page immediately following the title page. The copyright page should include your name and copyright date and is centered (left to right and top to bottom) in the middle of the page. The following is an example:

Copyright © 2016 by Evelyn McDevitt

Even though you technically own the copyright to your dissertation under copyright law, you can obtain greater protection by submitting a formal registration. Many CES programs require you to submit your doctoral study to ProQuest (see Chapter 10). ProQuest offers the option of applying for copyright. We encourage you to file the application for copyright because this will help protect your work and will document the completion of your dissertation.

Abstract

The abstract is a concise summary of your dissertation and can include the research problem, significance, research questions, research design, results,

A Comparison of Online and
Traditional Graduate Counseling Courses:
Learning Styles, Instructional Preferences,
and Educational Environment

by
Brandé Nicóle Flamez
MA, University of Texas at San Antonio, 2007
BA, University of Notre Dame, 2003

Dissertation Submitted in
Partial Fulfillment of the Requirements for
the Degree of Doctor of Philosophy
Texas A&M University–Corpus Christi

April 2, 2010

Figure 1.2
Example Title Page

recommendation for future research, and a statement on the implications of positive social change. In general, citations should be avoided in the abstract and the length should not exceed a page. Please check with the university and department for the specific requirements of what to include in the abstract.

Dedication (Optional)

The dedication section is usually optional. There are several types of dedications, and how this is written will depend on you and the persons to whom you are dedicating the work.

Acknowledgments (Optional)

The acknowledgments page, which is also optional, gives credit to all the individuals and groups who assisted you in this journey. Typically, this includes your committee members, other faculty, colleagues, family, and friends (see Chapter 10).

Table of Contents

Your table of contents is an outline of your dissertation and should be comprehensive in nature. The table of contents includes a title page, committee signature page, copyright, abstract, dedication (optional), acknowledgments (optional), list of tables and figures, Chapters 1–5 (the introduction, literature review, method, results, and discussion), references, and appendixes. You will want to include all headings and subheadings exactly as they appear in the text. Make sure to follow the *Publication Manual of the American Psychological Association* (6th ed.; American Psychological Association [APA], 2010) guidelines for your chapter headings. For more information, see page 62 in the APA *Publication Manual* (APA, 2010). Figure 1.3 provides an example of how you would organize your table of contents based on the heading levels.

List of Tables and Figures

You will be required to make a separate list of all the tables and figures you use throughout your dissertation. The list should include the number and

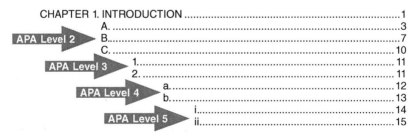

Figure 1.3
Example Table of Contents Based on the Heading Levels

full name of the table or figure that appears in the text. It is important to note that APA does not use the words *chart, illustration,* or *graph.* For more information on how to format tables and figures, see Chapter 5 in the APA *Publication Manual* (APA, 2010).

Chapter 1: Introduction

The introduction describes the topic of study and why this topic needs to be addressed. The introduction should draw the attention of the reader and, in many cases, describe the social implications of the study. This chapter should include background information summarizing the literature related to the scope of the study and identify the gap within the published research. You will also want to include why the study is needed (i.e., its relevance and potential implications). Background information is followed by a problem statement, purpose statement, significance of the study, research questions, theoretical perspective, methodology, basic definition of terms, assumptions, delimitations, limitations, and a summary. In the summary, you will also preview the next chapter for the reader. In Chapter 4 of *A Counselor's Guide to the Dissertation Process,* we review each of these components.

Chapter 2: Literature Review

The literature review is an exhaustive, up-to-date summation of research that you have read and reviewed to understand the problem under investigation. This section can include 30–50 references, mostly from peer-reviewed journals. It is hard to estimate the length of this chapter because it may vary depending on the specific topic being investigated and the design of the study, but Chapter 2 typically ranges from 25 to 60 pages. The literature review includes a discussion of the study's theoretical and conceptual framework and key variables and concepts, and it might include a historical overview of the problem and current trends. You will describe how other researchers have approached this problem and justify your rationale for the selection of variables. You will review the strengths and weaknesses of the previous studies, provide a critique of any controversial methodological analytics, and describe what needs to be studied. Because you are presenting information drawn from other researchers, you will use citations extensively in this chapter. It is important to note that you will want to avoid the overuse of direct quotations. In Chapter 5 of this book, we discuss the literature review in detail.

Chapter 3: Method

Chapter 3 presents a detailed discussion of specific steps that were involved to conduct the study, including data collection. This section will vary depending on the design (i.e., whether it is a quantitative, qualitative, or mixed-methods study). This chapter includes an introduction, description of the research design, sample, population, instrumentation, data collection procedures, data analysis, and limitations because of the design of the study, and summary. Chapter 7 of *A Counselor's Guide to the Dissertation Process* discusses the specific research methodologies and addresses ethical considerations of conducting research.

Chapter 4: Results

This chapter includes an introduction, data collection procedures, data analysis, and findings of the study. You provide readers with information regarding response rate and demographics. In Chapter 4, the emphasis is on the findings, which are reported in tables and figures. Chapter 9 of this book presents more detailed descriptions of this chapter of the dissertation.

Chapter 5: Discussion

This chapter includes a discussion, implications, limitations, suggestions for further research, and a conclusion. In this chapter, you provide a brief overview of the entire study. In the discussion section, you explain how your findings relate to the purpose of your study and to the findings of previous research on the topic. Under the implications section, you will describe the potential impact of positive social change. In the conclusion section, you provide your thoughts about the study, the findings, and the overall conclusions. Conclusions in this chapter differ from those in the fourth chapter of the dissertation because they are broader in scope and are drawn from the data analysis, previous research on the topic, and your own observations as a researcher.

Reference List

The reference list contains information that supports the relevance of your study and what has been published regarding your topic. You want to identify significant authors and the major journals recognized in your field. You will also be expected to reference primary sources (original articles or books) and avoid popular press opinion articles. The reference list should only include the works cited in your dissertation. In the past, you may have been asked to prepare a bibliography, which cites works for further reading. However, in the dissertation, you will only include a reference list and not a bibliography. Chapters 6 and 7 (pp. 169–224) in the APA *Publication Manual* (APA, 2010) address how to cite various references. A completed dissertation usually contains 60 to 100 entries.

Appendixes

As you begin writing your dissertation, you may come across important material that is too lengthy to include within the text. An example could be the inclusion of the 2016 CACREP Standards (CACREP, 2015). Rather than placing this within the text, you would put this in the appendix. You will want to place items in the appendixes in the order in which they appear in the text. See pages 38–39 in the APA *Publication Manual* (APA, 2010) on how to format appendixes. Also, remember to obtain permission for anything included in the appendix.

Curriculum Vitae

Although not common, some universities require students to submit a curriculum vita (CV) at the end of their dissertations. The CV is formatted in a basic outline form such as a resume or full-sentence form. If you are required to submit a CV, be selective of the information you chose to include because most universities limit students to one or two pages.

Roles and Responsibilities

Doctoral Student Versus Doctoral Candidate

Many students have asked us, "What is the difference between a doctoral student and a doctoral candidate?" The first 2 years of your program are devoted to completing required course work. During this stage, you are referred to as *doctoral student* or *PhD student.* Upon the successful completion of course work and comprehensive exams, the student becomes known as a *doctoral candidate.* At this stage, the student is ready to start the dissertation project and the majority of his or her time will be devoted to research and completing the dissertation. It is the doctoral candidate's responsibility to select a dissertation chair and, with the chair, identify committee members. It is also the doctoral candidate's responsibility to follow the timelines set forth by the committee and university, attend meetings with committee members, and submit all forms in proper sequence to the appropriate offices at the university.

Dissertation Chair or Adviser

You will work closely through all phases of your dissertation project with your dissertation chair, also known as the committee chair or dissertation adviser in some departments. You will meet regularly with your chair to determine when your dissertation proposal is ready for review. The chair is responsible for providing guidance and direction, monitoring and maintaining the academic standards of the university (e.g., content, research ethics), and overseeing the dissertation's contributions to the counseling profession. The chair will determine whether your proposal and dissertation are ready to advance to the next process and will monitor your progress from start to finish. The chair is also responsible for conducting the proposal and dissertation defense.

Dissertation Committee

After you have selected your dissertation chair, you will work in collaboration with him or her to select your committee members. A committee usually consists of three to five members, including the dissertation chair. Individuals who hold a doctoral degree from accredited universities are often allowed to serve on a committee. However, some universities specify whether the committee member must be part of the department, outside of the department but still within the university, or an external (nonuniversity) member. Some universities require only three committee members, and the third member is assigned to the student. Thus, it is important to find out the process at your university. Regardless of the process, we recommend that you search for members with a range of expertise. For example, you will want members who are knowledgeable about the content of your topic and the methodology you plan to use. A committee member works in collaboration with the chair to advise the doctoral candidate based on his or her expertise (e.g., content, methodology). Committee members are also responsible for evaluating the student's proposal, final dissertation, and oral defense. In Chapter 3 of this book, we discuss the roles of committee members and the selection process in more detail.

IRB

All students who conduct research studies that involve interviewing, testing, treating, surveying, or manipulating human participants or gathering archival data on human participants are required to have approval from the university's IRB before conducting any research. The IRB's responsibility is to review the student's application and make sure that the proposed research study complies with ethical standards. The IRB evaluates that the proposed data collection minimizes or eliminates risks to the participant. Chapter 7 of this book includes a more thorough discussion of the role of the IRB and ethics in research.

Summary

The journey of earning a PhD can be life changing. It requires your ability to plan, conduct, write, and defend original research. However, the journey also requires you to be aware of the personal challenges and uncertainties along the way. In this chapter, we discussed the important roles of commitment, stamina, and a positive mental attitude and provided you with strategies on how to overcome writer's block. We emphasized the unique aspects of writing a dissertation in a CES program and the potential to effect social change with your project. Although the structure and components of a dissertation can vary among disciplines, we covered the structure and components of typical doctoral dissertations. We described the major steps in the dissertation process and the roles and responsibilities of the student and dissertation committee members.

Now that you have an idea of what to expect when writing a dissertation, let's create a wellness program before you dive into your writing! After you have created a wellness plan, we will focus on the journey of completing a dissertation from start to finish.

Checklist

❏ Complete the graduate school accomplishments and disappointments activity.

❏ Create a list of dissertation guidelines and print them out.

❏ Become familiar with the dissertation process at your university.

❏ Gather any forms or guides your university may have that describe the dissertation process.

❏ Complete the following exercises:

Step 1: Think of your accomplishments in graduate school. Now think of the immediate feelings that accompanied the accomplishments and what sort of self-talk those feelings provoked. Take a moment to list at least three accomplishments and the feelings associated with each in the space provided.

Graduate School Accomplishments	*Feeling Associated With Each Accomplishment*
1. _____	_____
2. _____	_____
3. _____	_____

Step 2: Now reflect on any disappointments you have encountered in graduate school. List at least three disappointments and the feelings associated with each in the space provided.

Graduate School Disappointments	*Feeling Associated With Each Disappointment*
1. _____	_____
2. _____	_____
3. _____	_____

Step 3: Look at the feelings you listed under accomplishments and disappointments and compare the two columns. Under accomplishments, you may have listed feelings such as excited, proud, and happy. Under disappointments, you may have listed feelings such as frustrated, unhappy, and embarrassed. The lesson is that when people succeed, they are more optimistic about their competence and have a mind-set that is open to change, whereas when they are disappointed and believe that they have "failed," they are defensive and less open to change.

Step 4: Now that you have reflected on your accomplishments, discover how you can continue to be successful. For each accomplishment, answer the following questions:

Accomplishment 1:
How were you able to accomplish the goal?
What helped you be productive?
What worked well?

Accomplishment 2:
> How were you able to accomplish the goal?
> What helped you be productive?
> What worked well?

Accomplishment 3:
> How were you able to accomplish the goal?
> What helped you be productive?
> What worked well?

Step 5: Now list your disappointments and answer the following questions:

Disappointment 1:
> What did not work and why?
> What would you have done differently?
> What lesson did you learn from the disappointment?

Disappointment 2:
> What did not work and why?
> What would you have done differently?
> What lesson did you learn from the disappointment?

Disappointment 3:
> What did not work and why?
> What would you have done differently?
> What lesson did you learn from the disappointment?

After completing this stage of the exercise, we hope that you realize that you have the resources, strengths, knowledge, and potential to resolve your own problems. By focusing on the problems, we often lose sight of the strengths and resources that we possess. It is important to remember your strengths and how you can put them to work in solving any future problems that may arise during the dissertation process. Before you embark on your dissertation, let's create some dissertation guidelines.

Step 6: Think of five guidelines that would help improve the process of your dissertation journey. Examples might include "I will take care of myself during the dissertation process" and "I will embrace challenges that come my way." We encourage you to print out these guidelines and put them in a place where you can see them daily.

Guideline 1: _____

Guideline 2: _____

Guideline 3: _____

Guideline 4: _____

Guideline 5: _____

Additional Resources

Association for Counselor Education and Supervision. (n.d.). Graduate students. Retrieved from http://www.acesonline.net/graduate-students

Association for Support of Graduate Students. (2016). Home. Retrieved from http://asgs.org

Barnett, C. G. (2011). *The dissertation process: A step by step mentored guide.* Available from http://www.thedissertationprocess.com/products.htm

Miller, A. B. (2009). *Finishing your dissertation once and for all! How to overcome psychological barriers, get results, and move on with your life.* Washington, DC: American Psychological Association.

Chapter 2

Staying Well Throughout the Dissertation Process

The experiences of counseling and counselor education doctoral students are wonderful, brilliant privileges that few will have the chance to embark on. Students who choose any helping profession as their vocational identity are characteristically unique, especially counselors because they, not instruments or technology, are the mechanism for education, development, and change in others. There has been considerable evidence indicating that individuals who identify with the counseling profession tend to be healthier than the general population. However, as assignments, ambition, and obligations surmount, internal coping resources and social supports may not be as available as they once were, which may lead to a sense of fatigue, depletion, or even burnout. Yikes! However, there is good news: This does not have to be your narrative!

The fact that your dissertation process will be characterized by stress related to deadlines, output, mechanics of writing, and sleep are irrefutable. Yet the process will also be full of rewards as you overcome challenges, witness your professional development, grow your expertise, and complete your program requirements. You will probably experience several emotions, especially joy, exhilaration, and gratification. Regardless of the timeline for completion, methodology you implement, or composition of your committee, maintaining your wellness throughout the dissertation process is an imperative activity. As we discuss this simple, yet influential process, consider that effective wellness plans can be created alone, with just you accountable for content and process. Although these plans can work, we believe that the best wellness plans are going to be those that are developed with your dissertation chair or another important committee member with whom you will have routine contact during your dissertation journey. With this additional person or two involved in the process, you will increase not only the accountability but also the natural arc of your supportive network.

Maintaining your well-being during the dissertation process involves (a) understanding the graduate student experience from a holistic perspective, (b) developing a personal wellness plan, (c) evaluating your progress, and (d) rewarding yourself for successive accomplishments. Each of these activities is relatively easy to do and should not take away from any of your other dissertation-related activities. In fact, a little intentional self-care can go a long way for maintaining energy, focus, and a positive attitude. We will show you how. Not only will being intentional about your wellness provide you with a set of career-sustaining behaviors that will help you down the professional road, but your friends and family may also thank you for it!

Understanding the Graduate Student Experience From a Holistic Perspective

People are all multifaceted, synergistic beings whose traits, habits, and interpretations of the world are greater than the sum of the constituent parts. They experience a sense of wellness and well-being when there is balance among the many aspects of themselves. When these aspects of themselves are unimpeded, they flourish from within their personal expressions of uniqueness, creativity, meaningfulness, and connection with others. However, when people neglect some defining aspects of themselves, they experience distress and a sense of being unwell. This spiritual ache can be acute, lasting just a short time until their natural protective factors activate their resilience response, or long term and chronic in nature, making it a challenge to bounce back. In either case, people attain a sense of well-being by establishing, developing, and nurturing a lifestyle that promotes their optimal functioning in this moment, given the resources they can access. Fortunately, people do not have to "get well" all at once, because positive activities completed in one area of their lives will have a wellness-triggering effect on their overall level of wellness. In addition, people do not have to overhaul their whole lives because from this perspective, small changes are meaningful because they have the potential to (a) magnify into larger ones over time; (b) trigger other changes; and (c) inspire others, thereby strengthening the supportive network.

The concepts related to holism are the self-evident principles that undergird the counseling profession, and there is a further supposition that they define the lived experiences of everyone. Several researchers have submitted theories describing the holistic nature of the human experience and the factors that contribute to wellness (Dunn, 1959; Hettler, 1984; Myers & Sweeney, 2005; Roscoe, 2009; Seligman, 2011). You can probably discern the contributions of these holistic concepts from your course work, so the point of this discussion is not to take you on a theoretical exposition. Instead, we briefly present you with three frameworks (i.e., Adlerian life tasks, Hettler's [1984] wellness model, and Myers & Sweeney's [2005] Indivisible Self Model of Wellness) to conceptualize graduate student experiences that we have found useful when helping students to be proactive in their self-care so that they not only complete a dissertation but also finish well. Even though each of the frameworks can be readily understood with little more than a visual depiction, they are also complex enough to facilitate self-awareness and planning. As you read through them, consider not only which one makes the most sense for your experience but also which one would be the most useful for you as a support for brief wellness planning.

Adlerian Life Tasks

Adler (1931) and colleagues (Dreikurs & Mosak, 1967; Mansager & Gold, 2000; Mosak & Dreikurs, 1967/2000) proposed that people are at their best when they have a workable balance between the integrated, complimentary aspects of themselves that make them special, which are commonly referred to as *Adlerian life tasks*. As depicted in Figure 2.1, these life tasks are related to prosocial friendships, intimacy through loving relationships, occupational and work tasks (including pursuing a graduate degree), being able to get along with yourself (coping), and having a sense of spirituality. These factors are easy enough to conceptualize, and you can easily check your status. Consider that there is 100% of you and your energy, effort, and time. Now indicate how much of that 100% you dedicate to each life task. Most graduate students put an overwhelming majority of that percentage in the domain of work, which is typical as students endeavor to finish their programs. Give your initial ratings some reflection and then go back and decide if some adjustments are warranted. Once you have a reasonable indication if you are balanced (or not) across life tasks, you can consider which area is most important to you and where you could make a small adjustment in the future. Save that answer because you will need it in a bit.

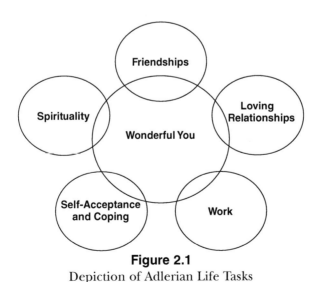

Figure 2.1
Depiction of Adlerian Life Tasks

Hettler's Wellness Model

Bill Hettler has made his life's work the general support of understanding and improving personal wellness (Hettler, 1984). His academic and personal experiences led him to surmise that meaningful contributions to a quality life occur across six dimensions: (a) social engagements with family and friends; (b) intellectually creative activities; (c) spiritual experiences that promote transcending oneself; (d) physical well-being; (e) experiencing positive emotions and effectively dealing with stress; and (f) occupation and work, including hobbies, a sense of spirituality, and meaning (see Figure 2.2). Hettler has provided free, public access to a number of assessments that evaluate wellness across these dimensions, and the LiveWell (https:// uhs.uwsp.edu/Other/livewell/) is particularly useful. The LiveWell is a 100-item self-assessment that asks questions related to each of the dimensions and, on average, takes approximately 10 minutes to complete. At the end, you get a summary report and visual depiction of your current degree of thriving in each dimension and overall. When you get to the end of the assessment, either print it out for your review or save it to a file on your computer because you will not be able to go back to it later.

Myers and Sweeney's Indivisible Self Model of Wellness

Myers and Sweeney (2005) used a data-driven approach to develop their model of factors contributing to overall wellness. Their analyses revealed five second-order factors or selves (Coping, Creative, Essential, Physical, and Social) that were integrated components, indivisible in their influence on total well-being.

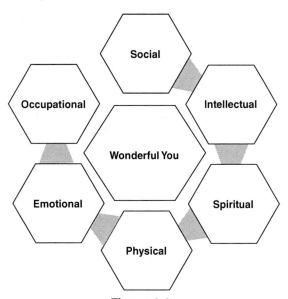

Figure 2.2
Depiction of Hettler's Wellness Model

Seventeen third-order factors of wellness (e.g., Stress Management, Realistic Beliefs, Self-Care, Spirituality, Gender Identity, Nutrition) are subsumed under each of the second-order factors (see Figure 2.3). To understand where you are on the wellness continuum for each of these 17 factors and overall, complete the Five Factor Wellness Inventory (Myers & Sweeney, 2005), which is offered for a nominal fee through Mind Garden (www.mindgarden.com/99-five-factor-wellness-inventory), as depicted in the Indivisible Self Model of Wellness. Mind Garden provides a report that has descriptive feedback, so you can decide which areas of wellness may be vulnerable for you during the dissertation process. Alternatively, you can take a more informal approach by (a) scaling your current level of wellness across each of the 17 third-order wellness factors using a scale ranging from 0 (*not well at all*) to 10 (*doing very well*), (b) scaling the degree of satisfaction with each domain from 0 (*not satisfied at all*) to 10 (*very satisfied*), (c) totaling the two values for each domain, and (d) using the resulting values to reflect on your priorities.

Regardless if you use one of these three models or have another conceptual compass that you use to find your direction, it is important to have a clear idea about what you hope to monitor, maintain, and promote during the dissertation process. You should also know that what emerges as important to you or a major influence on your well-being will likely be a fluid situation during the dissertation process. That's OK! It's logical. You are a complex person living in a complex system that is ever changing. It is a beautiful thing, but it is also best navigated with a reasonable, workable plan.

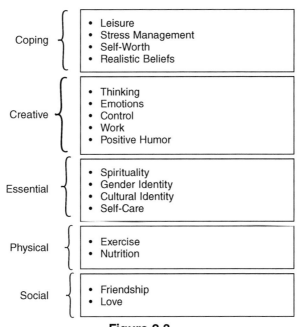

Figure 2.3
Depiction of Myers and Sweeney's Indivisible Self Model of Wellness

Developing a Personal Wellness Plan

There are a lot of ways to develop a wellness plan: Some are more informal in nature, requiring little more than a self-commitment or pact between you and your chair; others are more structured and formal, depicting specific strategies and measurable outcomes. Many individuals find plans that are more formal and specific to be the most helpful, but regardless of which route you choose, the best plans start by selecting one or a few areas for improvement. We do not recommend that you choose several or all areas of wellness because, let's face it, you are getting ready to be busy and now is not the time to set overwhelming or insurmountable goals that may be potentially discouraging. Remember, because wellness is a holistic, multifaceted construct, change or maintenance of wellness in one area of your life will contribute to your overall thriving, so once you have identified an aspect of wellness that you are comfortable paying attention to and fostering for the next month or so, it is time to make a plan.

Written wellness plans can be completed on your own or with your chair and are typically composed of five parts: (a) a personal definition of the wellness domain to be addressed; (b) a rating of your current satisfaction with yourself in this domain on a scale of 0–10; (c) commentary describing how focusing on this area may affect you during your dissertation project; (d) identification of interventions, including specific behavioral strategies that you will implement and resources that you will use; and (e) a personal estimation of how you will know when you are making progress toward wellness goals. The example wellness plan depicted in Appendix A shows the process that Sam, one of our students, engaged in; she decided that paying attention to leisure was going to be important during the dissertation process. Even without her assessment results, Sam recognized that she had let this important part of her life become diminished while completing course work and preparing for comprehensive examinations. The assessment results confirmed this, and Sam was a little emotional when talking about "just not having much fun, right now" yet believing that "this should be just as fun as it is challenging."

Sometimes identifying what areas of personal wellness may be helpful to address is not as intuitive as it was in the example of Sam. The good news is that some common domains tend to be of interest to counseling and counselor education students. Moreover, most students are well versed in the interventions, protocols, and anticipated outcomes within these domains, which we categorize as (a) priority and time management, (b) stress management, (c) staying social, and (d) fostering the physical. Because you have probably received formal training and supervision implementing these strategies with clients and students, we do not include an exhaustive survey. Instead, we provide a quick overview and citations for you to reference if needed.

Priority and Time Management

Even though people at this point in their academic career often know what a planner is, few view maintaining a to-do list as an ongoing process rather than an event. Like informed consent documents, your planner is a living thing that is constantly in play and requires revisiting, consultation, and editing to ensure best practice. Time management involves spreading out the myriad things that you have to do in your life over the span of a 24-hour day, a 168-hour week, or a longer period of time. Most people would have no problem with time management if the number of things they had to do were not constantly changing. Because the number of responsibilities you are accountable for is typically in flux, it is helpful to manage your priorities so that you direct your attention and energy to the most pressing activities within the context of available time. Developing these skills throughout the dissertation process can go a long way to maintaining your sense of well-being and general sense of control. Therefore, it is important to conceptualize the dissertation as a project with several subprojects, and you can increase the manageability by carefully sequencing the steps involved over time. Experts in time and priority management (Allen, 2001; Fiore, 2007; Morgenstern, 2004) have provided some great resources that are easy to understand and implement and not exhaustive to read.

Stress Management

Stress management is one area of wellness that as counselors, we are generally great at helping clients commit to and follow through with, but we are not as consistent ourselves. It's OK. It's normal. But consider the following: One of the most practical functions of a wellness plan is to encourage accountability for activities that will not only be beneficial to you but also be within the range of things you can realistically do. Stress management activities with a strong evidence base that may be worth considering include controlled breathing, journaling, brief meditation and other mindfulness activities, using positive self-talk, and increasing assertiveness (Regehr, Glancy, & Pitts, 2013; Richardson & Rothstein, 2008). If you are prone to being stressed and overwhelmed by large projects, then regularly using these skills may make meeting the demands of a dissertation project a more manageable and fulfilling experience.

Staying Social

One of the things we hear most about the graduate school experience is related to the struggle to stay socially engaged. Let's face it: There is only so much of you to go around and only so many hours in the day. If you are someone who draws a lot of energy and meaning from social interactions, it may be reasonable to plan on getting by with a little help from your friends, family, community groups, or any other supportive networks that are important to you. Planning to stay socially engaged can be as easy as conversations over text, FaceTime, or the telephone, but we recommend arranging things that are face-to-face if doable. There is just something powerful about the potential for relational connection when in the same physical space. Some other ideas may include attending peer group meetings or religious study groups, having date nights, or meeting for coffee or a meal. Whatever you choose, it should not be something that leaves you feeling drained or invalidated, but instead leaves you feeling energized and grateful for the moments shared.

Fostering the Physical

You have heard it a million times: You are what you eat. Well, every single time you heard it, it was true. Furthermore, an active lifestyle is strongly correlated with all sorts of wonderful outcomes, such as decreased anxiety (Conn, 2010), reduced risk for chronic disease (Oldridge, 2012), increased work productivity (Rongen, Robroek, van Lenthe, & Burdorf, 2013), and more self-esteem (Babic et al., 2014). Of course, this may not be the time to start training for your first triathlon; instead, make sure that you are giving your body the fuel that it needs to keep that beautiful brain of yours working at a high level and staying active so that you reap the benefits of staying connected to your body. We have had several students choose wellness plans in this domain, and they often include small, but meaningful, interventions such as making sure to drink a certain amount of water per day (not just coffee or shots of espresso); eating fruit and vegetables; or introducing short, moderate bouts of exercise. As a student, you can accomplish many of your activity-based goals through your college or university wellness center, which offers consultations to students, group fitness classes, or other incentive programs, all of which are paid for through your student fees.

Regardless of what approach you choose, we encourage you to put it in writing; include your chair or other people in your plan to promote and encourage accountability; and use the technology at your disposal, including the numerous free applications that will help with time management, brief meditations, social connection, and exercise routines. Of course, technology is only helpful if you use it, so make sure that the technological shoe fits before you wear it because ultimately this is about setting yourself up for success and with success comes reward.

Evaluating Your Progress

As with any good plan, regular and objective evaluation is a vital activity. This can be done by incorporating a satisfaction scale, or another measurable scale, into your wellness plan. If you are looking for something a little more visual or standardized, you can retake Hettler's LiveWell or the Five Factor Wellness Inventory and compare your results to previous ones. These evaluations can be done by yourself, but we encourage you to keep your chair in the loop because he or she can support, guide, and encourage you when needed.

There will be times when your plan may be just challenging enough to support your wellness and contribute to a sense of thriving. Other times, you may find that your plan is either too ambitious or not challenging enough given your current resources and support. In those times, it is important to decide if your plan is suitable the way that it is or if it could be amended to stimulate further progress. In any of these cases, it is important to be honest and compassionate with yourself so that you can make adjustments to your plan that will support you during the process.

Rewarding Yourself for Successive Accomplishments

Rewards are incredible things and should be a part of any wellness plan. From a behavioral perspective, if a desired activity is proximally followed by a commensurate reward, then that activity is increasingly likely to show up in similar situations. Simple, right? Well, if humans were all just the agents of stimulus-response chains, complex and sustained tasks such as completing a dissertation would be a piece of cake. However, when personality dispositions converge with pressure to achieve, unhelpful thought patterns emerge, such as "There is nothing special about what I have done," "What I have done is expected of students in my program," or "Others have done more than me." As a result, people can be tricked into plugging away at a daunting project without taking the time to acknowledge what they have done, treat themselves periodically for their efforts, and reflect on the nature of their progress. However, when students are intentional about doing these things, they tend to report feeling a greater sense of accomplishment and self-efficacy. For these reasons, we find that encouraging students to reward themselves is an imperative.

Although rewards can be anything that is safe and responsible, they typically occur across some common categories: (a) people you would like to spend more time with, (b) places you like to go, (c) things you like to do but do not often get to, (d) food and drinks, and (e) things you do not own but would like to. A great place to start is to identify or list at least a few examples within each category that you consider to be small, medium, and large rewards. As you move along your dissertation journey, you will meet many milestones; some will be small, some will be moderate, and others will be a big deal. In each instance, it is important to match your achievement with a reward that is proportionate to your effort. Sure, this may increase the chance that you will continue your efforts, but more notably, it will increase the chance that you develop an important career-sustaining behavior that will promote meaningful reflection and prevent burnout.

Summary

In this chapter, we discussed the importance of viewing your experience as a student from a holistic perspective. Being a student is just one aspect of your life, and to maintain your wellness throughout the dissertation experience, you will also need to be mindful of the other aspects. We also contended that through partnership with your chair, a mentor, or another colleague, you can develop a wellness plan that supports you not only starting your dissertation but also finishing it. By adopting a holistic framework, developing a wellness plan, evaluating your progress, and rewarding yourself, you can not only make it through your dissertation but also foster an important set of career-sustaining behaviors.

Checklist

- ❏ Choose a wellness theory that makes sense to you.
- ❏ Complete a wellness assessment.
- ❏ Schedule a meeting with your adviser to review the results and develop a wellness plan.
- ❏ Be consistent and kind to yourself throughout the dissertation process.
- ❏ Talk to your adviser about incorporating wellness monitoring as a part of your routine supervision.

Additional Resources

Hettler, B. (1984). Wellness: Encouraging a lifetime pursuit of excellence. *Health Values, 8,* 13–17.

Hettler, B. (2007). *LiveWell* [Measurement instrument]. Retrieved from https://uhs.uwsp.edu/Other/livewell/

Myers, J. E., & Sweeney, T. J. (2005). The indivisible self: An evidence-based model of wellness (reprint). *Journal of Individual Psychology, 61,* 269–279.

Myers, J. E., & Sweeney, T. J. (2014). *Five Factor Wellness Inventory.* Menlo Park, CA: Mind Garden. Available from www.mindgarden.com/99-five-factor-wellness-inventory

Roscoe, L. J. (2009). Wellness: A review of theory and measurement for counselors. *Journal of Counseling & Development, 87,* 216–226. doi:10.1002/j.1556-6678.2009.tb00570.x

Stamm, B. H. (2009). *Professional Quality of Life Scale.* Retrieved from www.proqol.org/ProQol_Test.html

Example of a Student Wellness Plan

1. **Domain:** Leisure—Activities that I do in my free time that contribute to a sense of having fun in life, not being *all work*, and enjoying the community that I live in with the people who give life meaning. Leisure activities are those during which time flies by because I am having fun and create a sense of zest and engagement with the playful side of life.

2. **Satisfaction with:** Leisure
   ❏ 1   ❏ 2   ❏ 3   ☒ 4   ❏ 5   ❏ 6   ❏ 7   ❏ 8   ❏ 9   ❏ 10

3. **Paying attention to and promoting leisure may affect my dissertation experience in the following ways:**
   a. Greater sense of self and balance between work and play.
   b. Increased awareness of the dissertation as one part of my life.
   c. Increased awareness of issues that counseling professionals need to develop career-sustaining behaviors.
   d. Greater connection with the people and places most important to me.

4. **Intervention:**
   Objective:
   a. Increase and maintain the amount of fun leisure activities that I engage in on a weekly basis throughout the dissertation experience.
   Strategies:
   a. Talk to family and friends to see what some of the fun things are that they have been wanting to do for a while but just haven't found the time. I will use this feedback and my own perspectives to make a checklist of fun things to do.
   b. Do one fun activity a week with family or friends.
   c. Do one fun activity a week by myself—it can be anything active or passive as long as it is enjoyable.
   d. Read things that are not related to my dissertation topic.
   e. Learn to cook two new dishes and have friends over to enjoy them.

5. I will know that I have made some progress when:
   a. My rating on the satisfaction scale has increased from a 4 to at least a 7.
   b. I have completed at least four of my strategy tasks.
   c. I perceive a greater sense of joy and connection with my life as a doctoral candidate.
   d. I can describe two ways that leisure is important in the lives of graduate students.

Chapter 3

Selecting the Dissertation Committee and Narrowing Down the Topic

Selecting your dissertation committee and narrowing down the topic can be exciting, challenging, and at times frustrating. There are myriad factors to consider when selecting your dissertation chair and committee. One rule of thumb when making this decision is to take your time. You should approach the selection of your committee as a process that involves first assessing what you need and what you are looking for and then meeting with faculty members to learn their style, interests, and expertise. You can also talk to current students and graduates of your program, but ultimately, honor your gut when making the final decision. We recommend considering your dissertation chair as your primary mentor, an individual who will guide you in making decisions throughout your career. Committee members, led by your chair, will also guide you through the dissertation process, provide you with recommendations after graduation, help you transition to your first job, offer advice during career changes, and introduce you to experts in the field. Also, do not forget about publishing opportunities! Your chair will generally be somebody you will collaborate with for the rest of your career. Although the two of you are not attached at the hip, you will never be too far away, especially when you need your chair the most.

Narrowing down your dissertation topic is a process in and of itself, and it involves an extensive time commitment, a high degree of thoughtful study, and active collaboration with other professionals in the counseling field. Therefore, it is really no wonder we needed to dedicate an entire chapter to selecting your committee and narrowing down your topic. To some degree, you might need a little luck to help you settle on a dissertation topic that truly reflects your research interests and sparks a research agenda that may span your entire career. We hope this chapter is that bit of luck you are looking for.

We begin this chapter with examples from three doctoral students, who discuss the process of selecting their dissertation chairs and committees. Next, we review some salient factors to consider during the selection process. We discuss the roles of the dissertation chair and committee members, along with issues that might arise when you work with a faculty team throughout your dissertation. We also provide suggestions on how to prevent and respond to problems that might occur.

There are multiple avenues you can follow to identify a dissertation topic. We hope the student examples we provide will help you gain some insight into this process. Before beginning your search for a topic, we suggest that you take stock of your personal/social life and inventory your knowledge related to research within the counseling profession and counselor education. This step is recommended as a check of your readiness to pursue a dissertation. The self-assessment serves as an inventory that reflects how prepared you are to begin your search. In this chapter, we provide a set of guidelines to help you select and narrow down a topic and an example that demonstrates how you and your chair might create a study after starting with a general topic.

How Do You Select a Committee?

Your dissertation committee, made up of faculty members, will play a significant role in the successful completion of your dissertation and your graduation. You will be working closely with your dissertation chair. You will meet regularly with your chair during each stage of this process because your chair will help you determine when your dissertation proposal is ready for review by the committee and ultimately guide you through the completion of your dissertation. Because of this close collaboration, we recommend you carefully select your dissertation chair and committee members. Examples of how three students arrived at selecting their dissertation chairs and committee members follow.

Student 1

My dissertation chair and committee members were selected based on the support I needed to complete my dissertation. Dr. Jain was selected as my dissertation chair because I knew she would greatly assist me throughout the whole dissertation process. This included supporting me by helping me develop my research questions, supporting me in providing feedback on my writing and formatting of each dissertation chapter, and supporting me through understanding what to prepare and expect for my proposal and defense. She served as a chair because she was a very seasoned professional, including being familiar with my population of interest, the treatment provided for this population, and the research methodology. She had led many previous dissertations serving as chair and seeing them to completion. All of these factors contributed to my selection of a dissertation chair. In regard to the other committee members, I chose Dr. Johnson as a committee member for his knowledge and experience working with this population and for his experience in research methodology. I wanted him to help me understand and select the appropriate instruments to use in measuring outcomes for this population, and for his understanding of various research designs and methods of analysis. I also chose Dr. Smith as a committee member for her knowledge and experience in using the intervention used in my study, which was valuable in guiding me to sustain fidelity in my treatment. I also chose her for her knowledge and expertise in APA writing and editing, and in seeing many other projects to completion.

Student 2

I selected my dissertation chair based on the professor's availability and willingness to work at my pace, content and research design knowledge, willingness to critique my study when necessary, and work ethic. I have to emphasize that our entire faculty had great knowledge and character; however, some had many responsibilities (e.g., leadership roles in ACA [American Counseling Association] and other professional organizations) for which they needed to allocate a great deal of time. My native language is not English; thus, my dissertation needed more work than a native speaker's research project. Because of time concerns, I had to find a professor who was flexible, a good editor, available, and knowledgeable. My chair also had studied my dissertation topic using a different population and had several published articles using the research design that I used in my study. I had two other departmental committee members. One of them had a very strong qualitative research background. I intentionally asked this professor to be a part of my committee because she was able to view findings from a different perspective. Lastly, I asked one of my professors who had great editing skills as well as time. Now thinking about this process, I realize that I followed a pragmatic strategy in selecting my dissertation chair and committee.

Student 3

Dr. Jain published several research projects using Theory X, Y, and Z as an intervention with high school students. Given her knowledge of the topic, she was the appropriate choice to serve as my dissertation chair. The committee was carefully selected from experienced faculty who worked with K–12 students.

These three students described how they selected their dissertation chairs and committees. You may have noticed the students had similar reasons for selecting their chairs and committees. However, there are some noticeable differences in what some of the students emphasized. To assist in your selection of a dissertation chair and committee, we suggest you review the roles of committee members and use these roles to help with the selection of both your chair and your committee.

Roles of Committee Members and the Selection Process

The roles and responsibilities of committee members, particularly your dissertation chair, are generally to provide the necessary direction and guidance to complete a dissertation, monitor and maintain the academic standards of the university and the program, and oversee the dissertation's contribution to the profession and the professional literature. How the committee functions and how individual members meet these general areas of responsibility will vary. It is assumed that committee members who have been reviewed and approved by the university's graduate office are familiar with their roles and responsibilities. Most programs require faculty approval for graduate status before they can serve on a doctoral committee.

The factors you will need to consider when selecting a dissertation committee parallel the roles of committee members, including those of the dissertation chair. If you are entering your doctoral program with a topic already in mind, selecting a chair and committee with knowledge about your topic might appear to be a seamless process. However, it would be wise for you to consider the factors listed in the following sections. These factors are likely to contribute to your success beyond the dissertation.

Knowledge of Research Topics and the Profession

If you have a topic in mind before beginning the program, you will most likely seek a dissertation chair and committee who have experience and publication records in the same domain. This is a natural phenomenon occurring in doctoral programs, including CES. Faculty advisers will suggest that you meet with professors who have research interests similar to your own. However, it is still up to you to review the research background and publication record of faculty before applying to a doctoral program. When considering who you want to select to be on your committee, you should take note of faculty members' knowledge of a wide range of research topics and the counseling profession. Your committee members will share their knowledge and provide resources to help you increase your knowledge and understanding of the status and future direction(s) of the counseling profession.

Mentorship Skills

Dissertation chairs and committee members not only serve as mentors while you matriculate through the program but also continue to take an interest in your development throughout your career. Mentorship covers a wide range of activities that go beyond providing guidance on the dissertation process. Four areas of mentorship are important to students in CES programs, particularly for those who intend to seek faculty positions after graduation: career planning, research, pedagogy, and supervision.

Career Planning

At the beginning of your program and throughout your career, your chair and committee members provide mentorship in career planning. Career planning mentorship is most evident during your final year as a doctoral student because your chair and committee members assist in your job search and in defining your career. Because your chair and committee are an integral part of your success, we recommend that you talk openly with these professionals about your plans for the future.

Research

Doctoral mentorship involves helping you develop a research identity and viewing yourself as a researcher. This is important for all graduates, whether you are planning to provide direct services in a clinical setting or planning to seek a university faculty position. Graduates seeking faculty positions will need to see themselves as researchers, a notion that is expected by universities hiring you to teach and conduct research. Choosing a chair and committee members who share your research interests will be especially helpful because these individuals can provide opportunities to collaborate on current and future projects.

Pedagogy

Because a significant number of graduates from CES programs seek university teaching positions, mentorship in pedagogy, along with gaining experience as a teaching assistant under the supervision of seasoned professors, is essential. Mentorship in pedagogy is also important if you plan to teach as an adjunct professor while fully engaged in a clinical position. When applying for teaching-related positions, you must clearly articulate both your pedagogical theory and teaching philosophy. Choosing a chair and committee who teach courses you are interested in, or whose teaching styles you seek to emulate in your own work as an educator, will help you develop your own pedagogical theory and teaching style.

Supervision

Mentorship in supervision is critical for doctoral students seeking direct service clinical positions after graduation. You will most likely be supervising beginning counselors in practicum and internship courses required in all CES graduate programs. Mentorship in supervision is also important if you intend to seek faculty positions that require skills in clinical supervision. This component may be especially salient if your dissertation topic involves clinical work in some capacity.

Professional Development

Dissertation chairs and committee members play an important role in your professional development. Their mentorship will facilitate your conference attendance, workshop participation, publication and research, membership in professional organizations, and advocacy and leadership skills. You might include individuals on your committee who have several years of clinical experience and are leaders in the profession, including working with licensure boards and professional organizations.

Research Expertise

Dissertation chairs and committee members are expected to possess expertise in research design, proposal writing, and other nuances of a dissertation. Your chair should have experience directing dissertations and serving on dissertation committees. In addition, your chair should possess a broad knowledge of dissertation topics in counseling and the behavioral sciences, data analysis procedures, and data reporting practices. We recommend selecting a chair and committee members who have experience conducting the research design you will use in your dissertation (e.g., quantitative, qualitative, mixed methods). Committee members also play a major role in helping you initiate and establish your own research agenda.

Editing and Writing Skills

It is not the responsibility or role of the dissertation chair to extensively edit and rewrite sections of your dissertation. Having to read a poorly written dissertation takes time away from assessing the content and quality of your study. Most chairs will not have the time to provide a complete edit of your work and, therefore, might refer you to an editor or to the writing center on campus. However, it is still important for the chair and committee members to flag writing errors found in your proposal. Perhaps you might inventory your writing strengths and weaknesses and discuss this with your dissertation chair, who could immediately direct you to individuals and services to address any concerns. Addressing this area is especially salient if you are an international student or if English is not your first language.

Time Management

It is important that throughout the dissertation process, your chair is available for face-to-face or electronic (e.g., Skype, web-based collaboration tools) meetings. Your chair will decide whether he or she will allow contact by phone, other than the office phone. Even though faculty members are busy, your dissertation chair should be able to commit the time necessary to help you develop your proposal and shepherd your dissertation to completion. Rather than deciding on a chair and committee members based on their perceived availability, assess them by their time management skills. Whether it is due to their prioritization of student needs or simply their use of good time management skills, active faculty members are often the ones who are most accessible to doctoral students. You may want to select a dissertation chair whose time management and organizational skills augment your own.

Relationship Skills

The relationship between you and your dissertation chair is one of the most important factors of your graduate education (Barnes, Williams, & Archer, 2010). When selecting a dissertation chair and committee, you should take note of the interpersonal style of faculty members, based on personal meetings, observation, and talking with others. Always keeping your best interests in mind, committee members have a responsibility to collaborate with you and each other.

Leadership and Management Skills

Anecdotal evidence indicates that you will probably experience several challenges while completing your dissertation. Your chair, on occasion, might need to use leadership and managerial skills to help you navigate problems involving committee members, university policies, office personnel, and other students. These experiences might help you develop and refine your own leadership and management skills.

In summary, dissertation chairs and committee members do play roles in the lives of doctoral students throughout and beyond the educational experiences. Students select committee members for a variety of reasons, including having brief conversations with peers, exploring salient factors associated with a faculty member's publication record, and interviewing faculty to determine whether they would be a good personal and professional fit. Selecting a committee is a difficult task because research does not support a selection model or specific list of what to look for in a committee. What works for you may not work for another student. Your readiness and personality will play major roles in your assessment and final selection of a committee. Heppner and Heppner (2004) cautioned students against making the following mistakes during the selection process: (a) choosing only supportive people, (b) avoiding a potential committee member who has been labeled as "difficult" by the rumor mill, (c) viewing faculty members' interests too narrowly, and (d) not consulting with your chair to determine if the constellation of committee members is appropriate before inviting them to serve. We hope the guidelines and recommendations will minimize the obstacles you will face during your doctoral experience and help you select committee members who will ultimately fulfill their role expectations. Therefore, we recommend that you consider the factors listed in the previous paragraphs that are important to you in selecting your committee.

Managing Committee Issues: Politics and Personalities

You should expect that issues will surface and that obstacles will need to be addressed while completing your dissertation. Issues of a political nature often surface among committee members, including your chair, while you are working on your study. The makeup of your committee, especially personality differences, can disrupt the dissertation process. These challenges necessitate that you use effective coping strategies and follow the advice of your chair, as appropriate, to help resolve difficulties that might arise.

In the following paragraphs, we discuss four examples of political and personality issues (competition and ego, availability, triangulation, and anger) and possible responses. We hope that you do not experience any of these challenges during the course of your program. We firmly believe that knowledge of potential issues can help you effectively cope with them should they occur.

Competition and Ego

Occasionally, a committee member, including your chair, can appear demanding by emphasizing perfection at every stage of the dissertation. When working with this personality type, there is little room for error because mistakes on your part will lead to criticism. If left alone, a student can become demoralized and even consider leaving the program. At some point, if the problem does not reside with your chair, he or she may need to step in by meeting with the full committee or individual committee members. In addition to personality issues, external factors, such as frustrating university policies, could explain a committee member's actions.

For example, university policies related to tenure and promotion can create a competitive environment in which faculty members compete for promotion and merit salary increases. In many cases, department chairs are asked to rank faculty members, top to bottom, of who should be considered for merit. Competition between faculty members can surface while serving together on a dissertation committee, particularly if they are pressured to demonstrate who knows the most about research or adheres to the highest standards. If a faculty member's ego, including your chair's, is based on being the best, the result can be the creation of a competitive climate, thereby raising havoc and affecting your committee and progress in completing the dissertation.

Your response: You should maintain contact with your dissertation chair, as appropriate, at all times. This necessitates providing regular updates of your progress toward completing your dissertation and interactions with committee members. You should inform your chair of any problems with committee members and expect your chair to help you make decisions on what to do. Your chair will likely give you advice on how to handle this situation, particularity if this problem surfaces early in the dissertation process. Your chair might provide advice such as "Take the high road on these matters and do not get involved with department politics," "Be patient and responsive by working to fix critiques given to you and try not to take them personally," or "Find time to interact with this committee member. Recognize his or her feedback as helpful and clarify the corrections he or she has suggested in a nondefensive manner. Always come prepared to meetings with the changes made as directed by the faculty member." If things become more upsetting after your attempts to make this work, your chair will be expected to intervene by talking to the committee member and removing the member if necessary. If the problem involves your chair, your first step is to talk with him or her directly. If the problem persists after talking with your chair, you may need to meet with the department chair. If your dissertation chair is also the department chair, you may need to bring your concerns to the dean of the college.

Availability

The availability of committee members is a perennial issue. Faculty are busy teaching classes, conducting their own research, publishing, attending meetings, serving on professional associations, preparing dossiers for promotion, and writing reports for annual reviews. Therefore, faculty members, including your dissertation chair, may not be able to meet with you or provide feedback in a timely manner. However, despite the myriad of responsibilities of faculty members, most individuals serving on dissertation committees do find the time to meet with their doctoral students and provide feedback on their written work. On occasion, a committee member might be unavailable and unwilling to meet with you based on political or personal reasons. Reclusive faculty members may lack interpersonal skills or struggle with their own personal issues (e.g., an addiction), thus limiting their availability or willingness to help. Personal issues such as these are serious and beyond your ability to change. Attempts at dealing with these cases often become political and legal.

Your response: This situation is beyond your purview. However, you must bring the issue to your chair's attention. Your chair may or may not know about the status of the faculty member's personal issues and will need to talk with the faculty member. Depending on the problem and its severity, your chair might work matters out with the faculty member or report the problem to the department chair. Ethics are paramount in situations such as these. If issues are irreconcilable or the committee member is unable or unwilling to fulfill his or her role, you might need to replace this individual and find another member to serve on your committee. Although these cases are rare, we encourage you to be assertive and work closely with your chair if you are to select a replacement. If your dissertation chair is the problem, you will need to first speak with your dissertation chair and then bring your concerns to the department chair or dean of the college.

Triangulation

You may find yourself caught in the middle of issues involving two committee members or your dissertation chair and a committee member. Triangulation could occur simply because both committee members are seeking your attention, approval, or admiration. In cases where there are differences of opinion about theory, data collection procedures, or data analysis, committee members may end up arguing, trying to prove to you who is right. When triangulation occurs, you are likely to feel uncomfortable with this difficult situation because you are caught in the middle.

Your response: This is an excellent opportunity to use your interpersonal skills. At first, you might attempt to go along with the adolescent behavior by remaining neutral and listening to the opinions of both committee members. You should balance attention between members and avoid taking sides at all costs. We encourage you to keep the concept of equifinality in mind: Try different strategies to defuse the situation (e.g., complimenting both parties on their helpfulness) or recognize the good points expressed by each committee member. If committee meetings continue to move off course because of triangulation, your dissertation chair, if he or she is not one of the parties involved, will need to step in and help both committee members refocus on their roles. If your chair fails to step forward, you should express your discomfort about being caught in the middle of squabbles and seek his or her advice on how you can meet with the two committee members with a third party present. If the dissertation chair is involved, you will need to address your concerns to the department chair or dean of the college. Changing dissertation chairs is always an option in cases like this.

Anger

Although everyone gets angry on occasion, an angry committee member can create a hostile environment during committee meetings and individual conversations, which will affect your dissertation progress. A committee member's anger could be political if he or she feels mistreated by the department or university. The committee member could take this anger out on you during committee meetings and in other situations in which university personnel are present. For example, because of transference, a committee member or your dissertation chair could express anger toward you as you might remind him or her of someone else in his or her life. Under these circumstances, you might feel confused by a committee member acting toward you in an angry fashion for unknown reasons.

Your response: In this case, it is best to share what you see occurring with your dissertation chair, as long as this person is not the culprit. Your chair may be able to provide insight related to the committee member's behavior, leading to a greater understanding of the context for the committee member's actions and emotions. This may help you avoid personalizing the committee member's expression of anger. If these concerns do not abate, your dissertation chair will need to intervene again. If your dissertation chair is the problem, follow protocol by first talking with him or her and then speaking with the department chair or college dean if problems are not resolved.

Recommendations for Addressing Political or Personality Issues

You will probably face some of the political and personality issues that involve members of your committee, including your chair. Most of these issues will have little to do with you or your topic of study. Regardless, how you respond to these issues will determine whether they continue to interfere with the completion of your dissertation and your graduation.

There are no evidence-based strategies for addressing issues among committee members. However, when these occasions arise, you should use the personal skills and response styles that are considered effective. Figure 3.1 includes a list of important personal characteristics for students who have to navigate issues involving committee members, including your dissertation chair. We encourage you to review these responses, build upon them, and use them as your interpersonal arsenal. In addition to using the personal response styles, you can use Joyner, Rouse, and Glatthorn's (2013) suggestions for preventing problems with your dissertation committee, including your dissertation chair. Several of Joyner et al.'s suggestions are included in the following list:

- First, select a dissertation chair and full committee who are compatible with one another and with you. You should review dissertations completed in the department, paying attention to committee member names that frequently occur and faculty members who regularly serve on committees together.

- Learn the ground rules of how the dissertation chair and full committee operate. If this information is not provided in a written format, you should talk to your department chair, faculty in your department, and other students.
- Avoid dropping in a committee member's office without an appointment. Most committee members will not appreciate you stopping by unannounced to distribute a completed chapter—or worse, your finished dissertation.
- Do not ask your dissertation chair or committee members to review a rough draft. If your draft is rough, it isn't ready for review. We highly encourage you to be sure all materials are free from grammatical and spelling errors.
- Keep your relationship with committee members, including your chair, professional. When contacting professors by phone, call their office. Many committee members consider their home or cell phones to be personal and require their permission to use them. When in doubt, we recommend taking a more formal stance to assure you do not inadvertently cross boundaries.
- Be respectful of committee members' time and work schedules. Do not give committee members three chapters of a dissertation before the Thanksgiving holiday, thinking that they will have this time to read your work during their break. Allow enough time for committee members to provide feedback on material. We recommend allotting at least 2 weeks for review, although this timeline will vary based on the amount of material and committee members' schedules.
- Be sure your dissertation chair approves everything before distributing material to your full committee. Do not surprise your chair. We are confident a chair will not appreciate being surprised.
- Stay in contact with your committee, even if it is a brief 10-minute contact to review your progress. If you happen to see a committee member outside of the university, however, do not provide dissertation updates unless he or she specifically asks you to do so. Do not surprise your committee members.
- Finally, use the recommended responses in Figure 3.1 when receiving feedback from committee members. Specifically, remember to use these in situations when the committee member's feedback is not what you expected. Clarify misunderstandings from a learner's perspective.

How Do Doctoral Students Select a Dissertation Topic?

Doctoral students follow a myriad of avenues, ranging from happenstance to tightly organized plans, that lead to selecting a dissertation topic. The process of selecting a topic depends on your professional experiences and the research background of your dissertation chair and committee. In the following paragraphs, two students' share their experiences in selecting a dissertation topic.

The Response Repertoire assesses your ability to use the 12 skills when responding to feedback. Please complete the brief self-rating by checking (√) by each skill, according to how you respond to your dissertation committee members, including your dissertation chair. Use the results to review your personal skills, reflecting on areas in which you could improve as well as those in which you excel.

Skill	Great	Good	OK	Could Be Better
Listening				
Acceptance of feedback				
Nondefensiveness				
Patience				
Ability to reframe				
Perseverance				
Tenacity				
Viewing feedback as helpful				
Clarifying				
Confronting				
Resilience				
Staying calm				

Figure 3.1
Managing Committee Problems: Response Repertoire

Student 4

My dissertation was titled *Reality Therapy With Youth in a Community Center: A Single-Case Research Design.* I selected my dissertation topic primarily based on two reasons: (1) from my personal experience and (2) from a review of the literature. The first reason includes my passion and experience for working with youth and adolescents, primarily youth involved in the juvenile justice system. From my experience providing counseling services to youth, and providing mental health screenings, I realized that many of the youth I served had significant mental health needs, yet had been underserved by mental health and school professionals. Many received no previous treatment. I wanted to find out if this was true for most individuals involved in the juvenile justice system. This leads me to my second reason for selecting this dissertation topic. I completed a review of the literature to further understand the mental health needs of this population, what treatments are available in serving this population, and . . . the potential of integrating reality therapy within rehabilitative programming for adolescents in a community center. The reason I chose reality therapy also stemmed from these two reasons as I enjoy using this approach and conceptualizing cases from this theoretical perspective, and also because I read about the effectiveness of using reality therapy and the recommendations of its use stated in the conclusion section of several research articles.

Student 5

I entered the doctoral program having completed several research projects, including a master's thesis, and having a few years of experience as a counselor. My background in research, as well as my understanding of the professional counseling literature, was solid, in my opinion. My goal was to complete the doctorate in a reasonable time period and pursue a position as a counselor educator. The direction I took to explore potential research topics was a thorough review of the literature, an assessment of my previous research endeavors to see if related studies were possible, attendance at conferences to keep up to date on "hot topics," a review of dissertations previously completed in the department, and lengthy discussions with peers who either had or were completing their dissertation. I decided on a topic that was modeled after a dissertation completed by a friend who recently graduated from the same department. The study was manageable and feasible, particularly from a time perspective since data could be collected and the study [could be] completed in less than a year or possibly a semester. The predictive study used a sample of freshman from classes at the university. Unfortunately, I had not been able to spend much time with my chair to discuss the study and had met with committee members only briefly. My chair raised some question when I set up a proposal meeting, but I was persistent and was allowed to present my proposal. The proposal meeting was uneventful, with committee members asking the expected questions related to research design, data analysis, and contributions to the literature. When asked to leave the meeting, I was calm but felt things were not quite right. When asked to return to the meeting and told that my proposal was not accepted, I was not surprised. Sage feedback was provided by my chair and committee members on their expectations of a doctoral study, blue-ribbon experimental research designs, and the importance of original investigations. I was provided information as to why my proposal did not reach an expected standard. It was recommended that I go back to the drawing board and conduct a more comprehensive review of the literature in order to identify an acceptable topic. It was also strongly suggested that I regularly meet and share progress being made and ideas with my chair and committee members. This last suggestion hit home as I realized I had done everything expected of someone searching for a dissertation topic, except communicate and discuss ideas with my chair and committee. This was my mistake and my fault. It taught me a good lesson. In looking back, it was the best thing that could have happened to me as a doctoral candidate during this time of my early career. Afterward I did spend a lot of time reading and working closely with my chair and full committee. The result, I am glad to say, was a solid dissertation subsequently published in a refereed journal.

These two cases demonstrate factors involved in selecting a topic to study. Student 4 entered the doctoral program with a clear idea of a population that he wanted to study, based on prior experiences. A review of the literature helped this student formulate a treatment plan. We will discuss the components of a literature review further in Chapter 5. This student eventually completed a quality dissertation by using previous professional experience, conducting a thorough literature review, and working hand in hand with the dissertation chair. (And by the way, the student's study was published in the ACA flagship journal, *Journal of Counseling & Development.*)

Student 5 entered the doctoral program with experience as a counselor and researcher. As the result of completing a master's thesis, she was familiar with many of the nuances of the dissertation process, including the proposal. This student carefully followed all of the guidelines suggested when searching for a dissertation topic. However, because the student wanted to complete the dissertation in a hurry, she failed to sufficiently interact with the dissertation chair and committee. The student subsequently recognized that mistake and realized that interacting with the chair and committee should have been a priority. But all's well that ends well, because the student produced a quality dissertation, with the findings published in a top-tier journal.

Self-Assessment Inventory

Your success in completing a dissertation begins with selecting a feasible topic. Several factors affect the topic you select. Personal/social factors and your knowledge about research, the counseling profession, and counselor education will influence the choice of your dissertation topic. It would be wise to be aware of these factors because they could also play a role in whether you complete a dissertation (see Figure 3.2). These factors relate to your readiness to start a dissertation and ultimately might determine your future as a PhD or an "all but dissertation" (ABD).

Personal/Social Factors

Personal/social factors likely to influence your progress include

- motivation (your reason for seeking the doctorate),
- time (the amount of time you have available and the amount of time you are willing to devote to your dissertation),
- stressors (e.g., finances, a full- or part-time job, legal issues, professional issues),
- relationships (e.g., spouse, children, parents, friends and peers), and
- support systems (e.g., family, friends, community, other doctoral students).

When students first approach a dissertation, we often hear, "I just want to finish!" Perhaps this reflects a lack of investment in selecting a dissertation topic. If true, there could be several reasons for this state of mind, including a lack of motivation, burnout, mounting finances, time pressure, or just pure exhaustion. The most alarming of these reasons is the lack of motivation, the internal driving force to complete the project that is necessary to ultimately graduate. Therefore, it could be important to check this out by assessing your desire to finish your degree before beginning the dissertation process.

The timing of beginning a dissertation is crucial because you will have just completed rigorous course work, practicum and internships, and a doctoral comprehensive examination. It is understandable that you would be ready for a break. Perhaps even a short break will be necessary—however, we emphasize taking only a *short* break. Talking to peers will help normalize your thoughts during these times. In addition, it might be helpful to talk with faculty members, mentors, graduates of the program, and professionals in the field. Faculty members are especially adept at understanding what you are going through because they have all been through this experience. New faculty members, in particular, may empathize with you because they recently completed and defended their own dissertations. We believe it is important to reflect on positive outcomes associated with completing a dissertation, including graduating, being competitive for employment opportunities, and

The Self-Assessment Inventory provides a review of your readiness to pursue a scholarly project such as writing a dissertation proposal and beginning the dissertation process. Using the following scale, rate yourself on the factors, total your scores, reflect on your readiness, and decide what you need to do to get ready.

Self-Rating Scale

1 = *I am not ready.*
2 = *I have a lot to do to get ready.*
3 = *I have a few things to do to get ready.*
4 = *I am ready.*
5 = *I am really ready.*

Factors	Self-Rating
1. Motivational level	
2. Knowledge searching a research topic	
3. Experience in conducting a literature review	
4. Extent of reading and critiquing journal articles	
5. Knowledge of "hot topics" in counseling	
6. Overall research experience	
7. Thesis experience	
8. Work on research projects or papers	
9. Discussing counseling topics with faculty	
10. Discussing counseling topics with students	
11. Discussing counseling topics with experts in the field	
12. Attending professional conferences	
13. Presenting at professional conferences	
14. Networking with other professionals	
15. Using dissertation abstracts	
16. Using research search engines	
17. Using EBSCOhost	
18. Using ERIC	
19. Using PsycLIT	
20. Using ProQuest	
21. Using PsycINFO	
22. Reading other dissertations	
23. Reading other dissertation proposals	
24. Energy	
25. Thoughts about the upcoming project	

Total Score _____

Scoring

112–125	Really ready
100–111	Ready
87–99	Need to do some work
75–86	Start getting ready
Under 75	You are not ready

Figure 3.2
The Self-Assessment Inventory

experiencing exciting life changes. Other compelling reasons for completing your dissertation include self-fulfillment, gaining expertise in a specific topic, understanding research, and contributing to the profession. Your motivation, the internal driving force for taking action, will determine the amount of effort you will put toward exploring dissertation topics, deciding on a dissertation topic, completing your study, and graduating. Therefore, we strongly recommend taking a personal inventory of your motivational level. It may also be helpful to write a list of your personal assets and gains that can take place as the result of completing your doctorate. Reviewing this list can be emboldening, particularly when your motivation begins to wane and challenges arise.

In addition to your motivational level, the time you have available and are willing to devote to reading and reviewing the literature will determine whether, when, and if you are able to arrive at a feasible topic. We believe it is necessary that you set aside generous amounts of time for researching, analyzing, and discussing several potential dissertation topics. Your search for a feasible dissertation topic needs to be a high priority. A strong will, determined attitude, and endless persistence will help you keep time commitments. Your success will be enhanced by your flexibility and resilience. These characteristics are especially important if you have a job prospect that requires you to graduate by a certain date or you are an international student with a limited number of years to complete your degree.

Your personal life stressors can influence whether you are able to select a dissertation topic and determine whether you will graduate. Stress-related factors are some of the reasons why only 50% of students entering a PhD program go on to obtain their doctorates, with the vast majority of students dropping out before the dissertation stage (Lovitts, 2001; R. L. Smith, Maroney, Nelson, Abel, & Abel, 2006). Stress-related factors include finances, full- or part-time employment, and school-related stressors. Most doctoral students admit to being stressed when starting a dissertation. If you completed a master's or educational specialist degree requiring a thesis, then you may experience less stress because of your familiarity with the process. The stressors of finances, work, and family, however, are constant among students, with intensity varying according to individual circumstances. We recommend completing an inventory of life stressors before selecting a dissertation topic (see Figure 3.3). Suggestions for taking care of yourself and mediating your stress levels are covered in Chapter 2 of this book.

Relationships, including those with other doctoral students, could play a role when selecting a dissertation topic. With other doctoral students, we suggest that you emphasize collaboration rather than making it a competition on who can be the first to identify a feasible topic. However, there are times when the competitive nature of peers might surface. Getting your dissertation approved, setting a proposal date, gaining IRB approval, completing the first three chapters, and setting your dissertation defense date are events in which students often compete with each other. It is the responsibility of

The Life Stress Scale inventories stress in 12 areas. Please complete the brief self-rating of your stress level of each stressor by checking (√) if the life stressor is major, a good amount, somewhat an issue, or very little. Use your ratings to reflect on what you might do to minimize or better cope with the stressors.

Points Scale

4 = *Major*
3 = *A good amount*
2 = *Some*
1 = *Very little*

Life Stressor	4 Points	3 Points	2 Points	1 Point
School				
Family				
Peers				
Social groups				
Finances				
Work				
Physical health				
Relatives				
Legal				
Worry				
Anxiety				
Mental health				

Subtotal _____   _____   _____   _____

(number of checks per column x points per column)

Total Score _____
(add the four column subtotals)

Scoring

42 or more   High stress
30–41   Medium stress
24–29   Low stress
12–23   Very low stress

Figure 3.3
Life Stress Scale

the department chair and faculty to create a collaborative culture, perhaps by having students work in small groups or using a doctoral cohort system.

The following advice has been passed on to doctoral students in a number of CES programs: While working on your dissertation, it is not a good time to start a relationship, end a relationship, get married, get a divorce, or start a family. Despite well-intentioned advice, we have seen students marry, remarry, divorce, start a family, break up with their significant other, get back together with their significant other, adopt children, take in family members, take pets into their family, foster dogs and cats, sell homes, buy homes, build homes, and experience heart-breaking loss. We stand amazed at the resilience and coping skills of the students who make it through a wide range of challenges, find a great dissertation topic, stick with it, and graduate. We still believe it helps to inventory your stressors before starting the dissertation process to gain an awareness of your current life challenges.

Family and friends can affect your ability to stay on task and ultimately complete a dissertation. We have seen incredible families that are involved and supportive of students. A number of families also let the students do their own thing, with minimal contact, but remain supportive. For most students, the immediate family is the primary source of support, with individual family members making sacrifices along the way. A family member might assume greater responsibility for raising children, caring for an aging parent, or handling household responsibilities so the student can focus on completing the dissertation. Talking with your family about the time needed to complete a dissertation can help prepare them and you for this journey. Family history, culture, belief system, religion, gender, employment, education, and genealogy are factors that can influence how well you and your family handle this stressful time. Friends, community support groups, church and other spiritual venues, social clubs, and community health and exercise centers also might play a supportive role during this time. It could be helpful to inventory your support system before starting this journey.

Knowledge

Knowledge is increased by education and life experiences. Some important areas of knowledge in your discipline include research, counseling, the counseling profession, and counselor education. Knowledge subtopics include

- knowledge of the literature,
- research expertise,
- conference participation,
- dissertation abstracts and proposals,
- IRB protocol, and
- research ethics.

We recommend that you assess your knowledge of the extant counseling literature and related behavioral sciences (e.g., psychology, social work, family therapy). Effectively reviewing the literature necessitates a familiarity with counseling and related professional journals. You are expected to have sufficient knowledge that goes beyond providing annotated bibliographies or a listing of journals and counseling texts. We recommend that you take an inventory of the literature reviews, article critiques, and studies that you have participated in during the past 2 years.

Assessing your research expertise involves reviewing the research courses you have completed and assessing the amount of knowledge retained. When assessing your research competence, you might also think about the past research courses and research texts that you have read. You should also consider the types of research designs and analytic procedures in which you have experience.

Most CES programs encourage students to participate in professional conferences as a strategy for gaining information on current research investigations, particularly areas considered "hot topics" in the counseling profession. In addition, conferences provide the opportunity to network with peers and seasoned researchers. If you have not taken advantage of these opportunities, you may be at a disadvantage when exploring the landscape of dissertation topics.

We recommend that you read several completed dissertations and dissertation proposals. We also recommend that you search the Dissertation Abstracts database available through your university's digital library portal, read dissertations and proposals completed in your department, and talk with faculty about how to obtain resources.

If not already covered in one of your research courses, you should become familiar with the purpose and policies of your university's IRB. It is also beneficial for you to seek access to completed IRB proposals to help you when writing your own IRB (see Chapter 7). You might ask your chair or committee members for examples of completed IRB proposals from the department. If you are fortunate to have a chair or committee member who is on the university IRB committee, please discuss your proposal with that faculty member. IRBs outline research ethics and generally require students to complete workshops or training in research ethics before submitting a proposal. In addition, we also recommend familiarity with the *ACA Code of Ethics* (ACA, 2014), paying close attention to the section on research ethics (Section G). The majority of doctoral students in the counseling profession will complete dissertations requiring access to human participants. Therefore, it is important to become familiar with the IRB on your campus.

Guidelines for Selecting a Dissertation Topic

How you will eventually decide on a dissertation topic will depend on your personal interests and experiences, your dissertation chair and committee, institutional policies and procedures, your initial ideas, and your projected timetable for graduation. During the dissertation topic selection process, we recommend that you review and consider assessing your knowledge about possible topics, the need for a study related to these topics, and the support for exploring topics.

Support From the Professional Literature

A complaint heard from some professors is that doctoral students are not reading enough. We recommend an extensive review of the literature, including journals (paper and electronic), books, dissertations, newsletters, conference proceedings, and government publications. Some doctoral students, when initiating a discussion of their dissertation topic, have stated, "Nobody has ever studied this before." We strongly recommend you avoid making this claim unless you have thoroughly reviewed the literature, including research published within and outside of the counseling field. By making a claim of originality, you might be waving a red flag to your chair, who will forever after question how, what, where, and whether you have conducted a thorough search.

Dissertation topics should have the support of the professional literature, including research findings in peer-reviewed journals. A good place to begin searching for a topic is to review professional journal articles and pay close attention to recommendations for future studies found at the conclusion of these articles.

Support From Your Dissertation Chair

Your dissertation chair is the single most important person who will guide you through your dissertation. Your chair will decide whether your dissertation topic is feasible and when your proposal is ready for your committee to review. You should meet with your dissertation chair early and often during your search for a topic. Your chair will provide advice on potential topics as well as how to conduct your search. You and your chair will brainstorm topics, eliminating those that are not feasible. Support from the professional literature and your dissertation chair are the two most important factors to keep in mind when searching for a dissertation topic.

Knowledge of the Topic

It makes good sense that you should have in-depth knowledge of the topics you consider as strong candidates for your dissertation. Your dissertation chair will expect you to demonstrate at least a moderate level of knowledge of these topics. Do not bring a topic to your chair that you have not researched or carefully examined.

Sustained Interest in the Topic

Students who enter the doctoral program with a dissertation topic often have a passion for that topic. If you are one of these students, then you need to ask yourself, "Am I interested in this topic enough to carry me through my dissertation?" Even if you select your topic during your 1st or 2nd year of the doctoral program, you will still need to assess how passionate you are about the topic. Whether you came to your program with a topic in mind or developed a specialized interest while in your program, you should discuss with your chair whether you have a sustaining interest in the topic.

Need for the Study

A comprehensive review of the literature will help you address the need for your study and provide citations to support your proposal. If you have dif-

"*Acceptance*" *Term Therapy*

ficulty stating a need for your study, continue to review published research articles in peer-reviewed journals and seek out textbook citations, conference presentation abstracts, and references by other researchers.

Contributions to the Profession/Society

Most doctoral students would like their dissertations to be something more than another hoop to jump through on their way to a doctorate. However, we caution you against being too grandiose. We encourage you to select a topic that will contribute, even in a small way, to the profession and society. Broad topics considered as grandiose can be narrowed down to feasible studies and still contribute. Perhaps your dissertation will be the beginning of a research agenda, which will allow you to contribute to the profession throughout your career.

We encourage you to review the example provided by Student 6 later in this chapter. If this student's general topic of interest (evidence-based treatments for all addictions) were possible, it would certainly contribute to the profession and society. As the student narrowed down the topic, the level of contribution seemed to lessen. Boundaries were tightened and the scope of the study became more limited. Ultimately, however, this student's study does contribute to a specific population of adolescents treated for alcohol use disorder.

Narrowing Down a Dissertation Topic

The process of narrowing down a dissertation topic can be one of the doctoral students' most frustrating experiences. However, it is one of the most important tasks during this journey. By not identifying a workable dissertation topic, you remain at a standstill and perhaps even are in danger of leaving the program. However, after narrowing down your topic to create a workable study, you increase your chances of completing a dissertation and ultimately the doctorate. The guidelines that follow are intended to help you secure a workable dissertation. If you are persistent and work closely with your dissertation chair, you can benefit from the use of these guidelines.

Limiting the Scope

The scope of a study refers to its breadth or range. Beginning doctoral students will often select a topic that is too broad and would take decades to complete. Topics with a broad scope (e.g., reducing substance abuse; increasing functional levels of young children with autism spectrum disorder; or increasing the number of graduates in science, technology, engineering, and mathematics [STEM] programs in the United States) involve years or even decades of research, and they often require government funding. The nature of the dissertation itself requires students to limit their scope. To help students determine the appropriate scope of a dissertation, Heppner and Heppner (2004) suggested that the dissertation represent a substantial amount of work and make a significant, publishable contribution to the literature or profession. When limiting the scope of your study, consider the availability of your sample, time needed to collect and analyze data, availability of needed resources, and variables you intend to assess. The process of narrowing down a study begins by considering your sample, research questions, and variables.

The Sample

Researchers often say, "No sample, no study." In our experience, students dislike this phrase because it usually means starting over, selecting a different research design, or modifying a topic. To avoid this, the student and dissertation chair can either explore another sample or modify the design of the study and thereby keep the same topic. For example, a dissertation that explores STEM programs across the United States would obviously include a sample size beyond the scope of a doctoral dissertation. Remember, your ultimate goal is to graduate. When narrowing down this topic, you would first limit it to one state and perhaps a select number of universities in that state. You might find that you can gather data from three universities who have students matriculating in STEM programs. The question that you will need to answer next is, "What do I want to find out about these students?"

Research Questions and Variables

Research questions help identify what it is you want to learn as the result of conducting this study. The research questions drive your dissertation and provide your chair and committee members with a clear picture and direction of the study. The variables investigated are included in your research questions. Your research questions further narrow your study by specifically stating what you want to find out about a phenomenon or sample. Your research questions and variables studied help you decide on a research design.

Research Design

Research questions help hone in on a research design. For example, if your research questions focus on the differences between students enrolled as STEM majors and non-STEM majors, you would use a quantitative design. You would also use a quantitative research design if you wanted to know whether relationships exist between STEM students' emotional intelligence, achievement motivation, and classroom performance. However, if you wanted to learn more about the experiences of STEM students, you would use a qualitative design. In this study, you would explore the lived experiences of STEM students. Your sample would be smaller, and you would gather data through individual interviews, focus groups, journaling, or observations. The questions you ask and the variables you are studying will determine your research methodology. You might also ask questions that necessitate a mixed-methods design, combining quantitative and qualitative research paradigms. Your dissertation chair and committee members will help you decide on a methodology that will address your research questions.

Time Considerations

Time considerations include the length of time needed to complete your proposal. You should consider the time needed to meet with the committee, gain approval of committee members, obtain IRB approval, gather qualitative or quantitative data, analyze data, report findings, and draw conclusions. Some students complete a dissertation in 1–2 years, whereas others take 3–4 years or more to finish. Your ability to manage time, willingness to stay on task, and tenacity level will determine how long it will take to complete your dissertation. In some cases, time constraints will be a factor in deciding on the design of your study. If you plan to conduct a longitudinal study following STEM students after graduation, your study will take several years to complete, so this would not be a good choice for a dissertation.

Feasibility of the Study

Narrowing down your study will determine its feasibility. A good question to ask is, "Will I be able to complete this study for my dissertation, considering time, resources, cost, and support?" We recommend having multiple conversations with your dissertation chair, committee members, and support groups to determine whether your study is feasible. By carefully narrowing down your topic and limiting the scope of your study, there is a strong possibility that your dissertation will end up being doable. Determining the feasibility of your study necessitates setting aside ample time, meeting regularly with your chair, gaining sample assurance, being able to measure variables, managing costs, and having the skills and resources to complete your investigation.

Example of Narrowing Down a Dissertation Topic

An example of a student and chair working together to narrow down a dissertation topic is presented in the following paragraphs. In this example, the student and chair work together to carve out a feasible dissertation topic. This example addresses the scope of the study, sample, research questions, variables under investigation, and research design.

Starting With a Broad Topic

At first, Student 6 wanted to research a broad dissertation topic:

> I am interested in examining effective treatment modalities for substance and process addictions. I would like to identify evidence-based models that can be utilized with individuals experiencing addictions. My premise is that all addictions follow a similar process, defined by a common set of symptoms and criteria. After identifying an effective treatment modality, I will recommend that professionals working with addictions infuse this model based upon my findings. These findings will be applicable to practitioners, thus contributing to research that focuses on alleviating addictions that are costly to society and harmful to families and the community. My topic is "A Treatment for Addictions."

The topic identified by this student, although highly relevant, starts out very general and will require the student and chair working together to narrow its scope. The student is passionate about contributing to a worldwide social problem. However, as it currently stands, the scope of this project is akin to investigating a cure for cancer.

Narrowing Down the Topic

The first step in managing this broad topic is pruning the **scope of the study**. By limiting the scope, the student and chair attempt to identify a niche within the topic that can be successfully researched considering time and other constraints of a doctoral dissertation. First, the student must address and clearly define the phenomenon of interest. It is obvious that the student will not be able to study all addictions because such a Herculean project is not plausible. The pruning process involves identifying and deciding what category of addictions (i.e., substance or process) will be the focus of the study. Once the student and chair make this decision, additional fine-tuning is needed because there are hundreds of substance and process addictions.

Next, the student and chair narrow the topic to substance addictions, with an emphasis on the study of alcohol. By completing this step, the student has **identified a general population,** individuals using alcohol, but not a **specific sample**. Therefore, the next step involves identifying **sample specifics**. The student will clarify sample demographics, such as age, gender, ethnicity, addiction status, degree of sobriety, and other related characteristics. Once a category of individuals targeted for the study has been identified (in this case, adolescents), the student and chair begin to state their **research questions**.

The student has identified adolescents with an alcohol addiction as the study sample, so the next step is to **delineate the sample**. At this stage, the student must provide concrete definitions related to the topic and the sample. The student must clearly define the general term *addiction*. The student may consider the term *substance misuse* for this study. However, the student uses the term *alcohol use disorder* because it is operationally defined by the *Diagnostic and Statistical Manual of Mental Disorders* (5th ed.; American Psychiatric Association, 2013).

The student now has identified a more specific sample to study. Throughout this process, the student and chair have discussed what the student wants to know about the sample or wants to do with the sample of adolescents experiencing a substance use disorder. The student's initial topic was finding or discovering an effective treatment for all addictions, and now the student has narrowed it to studying a treatment program for adolescents diagnosed with alcohol use disorder. The student's **research questions** will further clarify what he or she wants to find or discover. When writing research questions, the **variables** of the proposed study will need to be included. Variables will need to be clearly defined and measurable. Research questions will now guide the student in selecting a design most likely involving a treatment program.

Narrowing a broad topic to a feasible dissertation can be laborious. However, both the student and chair can experience a sense of satisfaction with their progress, along with a great sense of relief when a study seems possible. In this scenario, the student and chair moved toward an experimental design that included a treatment program for adolescents with alcohol use disorder. Of course, several specifics will still need to be ironed out, including defining the treatment program, selecting and measuring dependent variables, obtaining a control group, and deciding on a selection process for the sample.

Although this study fits with the student's research interests and is likely to be personally fulfilling, there could be obstacles in securing a large enough sample to conduct an experimental investigation. If the student is unable to secure a sufficient sample size, other avenues will need to be explored. For example, the student and chair could consider using a single-case or qualitative design with a smaller sample.

Summary

This chapter focused on two salient and exciting activities of the dissertation process. First, selecting a dissertation committee should be a thoughtful process beginning with choosing a chair and working jointly on selecting committee members. Several factors should be considered when selecting a committee. We provided suggestions on how to avoid (or at least successfully navigate) issues that might surface while working with your committee. Although we can provide sage advice, there are no guarantees that it will be a smooth ride, even if the roles of all participants are spelled out. Faculty members are busy and at times unavailable; they change university positions; and on occasion, they may disagree with each other or you. It is the chair's responsibility to iron out many of these issues and guide you through unanticipated changes in the committee makeup. You should be aware of university procedures if you change a committee member or chair, particularly in programs that assign students to an adviser upon acceptance into the doctoral program.

The process of deciding on and narrowing down a dissertation topic should be a joint activity involving your dissertation chair and committee members. Although your dissertation chair will be the key faculty member involved in this process, we also strongly recommend that you keep your committee members informed.

We stress the importance of completing a self-assessment inventory before searching for a dissertation topic. The purpose is to assess your readiness to embark upon the task of selecting a dissertation topic and putting together a dissertation proposal. During this process, you review your personal/social and knowledge factors.

Students who have been involved in the counseling profession, worked on prior research projects, presented at conferences, and collaborated with faculty have an experiential advantage when searching for a dissertation topic. Several students enter the doctoral program with research experience and a topic in mind. If this applies to you, we still recommend that you follow the suggestions presented on how to prune a broad topic to a feasible dissertation study. We provided guidelines in this chapter to help you search for a dissertation topic and narrow it down to a feasible study. Examples in this chapter are from students who have been through the process of selecting a committee, deciding on a research topic, and carving out a feasible study. We hope the suggested guidelines and examples provided will be helpful during your journey. Finally, be resilient, persevere, and remain confident in your chair, your committee, and your own abilities. We encourage you to be curious and enjoy the process!

Checklist

Committee Review

❏ Review department faculty web pages, examining their research publications and interests.
❏ Meet with faculty briefly to discuss general ideas of research interests.
❏ Talk with students working on their dissertations about their committee makeup.
❏ Review dissertations completed in the department, closely examining the committee makeup and faculty members who seem to work well together.

Narrowing Down the Topic

1. Select from one of the following topics:
   a. at-risk students,
   b. accreditation,
   c. multicultural competency,
   d. advocacy,
   e. evidence-based treatment, or
   f. couple and family counseling.
2. List the steps you would take to narrow down the topic you selected.
3. Reexamine the literature and dissertation abstracts to find studies associated with your topic.
4. Talk with your chair and committee members on how to make your topic into a feasible study for a dissertation.
5. Identify a sample for your study.
6. Identify variables to be examined in your study.
7. Develop a timeline for your study.

Additional Resources

Biggam, J. (2015). *Succeeding with your master's dissertation: A step-by-step handbook* (3rd ed.). Berkshire, England: Open University Press.

Graustein, J. S. (2013). *How to write an exceptional thesis or dissertation: A step-by-step guide from proposal to successful defense.* Ocala, FL: Atlantic Publishing Group.

Kringos, N. [TU Delft]. (2011, January 17). *Own your PhD project: How to take charge of your research* [Video file]. Retrieved from https://www.youtube.com/watch?v=q_rEqcO7hMY

Lani, J. [James Lani]. (2014, September 26). *Beginning your dissertation journey: Choosing your topic and selecting your committee* [Video file]. Retrieved from https://www.youtube.com/watch?v=YifW50Y7bQo

MyTake. (2016, March 19). *Tips for the PhD viva* [Video file]. Retrieved from https://www.youtube.com/watch?v=iH1LzFQl1Ms

Vithal, R., & Jansen, J. (2010). *Designing your first research proposal: A manual for researchers in education and the social sciences* (2nd ed.). Claremont, South Africa: Juta.

Chapter 4

Writing a Proposal

You are finally ready to write a proposal. You have completed part of this journey by selecting a dissertation topic, chair, and committee. This chapter guides you through the actual process of writing and completing a proposal so you can start the real work of conducting your study and completing the dissertation. First, you should check with your dissertation chair and committee faculty on their expectations and requirements of a proposal. You will find out that doctoral programs can vary in the format and style of dissertation proposals. In addition, your university's graduate office will have a lot to say about specifics related to style and format, such as margins, spacing, and pagination.

This chapter covers the three-chapter proposal and traditional proposal. Specific content areas within these proposals are examined. Research designs highlighted include quantitative, qualitative, mixed-methods, single-case, meta-analysis, and conceptual designs. Included within this chapter are full examples of quantitative and qualitative proposals.

Starting Out: Identifying What Constitutes a Proposal for Your Department

Now that you have selected your dissertation committee and narrowed down your topic, let's turn the focus toward writing your proposal. The first step you should take before writing your dissertation proposal is to determine what your chair, department, and institution expect in terms of style, format, and content. Your chair, department, and the institution typically follow similar dissertation proposal requirements in format and style. However, the structure of your dissertation proposal might vary from that of your peers enrolled in a similar program at another university. It is up to you to know, understand, and follow the format endorsed by your department. First, check with your chair about the style and format required for the proposal. Next, obtain copies of the doctoral handbooks published by your department and by the university's graduate office. These handbooks are usually available on the respective university websites.

Knowing and Understanding the Format Endorsed by Your Department and Institution

Your department probably requires one of the following style guides: the APA *Publication Manual* or *The Chicago Manual of Style*. The actual format of your proposal could vary because departments in CES use modifications of the traditional dissertation proposal. The style and format that you will use must be approved by the institution (i.e., the university's graduate office). You should not overlook the institutional requirements because mistakes in style and format could result in having the graduate office reject your request to propose or, worse, reject the proposal after it has been successfully presented to your committee. Guidelines for completing a dissertation proposal from a CES department handbook are provided in Table 4.1. The seven steps included in Table 4.1 can help guide you through the dissertation proposal process. This process begins with enrollment in a research seminar course designed to explore dissertation topics, develop a research proposal, and present the proposal to faculty members.

The graduate office at your university will also provide a handbook that more specifically states requirements related to the style and format of your dissertation and dissertation proposal. Examples of points emphasized within this handbook include

- margins,
- pagination,
- font,
- copyright procedures,
- page numbers,
- committee member page,
- copyright page,
- order of preliminary pages,
- spacing,
- abstract,
- acknowledgments,
- dedication,
- style, and
- submitting for publication.

The departmental handbook focuses on the content of the dissertation proposal and the completed dissertation, including the process involved for

Table 4.1
Example of a Department's Guidelines and
Formatting Recommendations for the Dissertation Proposal

Steps	Process
Step 1	
Enroll in a research seminar course.	Enroll in CNEP 6397 Research Seminar. A proposal for a research study is developed in the seminar. The student's research project should closely relate to a dissertation proposal and ultimately be presented to a doctoral committee.
Step 2	
Select a chair, doctoral committee, and topic.	Select your chair and committee. Select a topic for research closely aligned to counseling and counselor education.
Step 3	
Complete the Human Subjects Protection forms for the institutional review board.	If the intended research involves human subjects, the student must submit an application to the institutional review board.
Step 4	
Complete the dissertation proposal.	Secure a copy of the doctoral handbook from the College of Graduate Studies. Complete the proposal using the College of Graduate Studies guidelines for format and style and the departmental guidelines for content.
Step 5	
Schedule your proposal meeting.	Reserve a time for the proposal meeting with the department secretary (in consultation with committee members).
Step 6	
File proposal presentation with the College of Graduate Studies.	Once approval to present the written proposal is granted from the student's doctoral committee, permission to propose must be obtained from the College of Graduate Studies.
Step 7	
Distribute copies of proposal.	At least 2 weeks before the proposal meeting, the student distributes copies to all committee members and the College of Graduate Studies for distribution to its faculty representative. Questions or concerns from faculty are sent to the dissertation chair and student before the scheduled proposal meeting.
	All committee members and the College of Graduate Studies faculty representative are required to be present. The proposal presentation usually lasts approximately 1.5 hours. The procedure may vary, but a standard format includes introductions, introductory remarks by the student regarding the area of study, and an explanation of the proposed study. During the proposal, any faculty member may ask for clarifications and offer suggestions regarding the proposed study. At the conclusion of the proposal meeting, the student leaves the room, allowing the chair and committee members time to discuss the presentation and proposal. The student returns and is informed of the doctoral committee's recommendation(s) regarding the proposed study.

graduating. The format and style for dissertations and dissertation proposals set by the graduate office are provided to all doctoral programs throughout the university. The importance of becoming familiar with both departmental and institutional requirements related to your proposal and dissertation cannot be overemphasized.

Reviewing Similar Dissertations

Your chair and committee members might suggest that you review dissertations that have already been completed in the department. Reviewing department dissertations is an excellent idea because it will help you further understand what is expected of a proposal and dissertation specific to your department. Although completed dissertations will give you an example of what to expect, be careful not to repeat errors in formatting or style that might have slipped by the doctoral committee or graduate office. In addition, requirements may have changed, so make sure you are using the most recently published standards. When reviewing dissertations completed in your department, you might find studies that have focused on some of your interest areas, used methods appropriate for your study, and examined variables that catch your attention. Continue your search by reviewing the Dissertation Abstracts database, which you can access through your institution's online library portal.

The Dissertation Proposal Format: Traditional and Three-Chapter Proposals

CES departments might have more than one proposal format for you to consider. Two of the most widely used formats for writing a dissertation proposal are the traditional proposal format, which includes content related to the five chapters of a dissertation, and the three-chapter format, which emphasizes the first three chapters of a complete dissertation. Table 4.2 outlines what is included in a traditional dissertation proposal for a study using a quantitative paradigm; many CES doctoral programs follow this outline, with minor differences in the order of sections presented. CES doctoral programs can also use a three-chapter proposal format (see Table 4.2). The three-chapter proposal is longer and more detailed then the traditional proposal. However, when completed, it serves as the first three chapters of your dissertation. The three-chapter proposal includes the introduction to the study, the literature review, and the methodology (Joyner et al., 2013, p. 134).

It is important to be aware of your dissertation committee's format preferences for a dissertation proposal. If you and your committee decide to use a three-chapter proposal format, you will need to allow more time upfront to complete your proposal. However, once your committee accepts the proposal, you will have completed the first three chapters of your dissertation, which will allow time to concentrate on Chapters 4 and 5. Both the traditional

Table 4.2
Dissertation Proposal Formats

Traditional Proposal	Three-Chapter Proposal
Example quantitative study	
Introduction	Introduction
Problem statement	
Purpose statement	
Theoretical foundations	
Research questions	
Significance of the study	
Method	Literature review
Design	
Population and samples	
Instrumentation	
Data collection and analysis	
Basic assumptions	
Limitations	Method
Delimitations	
Definition of terms	

and three-chapter proposals include an introduction to the study, literature review, and the methodology of the study, with the three-chapter proposal consisting of full chapters that serve as the first chapters of the dissertation. Both proposals will often lead to a full five-chapter dissertation.

Introduction

The introduction of your dissertation proposal should be crafted in a manner that will attract the readers' interest. You are setting the stage for your study in the first several sentences. By using eye-catching lead sentences, you effectively build to your problem statement. In the introduction, you include citations and numerical data that support your study and emphasize the problem being addressed. However, be careful not to overwhelm readers with a long list of citations that distract from the content of your proposal. Creswell (2014) suggested following a deficiencies model when writing the introduction section. The deficiencies model includes studies that have attempted to address the problem, followed by deficiencies of previous research published on your topic. A concisely written problem statement, purpose statement, and significance of the study complete a major portion of your introduction. The introduction sections for traditional and three-chapter proposals follow similar formats. The introduction for a three-chapter proposal, however, is lengthier, consisting of three to four times the number of pages as compared with a traditional proposal.

Literature Review

Many dissertation proposals include a four- or five-page literature review in the introduction, which is often parceled under subheadings such as background of the study, significance of the study, and theoretical perspective. In the three-chapter proposal, the literature review is a chapter by itself and is equal in length to the second chapter of your dissertation, consisting of 30–40 pages, depending on the topic.

The literature review in the second chapter of a three-chapter dissertation proposal and the second chapter of your dissertation should include cited research and a discussion of findings that address the broad topic of your study. Cited research should include samples, designs, research questions, and variables germane to your investigation. Figure 4.1 illustrates how an inverted pyramid approach can help organize the second chapter of your proposal and dissertation. Studies included in the lower section of the inverted pyramid of Figure 4.1 will include research more specific to your study. The published articles reported in this section include recommendations for further research that could support your proposed study. (See Chapter 5 of this book for more detailed information on a literature review.)

Figure 4.1 uses addictions as an example of a broad topic. The literature review in this example begins with the inclusion of research findings on addictions. Research articles, statistics cited from government publications, and textbook information are included in this section. Because of the broad scope of this first section, it is important that you set boundaries on the

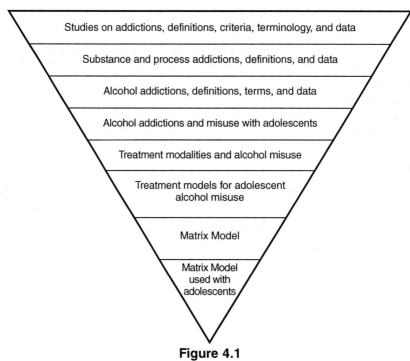

Figure 4.1
The Inverted Pyramid: Literature Review

number of studies you will include and the landscape of subject material you plan to cover. Be careful not to further extend your topic by including peripheral material not relevant to your study. Setting page limits and working from an outline will help organize your literature review. In the example provided in Figure 4.1, the literature review begins with the broad topic of addictions and then narrows in scope by including research on (a) substance and process addictions, (b) alcohol addictions, (c) alcohol addictions and misuse with adolescents, (d) treatment modalities and alcohol misuse, (e) treatment models for adolescent alcohol misuse, (f) Matrix Model, and (g) Matrix Model used with adolescents.

Method

The traditional and three-chapter dissertation proposals include the methodology used in your study. The method chapter of the three-chapter proposal is Chapter 3 of your dissertation. Only minor revisions, such as changing from future to past tense, will be necessary. Subtopics included under methodology are the same for both dissertation proposals. We will discuss the method section more in Chapter 7 of this book.

Review of Proposal Options

If you are given the choice of using proposal options, you should examine the advantages and disadvantages of a traditional dissertation proposal and the three-chapter proposal format. Students in CES doctoral programs have used both proposal options. The traditional dissertation proposal format has been used for a long time. It includes all the segments of a dissertation, except for reporting and discussing research findings. The three-chapter option covers the same landscape, but in more detail. If you decide to use a traditional proposal format, you might be able to set a proposal date before your peers who use the three-chapter proposal format. The traditional option proposal serves as the first chapter of your dissertation, whereas the three-chapter proposal option serves as the first three chapters of your dissertation.

Check with your dissertation chair regarding proposal options approved by the department. If several proposal options are used, obtain copies of the different proposals, talk with students who have used the proposal options, and discuss with your chair what might be best for you. Several factors, such as the design of your study, can influence your decision on which proposal format to follow.

An adaptation of the three-chapter proposal is a prospectus, which includes the completion of a professional article that accounts for the last two chapters of your dissertation. Students using this format will present their article submitted for publication at the dissertation defense.

You should explore the different dissertation proposal options early in your academic career. We suggest that you explore the dissertation proposal options available in CES departments before applying to doctoral programs, when first starting your doctoral program, and when getting ready to work on your dissertation proposal. If you have options, choose a format and topic that will enhance your research and writing skills as well as your career.

Dissertation Proposal and Research Designs

Doctoral graduates from CES programs have used a wide range of research designs as part of their dissertations. Research designs selected in a study vary based on the topic, sample, research questions, dissertation committee suggestions, and your expertise with research paradigms and methods of data analysis. You should let your research topic and research questions inform the design of your study. Additional variables such as the availability of a sample, your chair's interest and expertise, and your own timeline for graduation are factors that can influence the research design you select. We discourage students from first selecting a research design and subsequently a topic that fits that paradigm. Our advice is to select your topic, decide what it is that you want to find out, and then decide which research methodology is best suited for your study. Table 4.3 includes the outline of dissertation proposals representing qualitative and mixed-methods research designs.

Proposing a Qualitative Research Study

Table 4.3 provides an outline for structuring a qualitative dissertation proposal. Several sections in this example are similar to those of a traditional proposal (see Table 4.2), with both designs including an introduction con-

Table 4.3

Qualitative and Mixed-Methods Dissertation Proposal Formats

Example Qualitative Format	Example Mixed-Methods Format
Introduction	Introduction
Problem statement	Problem statement
Purpose statement	Purpose statement
Research questions	Research questions (quantitative, qualitative)
Grand tour question	Significance of the study
Subquestions	Literature review
Significance of the study	
Population and sample	
Data collection	Method
Data analysis	Sequence of designs data collection
Trustworthiness	Data analysis
Limitations	Data reporting
Definition of terms	Limitations
	Definition of terms
	Validity checking
	Measures
	Trustworthiness
	Member checking

sisting of a problem statement, purpose statement, and research questions. The procedures sections include data collection and data analysis. Unlike quantitative designs, however, qualitative research proposals include trustworthiness in addition to the role of the researcher, strategies for bracketing the researcher's experiences, and an appendix with several documents (e.g., interview questions, journal prompts, observation forms; Creswell, 2014).

Qualitative dissertations require a high level of creativity and thoughtful writing. The nuances of a qualitative study include the researcher's passion for the subject matter, with a section discussing personal bias and experiences. Qualitative research is time consuming and requires flexibility because changes often occur during the process of the investigation.

Proposing a Quantitative Research Study

Quantitative dissertation proposals follow a structure found in many of the behavioral science journals. Quantitative proposals emphasize the study's methodology and rules of scientific inquiry. Quantitative data consist of numbers that determine significant relationships or differences. If you like to work with numbers and are not easily discouraged by complicated statistical analyses, a quantitative research study is worth exploring. You will use computer software to analyze your data. Your chair and committee members will guide you through your data analyses.

Research questions, hypotheses, and variables are concepts emphasized in quantitative research. Your research questions need to be clearly stated, and your variables need to be measurable. It is important that you are specific on how you define and assess variables in your study. For example, if you are studying emotional intelligence, achievement motivation, and resilience, you should clearly articulate the meaning of each concept and how they are measured. Your dissertation proposal will vary slightly depending on whether you use an experimental or quasi-experimental design, determined by the possibility of random selection and on the ability to use a control group. In survey studies, you will collect data and analyze levels of correlation and degrees of predictability. Experimental and survey research should be well designed and include a theoretical perspective.

Proposing a Mixed-Methods Research Study

If you plan to use a mixed-methods research design, you are likely to develop a more comprehensive dissertation proposal because you will be working with both quantitative and qualitative research paradigms. Creswell (2014) emphasized the importance of a solid working relationship between the quantitative and qualitative research procedures in mixed-methods designs that begins with your introduction and continues throughout the data-gathering process, data analysis, reporting of findings, and discussions of implications. You should be able to provide a rationale for the sequencing of designs used in mixed-methods investigations. For example, in a mixed-methods study, Abel, Abel, and Smith (2012) researched the effects of a stress management program and further examined the attributions of participants who decreased their stress levels during treatment; the sequence they used was an experimental study (Phase 1), followed by a qualitative investigation (Phase 2) involving in-depth interviews with participants.

Several mixed-methods studies use a qualitative design for Phase 1. For example, consider a researcher who has created a new method of teaching Spanish that has proven to accelerate language learning among high school students. The researcher wants to see if the method will work with elementary school students but is not sure if they will be able to grasp the concepts. A qualitative design allows the researcher to implement this method with a small group of elementary-age students. In-depth data help determine if they understood the concepts. The qualitative phase also helps the researcher revise treatment before proceeding with an experimental investigation in Phase 2.

Table 4.3 provides an outline of a dissertation proposal using a mixed-methods design. Quantitative and qualitative designs include research questions, sampling procedures, data collection procedures, data analysis methods, and methods of discussing findings. In addition, a literature review is found in both qualitative and quantitative studies. When considering a mixed-methods study, it is important to assess your skills in both quantitative and qualitative research designs as well as your timeline for graduation.

Additional Research Designs and Example Dissertation Proposal Outlines

Students in CES doctoral programs have used a number of research designs. Work closely with your chair and committee members when deciding on what design you plan to use for your dissertation. In the following paragraphs, we discuss three additional designs: single-case research design, meta-analysis, and conceptual research design.

Single-Case Research Design

Single-case research designs in CES doctoral dissertations meet the criteria for a rigorous research methodology. The benefit of a single-case design is its ability to analyze data over time using a small sample. Data collection involves a series of phases, with participants being their own control group. The design uses quantitative and qualitative research questions, quantitative and qualitative data, and analysis appropriate for both data sets. The dissertation proposal is similar to a traditional proposal (see Table 4.2), with the exception of the methodology and results sections. An example of a dissertation proposal using a single-case research design follows:

1. Introduction
   a. Problem statement
   b. Purpose statement
2. Literature review
3. Method
   a. Single-case research design
   b. Phases of intervention
   c. Independent variable(s)
   d. Dependent variable(s)
   e. Measurements
   f. Data analysis

Students proposing a dissertation using a single-case research design should have a background in this methodology and be able to explain the procedures used during their dissertation defense.

Meta-Analysis

Meta-analysis is a method involving research synthesis. This design meticulously reviews primary research on a topic to integrate findings. A predetermined criterion determines the inclusion of studies. Emphasis is on consistency among research studies, including measures used, treatment protocol, and variables. Components of a meta-analysis dissertation proposal are included in the following two outlines. The first example outline includes

1. Introduction
   a. Problem statement
   b. Literature review of comparable meta-analyses
2. Conceptual framework
   a. Predictors
   b. Criteria
   c. Theoretical relationships among constructs, predictors, and criteria
3. Method
   a. Study retrieval
   b. Statistical methods
   c. Interpretation of results
   d. Hypothesis

A second example of a proposal using meta-analysis is as follows:

1. Introduction
   a. Problem statement
   b. Purpose statement
2. Method

a. Inclusion criteria
b. Literature review
c. Study coding
d. Data selection and extraction
e. Effect size calculation
f. Data aggregation procedures
g. Retrieval procedures

Conceptual Research Design: Theory Development

Conceptual research focuses on a set of concepts attempting to explain or describe a particular phenomenon. Research starts with the expression of a broad concept that the researcher has devoted a considerable amount of time thinking about, with the result being hunches and hypotheses. Theories produced using a conceptual research process are subsequently investigated using empirical studies. Because of its abstract nature, conceptual research proposals are less structured. The following proposal outline is used when combined with field research:

1. *Introduction*
   The researcher first discusses the problem at the broadest level (e.g., "What causes mental illness?"). The significance of the problem makes the case for why the topic is important and why people should care about the topic.
2. *Contextual Nature of the Study*
   The researcher places the problem in context. In the example of the cause of mental illness, the researcher would consider aspects of society, including family, friends, peers, work environment, religion, and other social systems.
3. *Literature Review*
   The literature review addresses the importance of the topic and discrepancies. Current theories are considered. Biological and chemical causes of mental illness would surface in this example.
4. *Method*
   The researcher often uses field research and relies on observational skills. The researcher thinks through what is known, observed, and written about the topic.
5. *Research Questions*
   After reading and contemplating about the topic, the researcher develops research questions. Additional ideas also surface through observation. Explanations and hypotheses are a response to the research questions.
6. *Development of Theory*
   The researcher develops and shares a theory as the result of reviewing the literature, observing, thinking about the concept, and responding to research questions. Theory, if possible, is tested with empirical studies.

The use of a conceptual research design for a dissertation proposal needs to fit with the dissertation preferences of the student and chair. Because of its abstract nature, it is important to set timelines when using this design.

Recommendations for Writing a Successful Proposal

As the wise adage goes, "By failing to prepare, you are preparing to fail." By careful planning, you have a good chance of overcoming obstacles and avoiding some of the common errors students make when writing their proposals. The proposal is your guiding document, and you refer to it throughout your dissertation. A weak or incomplete proposal will remain problematic throughout your study. Appendixes B and C include examples of quantitative and qualitative dissertation proposals from students who have successfully proposed and completed their dissertations. In the following sections, we provide 12 recommendations for writing a successful proposal, which emphasize planning ahead and avoiding common errors.

Outline Sections

The table of contents of your dissertation proposal outlines the major components of a dissertation. In this chapter, we presented the traditional and three-chapter dissertation proposal outlines. Each proposal includes several sections. Before writing, you should develop a working outline for each of the sections beginning with the headings (e.g., method), followed by the subheadings. Without an outline, you could drift off topic and lose valuable time. Be meticulous in your outline.

Set Parameters (Length and Scope)

When working on your dissertation proposal, you will set parameters for yourself and your study. Start by setting parameters related to the length and scope of your proposal. Chapter 3 of this book emphasized how to limit the scope of a topic. Consider this process to limit the scope of your proposal. After setting the number of pages for each section and the number of research studies involved in your literature review, you will begin to narrow the scope of your study. The average length of your proposal will range between 25 and 30 pages using a traditional format and between 65 and 70 pages using the three-chapter format.

Organize Resources and References

If you have a system of organizing resources and references that has worked for you in the past, please use it. However, realize that a dissertation covers more ground and includes a greater number of resources and references than papers required in your classes or your master's thesis. Thoughtful organization is the key to completing a dissertation proposal and the dissertation itself. This means first organizing yourself in terms of where and when you plan to work on your dissertation. Find a place that is comfortable and where you will not be disturbed. Chart out the times and days that you will work on your proposal and keep to a schedule. Your workplace should have few interruptions. Doctoral students have set up workstations in their garage, basement, shed, and even attic. Perhaps you have better options, and more than one. Having access to several workstations can be advantageous.

Being organized extends beyond time/space. Your organization of resources and references can affect the time you will spend working on your study. There are several software programs that will help you organize your resources. Find programs that are available at your university. Organize your references at the time you are citing them in your proposal. Do not wait to list references after completing the proposal because that can lead to frustration, loss of references, and lost time.

Use APA Style and Formatting

Your department, dissertation chair, library, and bookstore have copies of the latest edition of the APA *Publication Manual*. You will need to obtain a copy for yourself and become familiar with the style and formatting acceptable for professional writing. If your department uses a different style and formatting guide, such as *The Chicago Manual of Style*, be sure you have access to it. Using proper style and mechanics will save you significant amounts of time—and sanity—if you do it right the first time.

Follow Institutional Recommended Style and Formatting

In addition to the writing specifics set by professional organizations and your department, obtain copies of your institutional style and formatting handbook. The institution's handbook, produced by the graduate office, is usually available on their web page.

Use Available University Services

This is no time to be overly proud. Even the best writers have others proof their work. We strongly recommend that you use writing/editing services because they are often free or included as part of the university fees that you pay every semester.

Avoid Using Academically Inappropriate Sources

Keep your dissertation proposal at a professional level. The proposal is likely to be the first product your chair and committee members will review. Make a good first and lasting impression.

Remember to Proof Your Work

Read and reread your work before turning it in to your chair. The devil is in the details. It is often a small grammatical error that raises a red flag about your work.

Use Proper Grammar

Avoid run-on sentences and grammatical errors. It is recommended that you use short sentences.

Avoid Plagiarism

With so much information accessible on the Internet, plagiarism is a problem, particularly with the tendency to cut and paste and not reference. Remember that most departments have sophisticated anti-plagiarism software.

Successfully Address the Academic Challenge

There are certain times in your life when you will be challenged academically and professionally. Writing a dissertation is one of those times. However, remember that you have demonstrated unusual skill, tenacity, and perseverance to get this far. Use these same characteristics to address academic challenges presented during your dissertation.

Finally, Enjoy Yourself

You are poised to write a solid dissertation proposal. Your past success should provide all the confidence needed to complete this project. Because you have traversed this far and successfully handled stress along the way, it is time to enjoy the challenge and complete the journey.

Summary

This chapter initially covered housekeeping chores for you to follow, including knowing the dissertation proposal policies of your department and the university. These policies can easily be found on the respective web pages. We emphasized the importance of knowing the dissertation proposal format endorsed by the department. We discussed the advantages of the traditional and three-chapter dissertation proposal formats, and we covered the specific sections found within each dissertation proposal.

We also discussed qualitative, quantitative, and mixed-methods research designs, which are often used in dissertation studies, along with single-case, meta-analysis, and conceptual research designs. This chapter concluded with tips on writing a successful dissertation proposal, which emphasize the importance of planning and outlining your work. We provided examples of qualitative and quantitative dissertation proposals.

Checklist

❑ Check the department's recommended format and style for dissertation proposals. Does the department allow you to select one of the two formats discussed in this chapter?

❏ Obtain the doctoral program handbook from your department and from your graduate office. The handbooks should be available on the respective websites. Compare the information found in the handbooks, examining whether there are discrepancies.

❏ Use the inverted pyramid (see Figure 4.1) to narrow down your review of the literature, starting with your broad topic and including studies similar to your dissertation at the apex of the pyramid.

❏ Identify the research design(s) that could be used in your study. Discuss the designs with your dissertation chair and committee members.

❏ State your reason(s) for using a traditional dissertation proposal format and the three-chapter dissertation proposal format. Why use the traditional dissertation proposal format?

_____

_____

_____

_____

Why use the three-chapter dissertation proposal format?

_____

_____

_____

_____

❏ Briefly discuss/define the six research designs covered in this chapter.

Qualitative _____

Quantitative_____

Mixed methods _____

Single case _____

Meta-analysis _____

Conceptual _____

❏ Provide a self-assessment using the factors listed on the next page and plan for ways to move the factors marked as 1 (*could be better*) and 2 (*OK*) to ones marked as 3 (*good*) or 4 (*great*).

12 Self-Assessments

Rating scale: 4 = *great;* 3 = *good;* 2 = *OK;* 1 = *could be better*

Factors	Rating Scale			
1. Organizational skills	❏ 4	❏ 3	❏ 2	❏ 1
2. Grammar/writing	❏ 4	❏ 3	❏ 2	❏ 1
3. Literature search skills	❏ 4	❏ 3	❏ 2	❏ 1
4. Knowledge of research browsers	❏ 4	❏ 3	❏ 2	❏ 1
5. Knowledge of reference software (e.g., Zotero)	❏ 4	❏ 3	❏ 2	❏ 1
6. Use of dissertation abstracts	❏ 4	❏ 3	❏ 2	❏ 1
7. Knowledge of faculty expertise	❏ 4	❏ 3	❏ 2	❏ 1
8. Knowledge of dissertation proposal context	❏ 4	❏ 3	❏ 2	❏ 1
9. Knowledge of research designs	❏ 4	❏ 3	❏ 2	❏ 1
10. Assertiveness	❏ 4	❏ 3	❏ 2	❏ 1
11. Tenacity	❏ 4	❏ 3	❏ 2	❏ 1
12. Perseverance	❏ 4	❏ 3	❏ 2	❏ 1

Additional Resources

Flipp, C. [ChrisFlipp]. (2014, January 15). *Qualitative vs. quantitative* [Video file]. Retrieved from https://www.youtube.com/watch?v=2X-QSU6-hPU

Herr, K., & Anderson, G. L. (2015). *The action research dissertation: A guide for students and faculty* (2nd ed.). Thousand Oaks, CA: Sage.

Roberts, C. M. (2010). *The dissertation journey: A practical and comprehensive guide to planning, writing, and defending your dissertation* (2nd ed.). Thousand Oaks, CA: Corwin Press.

Scott, M.A. [M.A. Scott]. (2015, September 21). *Building the basic APA research proposal* [Video file]. Retrieved from https://www.youtube.com/watch?v=4QlcSJeII40

Smallwood, C. J. [Christopher Smallwood]. (2014, January 24). *A brief introduction to research designs: Quantitative, qualitative, and mixed methods* [Video file]. Retrieved from https://www.youtube.com/watch?v=XCUGlbQStRI

Appendix B

Example Quantitative Proposal

Herrero's (2014) quantitative dissertation proposal investigates the relationship among several strength-based factors that contribute to the academic success of college freshmen. Several specific research questions are included addressing the factors investigated.

Introduction

Every year millions of first-year college students eagerly begin their pursuit of a college degree in the hopes that it will lead them to desirable employment and successful lives. According to Snyder and Dillow (2013), enrollment for first-year college students "in all postsecondary degree-granting institutions increased by 39 percent from 1996 to 2010" (p. 24). There are a growing number of applicants wanting to enroll in college that makes the acceptance rate more competitive. Once in college, first-year students are met with complex challenges, which include personal and academic stressors. Making the transition from successfully completing high school to meeting expectations in college is difficult for first-year students. Many students manage to make the transition successfully, but others are not able to meet the demands of higher education. As a result, academic achievement eludes many first-year college students.

Conley (2007) defines college readiness as "the level of preparation a student needs in order to enroll and succeed—without remediation—in a credit-bearing general education course at a postsecondary institution that offers a baccalaureate degree or transfer to a baccalaureate program" (p. 5). Many first-year college students believe the mere fact they have been accepted by the institution implies they are college ready, possessing the skills and traits needed to successfully transition into college and achieve academic success. Upcraft, Gardner, and Barefoot (2005) provide a narrow definition of *first-year student success* ". . . (1) successful completion of courses taken in the first year and (2) continuing enrollment into the second year" (p. 8). Richardson, Abraham, and Bond (2012) state grade point average (GPA) is the most widely studied measure of undergraduate students' performance in college.

Tinto (2006) claims research findings on student retention supports efforts to promote student success. According to the National Center for Education Statistics (2010), the retention rates for first-time college freshmen returning in their second year varies from the highest rate of 84 percent in California to 63.3 percent in Alaska. With a retention rate of 73.3 percent, Texas ranks 33rd in student retention in the United States (NCES, 2010). The Planning and Institutional Research (PIR) Office at a regional public four-year university in South Texas reported a fall-to-fall retention rate of 57 percent for full-time, first-time bachelor's degree-seeking undergraduate students who entered the institution as freshmen in fall 2012. The institution's official fall 2012 enrollment for full-time, first-time bachelor's degree-seeking undergraduate students was 1,698 students, indicating an astounding 730 students did not return their sophomore year fall 2013.

A plethora of literature exists focusing on identifying factors that cause, predict, or contribute to student retention and attrition in college. The research established traditional academic factors such as high school grade point average (American College Testing [ACT], 2007; Atkinson & Geiser, 2009) and admissions test scores (ACT, 2007; Kobrin, Patterson, Shaw, Mattern, & Barbuti, 2008; Rothstein, 2004) as strong predictors of academic performance as measured by first year college grade point average. Many studies have attempted to identify nonacademic factors that bolster academic achievement among college students. According to the ACT (2007), nonacademic factors such as motivation, academic self-discipline, and self-regulation influence academic achievement. Other studies found hope (Snyder et al, 2002; Williams & Butler, 2010), emotional intelligence (Nelson & Nelson, 2003; Pritchard & Wilson, 2003; Sparkman, Maulding, & Roberts, 2012), academic self-efficacy (Chemers, Hu, & Garcia, 2001; Krumrei-Mancuso, Newton, Kim, & Wilcox, 2013), and optimism (Chemers, Hu, & Garcia, 2001) were predictive of first year grade point average, academic achievement, and retention.

A dearth of research has focused on the specific and unique strength-based factors of achievement motivation, hope, and resilience and how these three factors combine to predict academic success among first-year college students. Achievement motivation is defined as "the need to perform well or the striving for success, evidenced by persistence and effort in the face of difficulties" (McClelland, 1961, p. 36). Hope is defined as "the process of thinking about one's goals, along with the motivation to move towards those goals, and the ways to achieve those goals" (Snyder, 1995, p. 355). Masten, Best, and Garmezy (1990) define resilience as "the process of, capacity for, or outcome of successful adaptation despite challenging or threatening circumstances" (p. 426).

Statement of the Problem

Enrollment for first-year college students continues to increase; however, retention rates remain alarmingly low with as many as one in three first-year students not coming back their sophomore year. Research aimed at identifying nonacademic, strength-based factors that predict academic achievement can help first-year college students successfully make the transition from high school to college. This study seeks to extend the existing research that has been conducted on academic achievement by incorporating specific and unique, strength-based factors such as achievement motivation, hope, and resilience and examining how these three factors combine to predict academic success among first-year college students. Extant literature is limited related to the examination of the relationship among achievement motivation, hope, and resilience, and how they combine to predict academic achievement. This study addresses the gap in the literature.

Purpose of Study

The purpose of this study is to investigate the relationship among several strength-based factors that contribute to academic success. This research explores how achievement motivation, hope, and resilience combine to predict academic achievement of first-year college students enrolled in a Hispanic-serving institution. Identifying factors that contribute to academic success is important for helping students cope with the personal and academic stressors of transitioning to college. Furthermore, understanding the impact of nonacademic factors on academic achievement can lead to the development of strategies that can be utilized to help improve the performance and increase the retention of college freshmen.

Theoretical Foundations

Past and current studies of achievement motivation (McClelland, 1961; Wigfield & Eccles, 1992; 2000), hope (Snyder, 1995), and resilience (Richardson, 2002) offered a framework for this study of strength-based noncognitive factors related to academic performance of first-year college students. The conceptual framework of this study includes the following specific theories: achievement motivation theory (McClelland, 1961), expectancy-value theory (Wigfield & Eccles, 1992; 2000), hope theory (Snyder, 1995), and metatheory of resilience and resiliency (Richardson, 2002). First, McClelland's (1961) achievement motivation theory identifies a set of three distinct needs that are learned, acquired over time, and shaped by one's own life experiences: a need for achievement, a need for affiliation, and a need for power. Next, the expectancy-value theory posits achievement choice, performance, and persistence are influenced by expectancies and values (Eccles & Wigfield, 2002; Wigfield & Eccles, 2000).

In addition, Snyder's (1995) hope theory describes how pathways thinking and agency thinking allow individuals to set goals, develop specific strategies to reach their goals, and find the motivation to use those strategies to pursue their goals. Finally, metatheory of resilience and resiliency illustrates findings from three waves of resiliency inquiry: resilient characteristics of individuals are identified, process of acquiring those resilient qualities is recognized, and motivational force driving individuals toward self-actualization is discovered (Richardson, 2002).

Research Questions

This study seeks to determine the relationships among strength-based non-cognitive factors, achievement motivation, hope, and resilience, to facets of academic success among first-year college students. The following research questions will be investigated in this study:

1. What is the relationship between first-year students' achievement motivation and their academic performance as defined by grade point average?
2. What is the relationship between first-year students' hope and their academic success as defined by grade point average?
3. What is the relationship between first-year students' resilience and their academic success as defined by grade point average?
4. To what extent do achievement motivation, as measured by the Achievement Motivation Survey; hope, as measured by the Adult Trait Hope Scale; and resilience, as measured by the Brief Resilience Scale, of first-year college students in a Hispanic-serving institution predict academic achievement?
5. To what extent is there a difference in achievement motivation, as measured by the Achievement Motivation Survey, of first-year college students based on gender?
6. To what extent is there a difference in hope, as measured by the Adult Trait Hope Scale, of first-year college students based on gender?
7. To what extent is there a difference in resilience, as measured by the Brief Resilience Scale, of first-year college students based on gender?
8. To what extent is there a difference in achievement motivation, as measured by the Achievement Motivation Survey, of first-year college students based on ethnicity?
9. To what extent is there a difference in hope, as measured by the Adult Trait Hope Scale, of first-year college students based on ethnicity?
10. To what extent is there a difference in resilience, as measured by the Brief Resilience Scale, of first-year college students based on ethnicity?

Significance of Study

First-year college students face many challenges, and understanding what encourages academic achievement is important for helping them meet the expectations in their freshmen year in college. A large number of first-year college students are experiencing trouble in meeting those expectations, and research reflecting the needs of this population is imperative. The study has significance to school counselors, college counselors, counselor educators, college administrators, and educators by adding to the limited body of knowledge on the strength-based non-cognitive factors of achievement motivation, hope, and resilience of successful first-year college students.

From this study, the impact of strength-based non-cognitive factors on academic achievement, specifically achievement motivation, will be examined. Educators and school counselors can better position themselves to implement programs that can increase achievement motivation and improve the performance of students. Additionally, college counselors can draw on these findings to assist first-year college students adapt successfully to college life. Counselor educators can utilize results of this research to educate counselors-in-training about the unique challenges of first-year college students, the role school and college counselors play in helping students meet the challenges encountered in the first year of college and how interventions focused on strength-based non-cognitive factors can help improve the performance and increase the retention of first-year college students.

Furthermore, postsecondary educators can implement achievement motivation training programs designed to teach achievement thoughts and action strategies in an effort to increase students' need to achieve and academic achievement. In addition, the results help college administrators in their efforts to create retention strategies and help first-year college students meet the complex challenges of college.

Population and Samples

The population for this study will include first-year college students solicited from First Year Seminar (FYS) courses in the First Year Learning Communities Program (FYLCP) at a regional public four-year university in South Texas. Minimum age of the participants will be 18 years. Participants will be recruited by their seminar instructor during their scheduled FYS class. All instructors in the FYLCP will have the opportunity to solicit students in their respective classes. The seminar instructors will be contacted via a listserv used in the FYLCP for seminar instructors only. Instructors willing to seek volunteer participation from students will be provided with the necessary demographic forms, consent forms, and instruments. Sample size for this study is predicted to be 175 participants. This is an adequate sample size for sufficient power in a multiple regression analysis (Wampold & Freund, 1987).

Instrumentation

This study is a quantitative analysis of strength-based non-cognitive factors predictive of academic achievement of first-year college students. First-year college students choosing to participate will sign a consent form and complete a brief demographic questionnaire and three instruments, the Achievement Motivation Survey (Smith, 1972), the Adult Trait Hope Scale (Snyder et al., 1991), and the Brief Resilience Scale (Smith et al., 2008). The Achievement Motivation Survey measures achievement thinking, achievement behavior, and achievement motivation levels in relation to school, employment, family, community, and leisure time situations. The first set of items on the 48-item survey measures overall achievement motivation in terms of thinking and action and is answered using a 5-point Likert scale ranging from never to always. The Adult Trait Hope Scale measures a person's global level of hope. The scale consists of 12 items that comprise two subscales assessing agency (motivation to pursue goals) and pathways (strategies to achieve goals) and is answered using a 8-point Likert scale ranging from definitely false to definitely true. The Brief Resilience Scale is a 6-item scale that assesses resilience as the ability to bounce back or recover from stress and is answered using a 5-point Likert scale ranging from strongly disagree to strongly agree.

Cumulative grade point average (GPA) at the end of the participant's first year in college will be obtained as a measure of academic achievement. All incoming first-year students will be assigned a unique 9-character number known as their student identification number by the university. Participants will provide their student identification number on the demographic form granting the researcher access to their cumulative grade point average (GPA) at the end of the spring 2014 semester. A list of the students' identification numbers will be sent to the registrar's office for gathering of the cumulative grade point averages. Due to the need to match the participants' scores with their grade point averages, code numbers that can be linked to identifying information will be placed on the instruments; however, the list connecting identifying information with the code numbers will be kept in a locked file cabinet and stored in the researcher's locked office. All efforts will be made to keep data safe, secure, and confidential.

Data Analysis

Upon the receipt of the sufficient number of completed surveys required, the data will be collected and statistically analyzed. The predictor variables for this study will be measured by the scores on the instruments. The data will be screened for errors of entry, missing data, and checked for outliers, normality, linearity, and homoscedastic. Univariate, bivariate, and multivariate analyses will be conducted to meet the needs of this study. Frequencies, descriptive statistics, independent t-tests, a series of zero-ordered correlation coefficients, and regression analysis will be employed to evaluate relationships between and among the independent and dependent variables. The goal will be to determine the best linear combination of achievement motivation, hope, and resilience for predicting academic achievement as measured by cumulative GPA among first-year college students.

Basic Assumptions

The investigation is based on the following assumptions:

1. The instruments are reliable and valid and measure the constructs they purport to measure.
2. Participants will comprehend the concepts queried by the instruments and respond to questionnaires honestly and to the best of their ability.
3. Data will be collected responsibly and analyzed accurately.

Limitations

The limitations of this study include the following:

1. The study employs a convenience sample of students in the First Year Learning Communities Program enrolled in First Year Seminar courses at a public four-year university in South Texas making generalizability of the results to other populations difficult as the potential for demographic representation to be homogenous exists.
2. The scope of the study is narrowed by concentrating on only three of the many strength-based non-cognitive variables that might predict academic success: achievement motivation, hope, and resilience. The researcher does not imply that the variables under investigation are the only valid factors for predicting academic achievement of first-year college students.
3. Self-reported responses on questionnaires and surveys will be subject to response bias and increased error in reliability and validity.

Delimitations

The following delimitations are imposed on this study:

1. The population is delimited to first-year college students enrolled in First Year Seminar courses at a particular institution in South Texas.
2. The Achievement Motivation Survey (Smith, 1972) measures achievement motivation.
3. The Adult Trait Hope Scale (Snyder et al., 1991) measures hope.
4, The Brief Resilience Scale (Smith et al., 2008) measures resilience.

Definition of Terms

For the purposes of this study, the following definitions apply:

Achievement motivation: The need to perform well or the striving for success, evidenced by persistence and effort in the face of difficulties (McClelland, 1961, p. 36)

Achievement Motivation Theory: A theory of motivation identifying three learned motivators all individuals have: a need for achievement, a need for affiliation, and a need for power (McClelland, 1961)

Expectancy-Value Theory: A theory of motivation explaining how individuals' expectancies and values influence their achievement choice, performance, and persistence (Eccles & Wigfield, 2022; Wigfield & Eccles, 2000)

First year student: A student attending any institution for the first time at the level enrolled.

First Year Learning Communities Program (FYLCP): An innovative nationally recognized program at regional public four-year university in South Texas, which helps students make successful academic and social transitions from high school to the university

First Year Seminar: A small discussion-based course in which students and their instructors exchange ideas and information (Hunter & Linder, 2005)

Freshman: A first-year undergraduate student

Grade Point Average (GPA): A measure of scholastic achievement on a 4-point scale and computed by dividing the total number of grade points by the number of credits.

Hope: "The process of thinking about one's goals, along with the motivation to move towards those goals, and the ways to achieve those goals" (Snyder, 1995, p. 355)

Hope Theory: A theory of hope subdivided into four categories: goals (targets of mental action sequences), pathway thoughts (one's perceived capabilities at generating workable routes to desired goals), agency thoughts (the perceived capacity to use one's pathways so as to reach desired goals), and barriers (Snyder, Rand, & Sigmon, 2005).

Resilience: "The process of, capacity for, or outcome of successful adaptation despite challenging or threatening circumstances" (Masten, Best, & Garmezy, 1990, p. 426)

Metatheory of Resilience and Resiliency: A theory postulated as three waves of resiliency inquiry: identifying the resilient characteristics of individuals, recognizing the process of acquiring those resilient qualities, and discovering the motivational force driving individuals toward self-actualization (Richardson, 2002).

Persistence: A student's postsecondary education continuation behavior that leads to graduation

Retention: A measure of the number of full-time, first-time students who return to the institution the following year

Appendix C

Example Qualitative Proposal

DeLee's (2014) qualitative dissertation proposal explores the experiences of master's-level student counselors who participate in group supervision using the Awareness Wheel as a mode of feedback. One broad, central research question is followed by three subquestions.

Introduction

Group supervision is an essential component of counselor training as it provides a context for professional development. In group supervision, counselors discern and master counseling skills for themselves which benefit their clients. By building their skill set, they become effective while forging bonds with clients. This leads to operative and satisfying experiences for clients and counselors. Additionally, effective communication is essential in counseling. For counselors, it is imperative to learn how to communicate and to understand what is being communicated. Building effective communication skills can occur in the context of group supervision. The Awareness Wheel (Miller, Nunnally, & Wackman, 1975) provides a template for communicating that focuses on the counselor's own senses, thoughts, actions, feelings, and intentions. The purpose of this study is to comprehend the experience of master's-level practicum and internship students in group supervision that uses the Awareness Wheel as a communication tool.

Background Overview

Group supervision is required in counseling training programs that are accredited by the Council for Accreditation of Counseling and Related Educational Programs (CACREP, 2009). Group supervision is defined as

> . . . the regular meeting of a group of supervisees with a designated supervisor or supervisors, to monitor the quality of their work, and to further their understanding of themselves as clinicians, of the clients with whom they work, and of service delivery in general. (Bernard & Goodyear, 2009, p. 245)

A consistent and cohesive model for group supervision that lends itself to research, evaluation, and measurement is needed. Linton (2003) addressed the lack of empirical evidence regarding group supervision and its impact on counselors-in-training. However, the limited research on this topic has shown that group supervision has important benefits. These benefits include the opportunity for counselors-in-training to observe firsthand the application of different counseling approaches and receive helpful feedback (Linton, 2003). There remains, however, a dearth of research regarding group supervision, as well as an absence in consistent models for teaching the necessary and mandated skills.

Experiential learning has been shown to be most effective in acquiring new skills (Paladino, Minton, & Kern, 2011). Utilizing the Awareness Wheel in group supervision may provide counselors-in-training with needed consistency and a more complete model in which they can practice developing self-awareness by means of an experiential process. By providing feedback to one another in an experiential format that recognizes sensory data, thoughts, feelings, intentions, and actions, counselors-in-training may learn to conceptualize clients, cases, and problems in an organized consistent manner.

Communication is a vital to any relationship (Ekran, Özbay, Cihangir-Cankaya, & Terzi, 2012). For counselors, effective communication is necessary for performing the most basic of counseling skills. Basic counseling skills include the ability to listen carefully and effectively so that counselors can reflect a feeling, reflect meaning, and comment about the process of the counseling session (Ivey & Bradford-Ivey, 1999). These basic counseling skills require counselors to be cognizant of their own perspective as well as the perspective of the client.

To effectively communicate, it is helpful to have a healthy awareness of self (Miller, Nunnaly, & Wackman, 1975). Self-awareness has been defined as "awareness or knowledge of one's thoughts, emotions, and behaviors and can be considered a state" (Fenigstein, Scheier, & Buss, 1975, p. 522). Miller, Nunnaly, and Wackman (1975) state, "The first step in communication is identifying information you want to communicate to others . . . this information is often information about yourself" (p. 28). Self-awareness is key to effective communication because it requires the counselor to understand the worldview from which they operate, hopefully resulting in making more informed and clearer decisions where intentionality is apparent (Miller, Nunnally, & Wackman, 1975)

The counselors' style and the manner they are developing begin to form during their first clinical experiences in practicum and internship courses (Paladino, Minton, & Kern, 2011). Training counseling students in communication skills and developing self-awareness is a goal of practicum and internship courses. Increasing these skills and improving these abilities benefits them and improves clinical skills. Preparing counselors-in-training (CITs) to communicate in a way that accounts for their sensory data, emotions, thoughts, intentions, and behaviors has the possibility of helping them recognize the effect they have in the counseling session.

Additionally, having an opportunity to practice basic self-awareness at this early stage of clinical work might help CITs with important counseling issues such as interpersonal awareness, transference, countertransference, problem identification, and intentional intervention strategies. These skills are facilitated by greater interpersonal communication skills and are mandated by accreditation.

Statement of the Problem

Group supervision is widely practiced in counselor education but yields limited research. Exploring facets of group supervision in an effort to understand this supervisory modality is warranted. The need for new counselors to develop intentionality and basic counseling skills has been stated in the literature. New counselors struggle with intentionality and basic counseling skills, even as they approach graduation and enter into the profession (Gersten et al., 2013). This points to the need for effective supervision and a way to teach intentionality in particular. The Awareness Wheel provides a concrete way for the supervisor to assess the skills new counselors- in-training are developing in client awareness, intervention goals, and communications skills. It is important for supervisors to cultivate a relationship with the supervisee that allows for honesty between supervisor and supervisees. Training programs for counselors-in-training focusing on basic micro skills have shown to be effective in improving clinical awareness and skill sets (Duys & Hedstrom, 2000). Implementing a template for communication focusing on sensory data, thoughts, feelings, intentions, and actions in the context of supervision allows for an experiential opportunity to practice effective communication in the supervision group as well as in the counseling sessions under critique. Research exploring effective methods for providing group supervision as well as research about the development of self-awareness and communication in counselors-in-training is limited. Therefore, the research needs to be broadened in an effort to augment the knowledge base of new counselors and counselor educators and provide qualitative and quantitative evaluation. This increases the effectiveness of both.

Purpose of the Study

The purpose of this study is to contribute to the qualitative exploration of the experience of master's-level student counselors who participate in group supervision using the Awareness Wheel as a mode of feedback. As part of this study, students' experiences of giving and receiving feedback using a model of communication that focuses on skill building and awareness of sensory data, thoughts, feelings, actions, intentions, and future behaviors will be explored. Awareness of one's own sensory data, thoughts, feelings, actions, and future behaviors is important to the student counselors' ability to work effectively with clients.

Research Questions

The overarching research question is:

> What are the lived experiences of master's-level counselors-in-training (CITs) who participate in group supervision that utilizes the Awareness Wheel as communication tool when providing feedback?
> Sub-questions include: (a) how do CITs describe the experience of communicating using the Awareness Wheel, (b) how do CITs describe any impact of using the Awareness Wheel on case conceptualization, (c) how do CITs describe any impact of using the Awareness Wheel on their development as counselors or persons?

Significance of Study

The Council for the Accreditation of Counseling and Related Educational Programs (CACREP) encourages accredited programs to implement training focused on the development of self-awareness in order to enhance the counseling relationship (CACREP, 2009). Heightened self-awareness on the part of the counselor has been shown to positively impact the therapeutic relationship and effectiveness of counseling (Downs, 2000). Providing a setting in which counselors-in-training can develop and hone this skill without the pressure of working with a client appeared to be an important need.

Group supervision has been shown to be a helpful modality because it allows for group members to observe and learn from their supervisors and their peers (Linton, 2003). By utilizing the Awareness Wheel in this setting, students had an opportunity to learn via practice and observation. Additionally, this modality allowed for students to make mistakes and learn from those mistakes without the added pressure of being with a client.

Exploring the students' experiences when using this tool in group supervision provides the field with rich data regarding the supervision process, ways to develop self-awareness, and the developmental process of a CITs. In addition, it provides information about how CITs learn and use new communication skills. This information provides the profession with opportunities for continued research, as well as insight that will be useful when working with counselors-in-training. Additionally, it will add to the literature regarding group supervision practices, its significance in training, and possible quantitative measures for the future.

Population and Sample

The participants will include six master's-level CITs who agree to participate in the study and are fulfilling their requirements for clinical field work at a counseling and training clinic (CTC) located on a campus of a southwestern university in the United States. The CTC provides group and individual counseling to the public. The target number of participants is 5-7 CITs. The CITs completing their practicum and internship clinical work at the clinic will meet criteria for participation in the study. The criteria are that CITs must:

(a) be enrolled in a master's-level counseling program, (b) be enrolled in practicum or internship, and (c) be at least 19 years old.

Instrumentation

This is a qualitative study. A qualitative paradigm allows for an inductive process when exploring human experiences (Patton, 2002). Patton (2002) states, "Phenomenological analysis seeks to grasp and elucidate the meaning, structure, and essence of the lived experience of a phenomenon for a person or group of people" (p. 482). The phenomenological perspective focuses on the human experience of the phenomenon being studied (Creswell, 2009). This theoretical perspective is fitting for this study because the aim of the study is to understand CITs' experience of the Awareness Wheel in the context of group supervision. Interviews, journaling, field observation, and a focus group will be used to access the experience of the CITs. Exploring the process associated with awareness of self and effective communication requires a research paradigm that is inductive in nature and open to different human experiences while allowing themes to emerge that are similar across participants.

Group supervision utilizing the Awareness Wheel will begin during the first month of the semester and continue for eight consecutive weeks. The CITs will be taught the Awareness Wheel during the first meeting and asked to use the wheel as they provide feedback to their peers and as they present cases or issues to the group. After each group supervision meeting, the CITs will participate in reflective journaling. Upon completion of the eight weeks of group supervision, individual interviews and a focus group will be conducted.

Data Collection and Analysis

During the first week of the semester, the students at the clinic will be contacted face-to-face by the principal researcher and informed of the purposes of the study. They will be offered the opportunity to participate in the group supervision study and informed that their participation is voluntary. The students who agree to participate in the study will provide the principal researcher with days and times when they are available in order to establish a time for the group to meet. They will also be provided with an informed consent to review and return during the initial meeting. No student counselor at the clinic who is available at that time and wishes to participate will be excluded.

The principal researcher will hold an initial meeting with CITs who agree to participate in order to review the purposes of the study and the informed consent documents. Questions will be answered and the informed consents signed and obtained. The principal researcher will conduct group supervision using the Awareness Wheel for 8 weeks over the course of a semester. The supervision group will be in the CTC. Each supervision session will consist of a 2 hour group supervision meeting during which the students discuss clinical issues, professional development, personal awareness (as it relates to professional development), and any other client-related concerns. Students will be introduced to and asked to utilize the Awareness Wheel as a means of communicating with one another.

During the last 15–20 minutes of each supervision group session, participants will journal their experience using the following prompts:

1. My experience of today's group supervision was . . .
2. How did today's group supervision impact your conceptualization of clients or cases?
3. How did today's group supervision impact your conceptualization of yourself as a counselor?

Each participant will create a pseudonym that will be used to identify the journals. The journals will be collected and stored in a locked cabinet. The pseudonyms will be used on all data collected during the study. Throughout the entirety of the study, the researcher will take field notes in order to reflect upon the process, make observations, and note actions taken as the supervisor. In addition, the researcher will record her reactions, thoughts, and experiences in the supervision sessions.

Following the final group supervision, a semi-structured interview will be conducted with each research participant. Participants will be asked the following:

1. What was your experience of using the Awareness Wheel in group supervision?
2. In what ways, if any, did using the Awareness Wheel help you communicate with your peers?
3. In what ways, if any, did hearing feedback that was provided using the Awareness Wheel helps you to receive it?
4. In what ways, if any, did using the Awareness Wheel help you conceptualize client cases/issues?
5. In what ways, if any, did using the Awareness Wheel impact you as a counselor?
6. Please describe any ways in which using the Awareness Wheel might have impacted you personally.

Each interview will be audiotaped and transcribed for the purpose of analysis. Any identifying information will be removed from the transcription in order to protect participant confidentiality, and pseudonyms will be utilized to identify each transcript. Each interview will take place at the CTC, lasting approximately one hour, and will be audio recorded

Analysis is an ongoing process in which the researcher goes through the data multiple times. Creswell (2007) depicts data analysis as being similar to a spiral. At the beginning of the study, the researcher will describe her experience with the Awareness Wheel, a process known as bracketing (Moustakas,

1994; Creswell, 2007). In order for the focus of the research to be on the participants and their experience, it will be imperative for the researcher to bracket her experience from that of the subjects for the purpose of enhancing credibility of the study. In this case, the spiral-like nature of research analysis resembles a double helix where analysis of the subjects and researcher are separated but connected.

Throughout the study, the researcher will be immersed in the data by reviewing the journal entries and making her own observations about the process. Upon completion of the 8 weeks of group supervision, the researcher will review the journal entries, listen to the interviews, and identify emerging themes. The participants will be asked to participate in a focus group to review the initial themes found in the interviews and journals. The participants will be asked to provide their thoughts on the initial themes. They will be offered the opportunity to discuss any questions or thoughts they had about the experience of using the Awareness Wheel as part of the group supervision process.

Following the focus group, the researcher will transcribe the individual interviews and the focus group recording. Once the interviews and focus group are transcribed, the researcher will engage in a step called horizontalization (Moustakas, 1994) in which the researcher reviews the data by listening to the interviews, reading the transcriptions, reading the journals, and taking note of statements or phrases which lend insight into the lived experiences of participants. The researcher will read through the transcribed interviews and journals and highlight those words and phrases that elucidate the research question being asked.

The data from the group along with the individual interview transcriptions will be reanalyzed for units of meaning. Then, clusters of meaning will be developed in order to facilitate the researcher in detecting themes as they emerge from the data (Hays & Wood, 2011). Clusters of meaning are identified when the researcher looks for meaning that is static across the initial statements identified (Hays & Wood, 2011; Moustakas, 1994). Once the clusters of meaning are identified, then the researcher will look for textural descriptions of the phenomenon (Hays & Wood, 2011; Moustakas, 1994). These descriptions can provide rich information and illuminate the experiences of participants (Hays & Wood, 2011). These descriptions will be used to provide the researcher with a clearer understanding of the experience of the individual participants and the experience across participants. Themes in the data will be constructed from the clusters of meaning and textural descriptions. Throughout the study and the data analysis process, the researcher will make certain to write about her own experience as it relates to the phenomenon of study (Moustakas, 1994). This will enable the data to be analyzed on several concentric levels and from a variety of perspectives, both from an individual standpoint and from a process standpoint.

Moustakas (1994) discussed three important strategies utilized here to strengthen trustworthiness of the study. Triangulation of data utilizes multiple sources of data to explore the phenomenon of interest (Creswell, 2007). Having multiple sources of data provides credibility to the themes identified. This triangulation of data analysis provides the framework for the helix or spiral described by Creswell (2007). Going across data or horizontally through data provides a three-dimensional mode of analysis. For this study the (three) sources of data are journal entries, the focus group, and interviews. Member checking will be utilized in two ways. First, participant transcriptions will be provided to each CIT in order that changes can be made to accurately reflect experiences. In addition, initial themes will be presented to the focus group, which again provides an opportunity for participants to add, counter, and include additional information. The transcriptions will be submitted to each CIT electronically and the CIT will review the transcriptions and make any changes to accurately reflect their experience. Member checking will serve as a way to validate the interpretation of the data made by the researcher (Creswell, 2007). Interviews, journals, and the focus group can provide thick, rich descriptions of participants' experiences. Finally, making certain the researcher will provide a thick description of the phenomenon by staying true to the participant's statements of their experience and checking that description with participants allows for a clearer and richer account of the phenomenon (Hays & Wood, 2011; Creswell, 2007).

All recordings and transcriptions will be kept in a secure cabinet in the home of the researcher for the duration of the study and will be kept for 3 years beyond the successful defense of the dissertation. The data will be destroyed by the researcher three years after the dissertation defense.

Basic Assumption

Basic assumptions before beginning the study are that using the Awareness Wheel as a template for communication will increase counselor self-awareness and improve communication skills. The Awareness Wheel helps identify one's own sensory data, feelings, intentions, thoughts, and actions and thereby enhances effective communication, rapport, and therapeutic alliance because it takes into account the importance of the person who is doing the communicating. Further, it is assumed that this experience will provoke personal and professional development within the student, in turn increasing competence and confidence for students. Additionally, it is assumed that those who elect to participate will do so fully and that they will provide honest information about their experiences.

Researcher Bias

I have implemented the Awareness Wheel in both my professional and personal life. On a professional level, I have used it when working with CITs who have verbalized issues with their co-counselor. I have found this intervention to be helpful as it outlines for students their own data, thoughts, actions, feelings, and intentions as it relates to the issue presented and helps them take responsibility for themselves and communicate with their co-counselor.

Additionally, I have found this tool helped me as a clinician as I communicate via this model with my clients. I am able to build a strong therapeutic relationship with less effort and in a short period of time. The tool enhances both communicating and listening. On a personal level, I have used this tool in many areas to help with my own self-awareness as it relates to professional and personal growth, responsibility, and interpersonal meaning.

Limitations

A significant limitation associated with this study is that I, the researcher, will be the group supervisor. Patton (2002) discussed how interviews can have an impact on the emotional state of the research participants, resulting in distorted responses, self-serving responses, and error in recall. I recognize that the students might feel compelled to behave or share their experiences in an uncharacteristic manner. I will attempt to avoid this by analyzing numerous points of data across participants and by utilizing an external interviewer for individual interviews. Another limitation is the limited range of research participants. The research participants will be from a counseling program at a university in South Texas. They will have been accepted to complete their practicum or internship at the Counseling and Training Clinic.

Definitions and Key Terms

Awareness Wheel (the Wheel): The communication model to be used throughout the study. The Awareness Wheel focuses on sensory data actions, thoughts, feelings, and intentions thus focusing on the whole person as the source of communicating and listening (Miller & Miller, 2011).

Counseling and Training Clinic (CTC): The location of the study. Located on the university campus, the CTC is staffed by master's-level counselors-in-training and provides individual and group counseling to the community.

Counselor-in-training (CIT): Masters-level students participating in their required clinical work for their degree. These students are registered in practicum or internship courses.

Listening Cycle: The Listening Cycle is a model used in conjunction with the Awareness Wheel and in no way is separate from the Awareness Wheel. The Listening Cycle facilitates awareness for the person communicating their experience on the Awareness Wheel. The Listening Cycle provides a model for aiding the person on the large skill mat in uncovering their experience.

Supervision: "An intervention provided by a more senior member of a profession to a more junior member of the same profession" (Bernard & Goodyear, 2009, p.7).

> ***Supervisor:*** The senior member of the profession responsible for moni-
> toring the junior member in all areas of clinical work and profes-
> sional development (Bernard & Goodyear, 2009).
>
> ***Group Supervision:*** The regular meeting of multiple supervisees with a
> supervisor who monitors the quality of their clinical work and assists
> them in developing as a clinician (Bernard & Goodyear, 2009).

Summary

The purpose of this study is to uncover the lived experience of CITs utilizing the Awareness Wheel in the context of group supervision. A qualitative
methodology is appropriate for this study as it allows the researcher to explore the experience of the research participants in an inductive manner.
Weekly supervision will be provided for 8 weeks during the fall semester
with the Awareness Wheel being used as the template for communicating
during supervision.

Chapter 5

The Literature Review

Among the many components of a dissertation project, the literature review is often the most dreaded. Students often refer to the dissertation process as a *beast of burden*, and they are usually not referring to writing the results section. It is the literature review that is frustrating and seems to take so long to complete. The good news is that in this chapter, we offer some tips to make the literature review bearable, and maybe even enjoyable. Also, this project can become less intimidating when you have a structured and systematic guide to follow. In this chapter, we provide you with an overview of core components, key activities, and practical approaches that will help you get organized and complete this important part of your dissertation.

Literature Review as the Formal Context for Your Project

According to Machi and McEvoy (2012), the literature review of your dissertation "presents a logically argued case founded on a comprehensive understanding of the current state of knowledge about a topic of study" (p. 4). From a practical perspective, we suggest that you use this opportunity to transition your topic from something personal to you to something professional that indicates its relevance. Once you present readers with an overview of relevant issues, constructs, and empirical findings, you establish your literature review as the formal context of your project. This further clarifies your study among committee members. Before we get into the specific components and processes associated with writing your literature review, let's go ahead and address questions posed by students and colleagues.

Where Do I Even Start?

Beginning with the end in mind is a good place to start. Well-developed statements about the problem under investigation, your research questions, and the significance of your study will tell you where you will eventually end. Therefore, the task is to establish a road map for readers to help them get there with you. Just like a road map uses landmarks between where you are and where you want to go, your literature review uses important topics and historical findings as landmarks to help readers understand your project and the problem under investigation.

What Reference Sources Are Appropriate for a Dissertation?

Most of what you would consider reasonable is appropriate for inclusion in a dissertation, but in general, citing dictionaries, encyclopedia entries, unmoderated blogs or web content, textbooks, newsletters, and other non-peer-reviewed resources is not always advisable. Instead, we encourage you to focus your efforts on including published peer-reviewed articles, primary and seminal books, monographs and unpublished empirical reports, working papers, government documents, dissertations/theses, association-sponsored seminars, and face-to-face training programs.

How Long Should My Literature Review Be?

That one is tricky. With so many dissertation formats currently implemented in counselor education programs, using a standard rule of thumb, such as 20–30 pages, although less ambiguous, would be misleading. Completing a literature review is about explicating the nature of your topic while providing a context for the importance and relevance of your project. After outlining the hierarchy of ideas with your dissertation chair, you will have a better idea of the length of your literature review.

How Many References Should Be Cited?

At least 100. Just kidding! Again, just as with the length of your literature review, your reference citations should be representative of the historical and contemporary status of your population, topic, and related constructs. To achieve this, you will need to include citations of seminal works, peer-reviewed journal articles, book chapters, and other documents that span a reasonable amount of time. For example, should a dissertation evaluating a wellness intervention overview and cite the works of Aristotle? Maybe. It just depends on the arc you are developing. We encourage you to focus on including references that are seminal to the topic being investigated and imperative to establishing a working context for your readers. This might be done in 30 references or it could take 130 references. An arbitrary number may be misleading and not honor the uniqueness of your project.

Can You Help Me Get Started?

The answer to this question is "Yes." Starting and completing your literature review can be better approached by putting into motion the concepts and structure that we discuss in this chapter. You may find it helpful to make notes in the margins and plan the components of your literature review as we go along. Let's get started by depicting a step-by-step approach you can use and then review the typical components of a literature review section.

Five Steps to Completing Your Literature Review

Step 1: Establish Your Conceptual Framework

Establishing a conceptual framework for your dissertation, including the literature review, may be one of those critical aspects affecting the success of your study. We have found that this aspect of project development is often underdeveloped or even overlooked. Your conceptual framework is the theoretical lens that will guide your thinking throughout the dissertation. We have heard this referred to as a researcher's epistemology, theoretical worldview, and the blueprint of the project. From this blueprint, your design, method, analysis, and interpretation should follow. Just like any other blueprint, it defines the structure and provides depictions of aspects relevant to understanding the overall design, but does not get into the minutiae of the project. Similarly, your framework should identify the overarching theory, identify and briefly describe relevant concepts, and make a statement about how these fit with your project.

Consider the example of a qualitative investigator wanting to understand counseling students' perceptions of institutional pressure to compromise personal safety and ethical scope of practice to complete direct contact hours during practicum and internship experiences (controversial, we know). The author of such a dissertation might establish a conceptual framework by using constructivist thinking, based on the premise that critiques institutionalized norms and informal policies as a product of socially negotiated power. The conceptual framework may guide a narrative inquiry methodology and implement a creative analytic practice to evaluate data. Alternatively, someone implementing an empathic development program among counseling students may adopt a conceptual framework with a modern, positivistic perspective. From this perspective, knowledge is generated from inferences about the ways that observed phenomena respond to well-controlled manipulations, which allows the researcher to test hypotheses and determine magnitudes of relations. With this framework in mind, the researcher could select an experimental design with randomization and implement statistical and practical significance-testing approaches to infer the effectiveness of the program. In either case, the conceptual framework can support the student's dissertation and help the reader further understand the context of his or her study. Whether it is formally written into the literature review section of your dissertation or just informs and guides you, a conceptual framework can help transform your thinking about your topic of study.

Step 2: Develop an Outline

With a framework in hand, it is time to develop an outline of your literature review. Although it can be tempting to passionately dive headlong into writing, we encourage you to take the time to develop a road map for three general areas: the introduction, body, and summary sections of the literature review. Of course, if your college or department has a template for students, please follow their suggestions. There is no reason to reinvent the wheel, if the wheel gets you where you need to go. Machi and McEvoy (2012) discussed how to conceptualize the content of these three sections. Let's take a look at each of these three sections and talk about the content that should be included in your outline.

The introduction is pretty straightforward. The outline that you develop for this section should (a) introduce readers to the section; (b) restate the study topic; (c) situate the study in a context that establishes relevance; (d) restate why your project is significant and what the implications could mean for counselors, counseling students, or counselor educators; (e) indicate why the absence of knowledge you are generating is a problem; and (f) present the organization of the material that will be presented in the body. Each of these six components can range from a few sentences to a few paragraphs, whatever it takes to build a logical lead-in that appeals to the emotional nature of your topic and stimulates a sense that action is warranted.

The body of your literature review will provide readers with an overview of the major and contemporary movements, contributors, constructs, issues, and state of affairs related to the study. We recommend using headings to represent your major topics and the subordinate information in a way that is logical and builds the arc of your argument. The overall outline should look like an inverted triangle moving from the broad, general content associated with your topic to the specific information directly related to your project. Likewise, you should implement an inverted triangle approach for each major topic area. In this way, you will use bullets or APA formatted headings to establish a series of inverted triangles within an inverted triangle—everything moves from the broad to the specific, even within the content subsections.

The summary section will provide a grand statement, hitting the high points of what you have reviewed so far. You should plan to inform the readers what you have already told them and bring together the incredible amount of material you have presented in a way that is succinct and meaningful. Following your summary is your chance to propose a call to action. An example for counselors may include "Therefore, based on the increasing costs to individuals and society, it is a prudent activity for counselors to identify treatment protocols that expedite recovery processes and reduce the length of stay in long-term care facilities." An example for counselor education students may include "Given the critical need for professional counselors who specialize in child and adolescent behavioral health, counselor educators are called to identify and evaluate training programs that promote competence in evidence-based practices." Finally, you will need to plan on the best approach to discuss the implications of your project for influencing the state of the literature and common practice for counselors and counselor educators. Appendix D presents an example of one of our literature review outlines, which clearly contains an introduction, body, and summary. With such an outline in hand, you will be prepared to complete your systematic search.

Step 3: Complete a Systematic Search

OK. You have a framework and an outline. What next? Well, first of all, promptly administer yourself a pat on the back because you are incredibly ahead of the game at this point. Many people just dive headlong into Google Scholar or PsycINFO and start searching for buzz words or general constructs such as *depression* or *trauma*. That approach lends itself to a certain degree of usefulness when completing course papers, and some students may survive a dissertation that way, but we suggest that you try a targeted, systematic approach, which perhaps will yield a greater quality of results and save you time in the long run. When you start your search with a framework and outline as your guides, you are *beginning with the end in mind* and can focus your time and effort on specific topic areas, constructs, outcomes, or categories of inquiry that support your developing argument. Part of beginning with the end in mind involves getting organized, so figure out if you are someone who prefers electronic documents, someone who would rather have hard copies of everything, or a combination the two. We find that although hard copies are an easier read at times, the convenience, accessibility, and reliability of electronic documents is unparalleled, especially when using web-based platforms such as Google Drive or Dropbox, which can be installed onto your computer and accessed from any number of devices, including smartphones. Within these platforms, you can create a series of folders that are either modeled after your outline or organized according to some other theme of your choosing.

The next aspect of implementing a systematic search is deciding what sources are relevant to each of your major sections. For example, a section in your literature review about integrating wellness within counselor education may draw from the many notable peer-reviewed journal articles published in *Counselor Education and Supervision* and *The Clinical Supervisor* or peer-reviewed conference presentations by counseling experts who provide workshops in the Association for Counselor Education and Supervision conference circuit. By contrast, a review of cognitive theory for the treatment of social phobia may draw primarily from scholarly books associated with the Beck Institute, such as Albano and DiBartolo (2007), Beck (2011), and Clark and Beck (2010). We recommend taking your outline and matching potential authors and sources to your topics that are more likely to yield your materials so that your search is focused. From there, it is time to start searching and retrieving your documents.

A systematic search of published literature is an effort to identify and include a population of source materials representative of the topics that you will address. Characteristically, this search endeavor is thorough, recursive, and exhaustive and will initially be exploratory in nature before becoming more targeted. Therefore, we recommend that you keep documentation of your search strategy in case your dissertation chair or a publication outlet requests it. Although there are a multitude of strategies that have been recommended for identifying studies for inclusion (see White, 2007), we suggest that you can find most of what you will be looking for through (a) primary texts, (b) electronic database searches, (c) journal-specific searches, (d) hand searches, (e) footnote chasing, and (f) consultation. In each case, your strategy should be implemented to obtain all available published reports (white paper literature) as well as those unpublished documents (grey literature) that may contribute to a more accurate depiction of your treatments, interventions, constructs, or theories. In the following sections, we discuss these sources and strategies to help you be successful when using them.

Primary Texts

Primary texts, also referred to as primary sources, are the original works by authors that we have all come to know and love. Of course, these may represent the theoretical pieces of individuals such as Freud, Adler, Maslow, and Rogers, but they are also technical manuals and treatment protocols developed by master practitioners, such as Cohen, Mannarino, and Deblinger (2017); Kendall, Crawley, Benjamin, and Mauro (2013); and Linehan (2015). Unlike survey texts that depict secondhand accounts of theories or interventions, primary texts provide unfiltered access to scientific thought and scholarly products during the time when they were developed. In this way, they depict a truer portrayal of terminology, concepts, constructs, and practices than is available through secondary works. Therefore, primary texts are considered more reputable and distinguished references than their secondary counterparts. College or university libraries have primary texts on the shelves or can retrieve them for you using interlibrary loan.

Electronic Databases Searches

With so many databases available, a good guideline is to choose ones with content relevant to your disciplinary scope and availability of access. You may not be aware of this, but each bibliographic database has a series of target disciplines within its scope of coverage that you should consider. For example, databases such as PsycINFO and Academic Search Complete both contain behavioral and mental health documents; however, Academic Search Complete also contains abstracts for documents in related fields such as ethnic and cultural studies, women's studies, and theology, which may extend the yield of a search. Given the difficulties of the pay-for-access system of publication abstracting and indexing, you should consider whether you have access to a database; what time frame is covered within your access; if that access includes documents from another language or country; and whether it includes unpublished documents, such as dissertations, theses, or government reports. Even though you may not have electronic access to search results, you will likely be linked to items that can be retrieved through hand searching your library stacks or making an interlibrary loan request. When conducting your search, we recommend using search terms and variations of search terms that target your topic, relevant constructs, population of interest, and intervention. Furthermore, using Boolean operators can help you narrow or broaden your search strategies. For example, placing AND between two terms will yield only documents that are relevant to both of those terms. By contrast, inserting OR between two or more search terms can be useful in cases when several synonyms for a concept are frequently used, such as in the phrase *children OR adolescents OR youth.* For example, for a project on treating social phobia with cognitive behavior therapy (CBT), you could use the following search strings to identify the topic, intervention, and dependent variable: social phobia AND social anxiety, CBT OR cognitive therapy, and anxiety OR stress.

Journal-Specific Searches

As great of a gift as large database abstracting is, it is also not a perfect strategy: It will almost always miss something that is pertinent to your topic. For example, your library may subscribe to PsycINFO but not have access to the *Counseling Outcome Research and Evaluation* journal because it was not added on to their subscription. Therefore, we consider journal-specific searches as a prudent addition to any systematic strategy to locate relevant documents. With this in mind, completing a search for candidate articles requires some familiarity with what journals tend to publish articles related to your topic. Most often, counseling and counselor education students are encouraged to pursue flagship journals (e.g., *Journal of Counseling & Development*), specialty publications (e.g., *Counseling Outcome Research and Evaluation*), and topic-specific journals (e.g., *Counselor Education and Supervision*) to promote a comprehensive, recursive yield of candidate articles. Because of increasing access to peer-reviewed publications, searching specific journals for candidate articles can be done easily through online access, so if you are having trouble getting started in this area, contact your librarian. They usually love their work and are full of amazing tips and resources.

Hand Searches

As previously mentioned, not every library will have access to every journal within their databases. Oftentimes, the reason for this is that journal access can be very expensive, but it is possible that your college or university already has a paper subscription to the journal, which means searching through the stacks by hand may be your best bet. Even though this can be time consuming, it is also a very intimate way to make contact with your sources. One of the major advantages of this strategy is that with hand searches, you can often see the topical and authorship trends that occur within and across issues of a publication over time. It is likely that a hand search of relevant publications over the span of 5, 10, or 20 years will spur along useful insights and perspectives that may help you shape the context of your study in meaningful ways that may not be available through database searching alone.

Footnote Chasing

Footnote chasing, also referred to as *reference mining,* denotes the skillful use of primary text and article footnotes or previous authors' reference lists to identify relevant resources to include in your project. The strength of this approach lies in the fact that previous experts in your topic area may have already identified relevant literature and presented you with a foundation of information that is readily accessible by identifying primary studies related to your topic. This may seem like an extra step, but it is fairly easy to comb through a small series of reference lists when compared with thousands of returned results from just one database search. Common sources of footnote chasing include primary studies, educational or treatment manuals, and reference lists of meta-analyses.

Consultation

Students writing a dissertation or other capstone research rarely are experts on their topics. However, they are becoming experts. Therefore, it is important to consult with experts who can support your content and the conceptualization of your study. Ideal targets for consultation are individuals who have developed or pioneered the particular field you are investigating, general topic experts, colleagues with in-depth knowledge of your content area, and your faculty chair or adviser. Communication with these individuals can help you identify additional studies or confirm that you have reached a sufficient degree of depth and breadth of content for your literature review.

As you find resources during your systematic search, it is important to save anything that may be usable. It will not take long for you to believe that you have scoured the professional literature, so it is up to you, your chair, and your committee members to decide how exhaustive your search should be. Much of that determination will be a function of the type of project you have selected, the amount of literature needed to situate readers in the context of the study, and institutional precedent.

Step 4: Organize Your Resources

As you start collecting and collating your resources, it is important to develop a system for organizing the incredible amount of material you will pull together. Many of us writing this book and likely some of your faculty members completed our dissertations in a time when we kept hard copies of articles that we printed out or ran off at our libraries, and when we could not afford more copies, we took notes on legal pads. We had these large, compendious files organized by topic that, although impressive to look at, were cumbersome to pour through and likely a fire hazard. You are, of course, still able to use this more traditional method, but we encourage students to use the many (and often free) resources that allow you to easily organize and access your sources in PDF or HTML files. We will briefly identify and describe three categories of downloadable software: web-based storage, programs commonly linked with university libraries, and more advanced online programs. Each program type allows for individualizing how you organize and access your collected materials in a way that makes sense to you and promotes ease of access. As we survey some of your options, consider the following key questions: What level of technology are you OK with? How many devices do you want to access your material from? and Overall, what seems most intuitive for you in terms of layout?

If you have made it this far in your graduate program and have not heard of Dropbox or Google Drive, prepare to have your mind blown. Both platforms offer plenty of free storage for users and allow you to access and edit files using many devices, including computers, tablets, and smartphones. Each is basically a blank canvas that you create folders in and upload content into. The blank canvas format lends itself nicely to creating a series of folders that reflect the content and flow of the outline you have created for your literature review. For example, you can include a folder for each of your major sections, and then within those, you can have additional folders that reflect the subordinate topics, constructs, contributors, and so forth. The good news about programs such as Dropbox and Google Drive is that they offer a substantial amount of digital storage for free, so you can have duplicate documents in each section, which allows for collaboration on documents by you and your dissertation chair, and desktop-to-desktop file syncing promotes functionality that is often referenced as the industry standard.

Another class of resources that you can use are programs commonly linked with university libraries, such as RefWorks, EndNote, and Zotero. Each of these allows you to integrate directly from your library search engines to your document storage platform. In practice, as you find documents of interest to you, you send them to a folder within your university's search engine where you can select to export them to the document manager with little more than a click of a button, which makes compiling and collating your materials almost effortless. It is important to know that most academic institutions are not affiliated with every one of these document managers, so it is important to look for yourself or ask the librarian before completing the registration process. One of the great features of this class of document management programs is they often include a function to delete duplicates—when you are dealing with hundreds of resources, this is a real gift. These programs allow you to categorize articles by topic and customize the way you access your articles, and they offer great customer service nearly around the clock. In addition, these programs will almost always produce reference lists for you in APA publication format, but you should always go back and check that the nuances, such as inclusion of issue numbers and digital object identifiers, are accurate. One thing to consider is that if the program you use is included with your academic fees, it may not be available to you after graduation without paying for access. Also, some of these programs do not offer offline access, so if that is important to you, selecting one that does (e.g., Zotero) may be a prudent choice.

The more advanced online programs include options such as Mendeley, OpenDocMan, and ZohoDocs. These programs allow for a greater degree of integration and importing from the web, library databases, and files from your hard drive. Your library of documents can be sorted by authors, title, year, or publication source. Once your documents are in the document manager library, these programs often allow you to highlight PDFs and place keyword tags on your documents, allowing you to search for clusters of similar documents using topic searches (e.g., Adler, children, CBT). Within the programs, you can add notations on the PDFs that can be viewed by you or other collaborators, such as your dissertation chair and committee members. These programs are often integrated with Microsoft Word through free plug-ins so that you can easily insert citations and references on the fly. These programs may take a little bit of adjustment as you become familiar with the platform, but once you are settled into the format, the resulting product is a high-powered platform that can easily handle an incredible amount of resources that are easy to search, retrieve, and share. Although many of these programs are free, some publishers do charge a modest fee.

Regardless of which platform you choose, you will find yourself surrounded by the theoretical and empirical trappings of a topic expert. By this time, you have your framework, an outline, and all the materials associated with your project, and at this point, there is only one last preparation you can make—plug in your laptop.

Step 5: Start Writing!

You may never be more prepared to start writing then you are at this point in the project. Of course, there will be mental blocks that come and go when writing your literature review, but you will overcome these and find success at the end of the journey. We are now going to cover some of the common components that you will need to address in your literature review. It is worth noting that the process will be multifaceted. Sometimes you will need support from your chair and committee members, and other times you will perform at your highest level when just left to do your own thing. In either case, it is important to be consistent with your writing by scheduling time to write each week, preferably at least a few days. Even if it is just a paragraph or two, keep plugging away because writing is a skill and writing a dissertation is unlike the term papers or comprehensive exams you have previously encountered. Also, it is important to schedule meetings with your chair and committee members to review your progress, develop stylistic writing mechanics, and edit as needed. Keep your expectations realistic because you will probably go through multiple rounds of revisions. During this process, you will want to make sure to include the following core components in your literature review.

Core Components of a Literature Review

All dissertation literature reviews share commonalities that authors implement to develop a case for their topics' importance and craft an argument that creates the context of the study. The most prominent components of a literature review are (a) an introduction, (b) overview statements, (c) a series of headings that represent your conceptual framework, (d) general and specific reviews, (e) a critique of previous literature, (f) meaningful synthesis of concepts and evidence, (g) transitions between concepts and sections, and (h) a summary. Each of these components contribute to the overall literature review in a synergistic way, so it is important to include all of them as part of your project. Let's take a look at each component in greater detail and demystify exactly what they are and why they are important.

Introduction

Before launching into the review of a topic, it is important to present the readers with a general introduction. Think of the introduction as your first impression to the deeper thesis of your study. With that in mind, you can apply structure to your content to provide the reader with a road map for the journey ahead. With a well-written introduction, you can perhaps make a great impression that fosters interest and creates momentum. At a minimum, the introduction to your literature review should include (a) an opening statement, (b) statements that place forthcoming material into context, and (c) the organization of topics. In general, you should avoid introductions that are vague, simply restate your project's purpose, reference a dictionary definition, or provide an extensive boring historical review of your topic. Instead, be specific and provide a bridge for readers.

Overview Statements

Overview statements provide the reader with a general depiction of forthcoming content. Because literature reviews can include a considerable amount of content, overview statements are used to introduce the reader to important topics and transitions. You can think of this as analogous to setting the agenda within a counseling session where we provide clients a general road map to therapy. The following is an example overview statement for a project using CBT with adolescents who have social phobia:

In the following section, I will present some critical information for understanding the empirical evidence that supports the use of CBT as a first-line treatment for social phobia among adolescents. Initially, I will discuss CBT as an intervention for the anxiety symptoms, and then transition to dialogue specifically related to treating social phobia and the co-occurring depression symptoms that tend to accompany the disorder. Within each of these broader categories of evidence, I will report findings from primary studies, meta-analysis, and investigations of participant characteristics that appear to moderate treatment effect. Finally, this discussion will conclude with a synthesis of this information that depicts the current state of evidence for treating social phobia among adolescents with the intention to depict indications for best practice and areas of best practice that are currently unclear.

Series of Headings That Represent Your Conceptual Framework

Headings will help you to organize ideas you believe are important for understanding your project while also providing the reader with a format to follow. When done effectively, your use of headings will accomplish important things. Foremost, it will provide readers with a reference to the key points of your project, such as the overarching theories, major concepts, philosophical movements, and categories of empirical evidence. In addition, headings provide readers with a road map they can use to anticipate and track progress, establish context, and further engage in your study. In the example of describing the evidence for CBT with adolescents who have social phobia, after your first-level heading, subheadings could illustrate categories of dependent variables, sources of evidence, and nuances of findings. As a rule of thumb, you want to have at least two subheadings under each major heading. If two subheadings are not possible, you probably will not need any.

General and Specific Reviews

General reviews of the existing literature will provide the reader with a broad overview of information related to your topic. This can include a discussion of thematic material that has been developed over time or a review of paradigms of inquiry that have been used with similar studies. By contrast, specific reviews target explicit details related to your topic that are imperative to developing context. For example, a general review within a study evaluating the use of a CBT intervention for treating social phobia among adolescents may depict historical approaches to treating social phobia across major theoretical paradigms. By contrast, a more specific review may depict the current states of cognitive conceptualization, which include specific treatment targets and interventions.

Critique of Previous Literature

Whether providing a general or specific literature review, you will be expected to critique previous studies and the literature on your topic in general. Sometimes, students spend so much time and effort pouring through databases and library stacks just to compile the literature review that they forget how the studies are connected. Dissertation committee members may not be experts on your topic and may not understand the inner workings of your subject. Therefore, it is imperative that as the author, you not only connect the dots for your readers but also compare and contrast the dots themselves and evaluate the ways they fit together. This is accomplished by organizing literature findings in a meaningful way, interpreting information, and then unequivocally evaluating the merit of what you have uncovered. Your critique might include other critical reviews of your topic, an inspection of effect size, relevance of clinical anecdotes, consistency with established theories, and even your personal perspective when grounded in a logical formulation of the problem.

Meaningful Synthesis of Concepts and Evidence

Just as you will compare and contrast concepts and evidence through critique, you will also need to consolidate all the information meaningfully through statements that synthesize your content. Meaningful syntheses of concepts and evidence will combine the frameworks, facts, and critique to provide your summative position on a topic. Doing so helps the reader not only tie all your content together but also understand your position, which is imperative for establishing context and need for your project. These statements tend to start with prepositions such as *overall*, *taken together*, or *generally speaking*, which cue the reader that you are going to integrate your content into a personal position statement.

Transitions Between Concepts and Sections

Transitions join thoughts together across paragraphs and sections of a literature review. When used effectively, transitions reduce the perception that you are jumping from topic to topic. Transitions increase the flow across a document. Whether used within sections or between them, transitions are the ways that you can show logical relationships between a myriad of concepts. For example, you may have noticed that the previous section about synthesis started with a sentence that tied it to critiques; that sentence is an example of a transition that bridges separate but related content. There is nothing incredibly special about that sentence, but it promotes flow and readability by establishing a link from the preceding material. Within sections, you can do this with a simple sentence at the beginning of a paragraph that links it to the previous paragraph, as used in the critique-synthesis example. Alternatively, you can also use a sentence at the end of the paragraph that cues the reader to what is forthcoming. For example, now is a good time to mention that some of the most important transitions you use will be summary statements.

Summary

Within writing composition classes, there is a frequently used adage to represent the writing process, which is important to keep in mind when preparing your literature review section: Tell them what you are going to tell them, tell them, and then tell them what you have told them. We have observed that many students handily address the first two steps (writing the introduction and the body) but forget to provide summaries of content across major sections and the entire literature review itself. Summaries of major sections not only provide an opportunity to consolidate important concepts, procedures, propositions, or evidence but also function as transitions for subsequent information. Alternatively, the overall summary for your literature review itself is your chance to ride off into the sunset on the back of the many ways that you have defined and clarified relevant issues; summarized findings of previous investigations; and identified contractions, relationships, and gaps, while also suggesting the next steps for solving the problem. This summary should be concise yet inclusive, and it should meaningfully transition the reader to your method section in a clear, logical way.

Summary

Well, there you go! We have provided a concise overview of some prominent components that authors use to showcase the importance of their topics and establish the context of their studies. An important consideration to keep in mind is that these eight components overlap and are often not exclusive in their presentation. For example, as we previously mentioned, a summary can function as a transition. The main takeaway may be that each of the components will contribute to your literature review in a synergistic manner and support your study.

Checklist

- ❏ Meet with your chair to identify and review expectations for the literature review.
- ❏ Establish your conceptual framework.
- ❏ Develop an outline using headings as your guide.
- ❏ Complete a systematic search of the literature.
- ❏ Organize your resources.
- ❏ Start writing!
- ❏ Check in routinely with your chair and use the resources available to you through your university for proofing and editing.

Additional Resources

Boland, A., Cherry, G., & Dickson, R. (2013). *Doing a systematic review: A student's guide.* Thousand Oaks, CA: Sage.

Machi, L. A., & McEvoy, B. (2016). *The literature review: Six steps to success* (3rd ed.). Thousand Oaks, CA: Sage.

Onwuegbuzie, A. J., & Frels, R. (2016). *Seven steps to a comprehensive literature review: A multimodal and cultural approach.* Thousand Oaks, CA: Sage.

Example of a Literature Review Outline

I. Introduction
  a. Opening statement
  b. Restatement of study topic
  c. Establishing context within a counseling and training clinic as well as the profession at large
  d. Restatement of significance
  e. Restating importance of project niche
  f. Organization of material within chapter
II. Theoretical Framework
  a. Holistic, developmental perspective with self-determination as a core feature
  b. Postpositivistic perspective of scientific inquiry
III. Supervision of Counselors
  a. Definition of construct and practice
  b. Importance to counselor development
  c. Historical development of practice to point of commonplace activity
  d. Process of developing clinical skills within supervision
    i. Nondirective versus micro skills
    ii. Medical model of training versus strength-based approaches
    iii. Parallel process
  e. Measuring clinical skills
    i. Inventories available
    ii. Counseling Skills Scale
  f. Integrative models
    i. Trends in development
    ii. Functional purpose
IV. Wellness Within the Counseling Profession
  a. Historical development of construct
    i. Large groups such as American Medical Association, World Health Organization, and American Counseling Association

        ii. Aristotle
       iii. Adler
       iv. Hettler
        v. Myers, Sweeney, & Witmer, 2000
       vi. Myers & Sweeney, 2005
      vii. Roscoe, 2009
     viii. Reese & Myers, 2012
      ix. Barden, Conley, & Young, 2015
  b. Emergence in clinical setting
        i. Adler
       ii. Myers, Sweeney, & Witmer, 2000
  c. Representation in counselor education and supervision
        i. American Counseling Association
       ii. Council for Accreditation of Counseling and Related Educational Programs
      iii. Problem of wellness maintenance in practice
        1. Burnout
        2. Vicarious trauma
        3. "Over-giving of self"

   V. Supervision Models That Infuse Wellness Concepts
  a. Some examples
        i. Stoltenberg & NcNeill, 2009
       ii. Foy & Breunlin, 1995
      iii. Smith, 2001
  b. Wellness Model of Supervision (WELMS; Lenz & Smith, 2010)

  VI. Student Learning Outcomes
  a. Definition
  b. Purpose
  c. Controversy surrounding difficulty in measuring student learning outcomes
  d. Development of student learning outcomes that indicate personal and professional monitoring of students

  VII. Evidence-Based Practices
  a. In counseling
        i. Justification and rationale
       ii. Trends
  b. In supervision
        i. Generally, not "outcome research" but instead analysis of what models tend to include and boast about
       ii. Paucity statement

  VIII. Implication of the WELMS for Student Learning Outcomes and Evidence-Based Supervision in Counselor Education
  a. Provides a quantifiable measure for student learning outcomes related to wellness

      i. Expansion of construct
     ii. Measurable maintenance or development using Five Factor Wellness Inventory
   b. Provide quantifiable evidence for counseling skill development
      i. Counseling Skills Scale
IX. Summary

Chapter 6

Creating the Problem Statement, Purpose Statement, and Research Questions

Congratulations! You have conquered the literature review and are moving right along! In this chapter, we begin by discussing problem and purpose statements, sharing examples, and examining differences. Also in this chapter, we discuss research questions and hypotheses, with example research questions provided for qualitative, quantitative, and mixed-methods designs.

With the support of your dissertation chair and committee, you are now ready to complete important components of your dissertation proposal. By identifying a researchable problem, you have laid the groundwork to complete a problem statement, which leads to the purpose statement and your research questions. You can breathe a sigh of relief when completing this part of your proposal because these sections will drive your dissertation, including the design of your study. Your dissertation chair and committee members, being familiar with the three commonly used research designs (i.e., qualitative, quantitative, and mixed methods), will provide you with the guidance needed to complete the method section of your proposal.

Problem Statement

The first step in creating a dissertation proposal is to identify the problem that you would like to address. This task can be daunting, particularly when narrowing a broad topic into a workable study. However, you must be able to write a clear problem statement for several reasons. First, you, as the researcher, must understand what the problem is that you plan to investigate. Second, people who read your proposal, particularly your dissertation committee, need to understand the problem. Third, a clear problem statement is necessary because it drives your purpose statement and describes how you will address the problem. The problem statement is the foundation of a study. It informs readers why you want to design and implement a research project.

The problem statement evolves as you narrow down a broad topic. The broad topic is an overarching concern, often a societal problem bantered about using everyday language (e.g., Why can't high school graduates read?). This topic is too broad for a dissertation study and would need to be reduced in scope for it to become a feasible research project.

The introduction section of a dissertation proposal includes a number of issues related to a macro problem. For the broad topic of why high school graduates cannot read, related issues might include the following: Why are students graduating from high school with less than a 12th-grade reading level? Why are high school graduates unemployable? Why can't they read a job application? and Why are they not learning how to read in high school? Issues related to an overall problem often are part of the narrowing process that leads to your problem statement.

Addressing a Gap in the Literature

Problem statements often address gaps in the literature. An example of a gap in the literature is that few studies have investigated a salient topic and the findings from extent research are spurious. Another gap involves the use of limited samples because the researcher only tested college students enrolled in psychology classes. Studies attempting to gather normative data for assessments of achievement, intelligence, and mental health frequently omit diverse populations. Topics that you have thought of for a dissertation may have been studied using samples from an Anglo population, thus inviting you to study a more diverse population.

Well-designed studies can lead to a series of investigations often establishing one's research agenda. Researchers will often recommend additional investigations of a topic using different variables. Perhaps salient variables were omitted in extant studies. Emotional intelligence, for example, was absent in the early studies predicting achievement. In more recent studies, emotional intelligence has proved to be a significant predictor of achievement when included as a variable. The initial studies examining high school attrition focused on student and teacher variables, but more recent investigations have included examining parental support and student assets and have found these variables to be significant. Early studies on college student attrition focused on the characteristics of university students and teachers, but later studies investigated the university structure, climate, and support systems and found these variables to be significant predictors of attrition.

By extensively reviewing the literature, you will find several gaps related to your topic. A gap in the literature might be a variable overlooked, a sample not investigated, or a general lack of research related to your topic.

Framing the Problem Statement

Lead sentences, citations, and information in the introduction will frame your problem statement. Therefore, how you construct sentences leading up to your problem statement is important. A global problem, broad in nature, is included in the first paragraph of your introduction, often with data emphasizing the severity of the problem. Narrowing the global problem leads to a more specific problem statement that your study will address. The problem statement is often presented in a brief paragraph under the heading Problem Statement or embedded at the conclusion of your introduction.

Example Problem Statements

Qualitative Problem Statement

The problem statement in DeLee's (2014) qualitative study suggests an exploratory study. The statement is framed by a discussion of issues, followed by a specific problem to be investigated. DeLee's qualitative problem statement is as follows:

> The counselors' style and the manner they are developing begin to form during their first clinical experiences in practicum and internship courses (Paladino, Minton, & Kern, 2011). Training counseling students in communication skills and developing self-awareness is a goal of practicum and internship courses. Increasing these skills and improving these abilities benefits them and improves clinical skills. Preparing counselors-in-training (CITs) to communicate in a way that accounts for their sensory data, emotions, thoughts, intentions, and behaviors has the possibility of helping them recognize the effect they have in the counseling session.
>
> Additionally, having an opportunity to practice basic self-awareness at this early stage of clinical work might help CITs with important counseling issues such as interpersonal awareness, transference, countertransference, problem identification, and intentional intervention strategies. These skills are facilitated by greater interpersonal communication and are mandated by accreditation.
>
> Group supervision is widely practiced in counselor education but yields limited research. The need for newly trained counselors to develop intentionality and basic counseling skills has been discussed through the literature. New counselors struggle with intentionality and basic counseling skills, even as they approach graduation and enter into the profession (Gersten et al., 2013). This points to the need for effective supervision and a method of teaching intentionality in particular.
>
> The Awareness Wheel provides a concrete way for the supervisor to assess the skills new counselors-in-training are developing in client awareness, intervention goals, and communications skills. It is important for supervisors to cultivate a relationship with the supervisee that allows for honesty between supervisor and supervisees. Training programs for counselors-in-training focusing on basic microskills have shown to be effective in improving clinical awareness and skill sets (Duys & Hedstrom, 2000). Implementing a template for communication focusing on sensory data, thoughts, feelings, intentions, and actions in the context of supervision allows an experiential opportunity to practice effective communication in the supervision group as well as in the counseling sessions under critique. Research exploring effective methods for providing group supervision as well as research about the development of self-awareness and communication in counselors-in-training is limited.

Quantitative Problem Statement

Froeschle's (2005) quantitative experiment used a random selection process and a control group. The problem statement is framed around the fact there are few studies investigating this sample using a solution-focused treatment program. Froeschle's quantitative problem statement is as follows:

As adolescent females mature, they seek to establish a unique identity and autonomy from their parents. Negative influences and a lack of proper role models can affect their choices made about drinking, drugs, and smoking. Females are abusing prescription and illegal drugs at alarming rates and differences between rates of male and female addictions is now minimal (Najavits, 2002). Research has indicated that school based programs have the potential to reduce drug use among mixed groups of males and females (Black, Tobler & Sciacca, 1998; Botvin, Baker, Dusenbury, Tortu & Botvin, 1990; Pentz, Trebow, Hansen, Mackinnon & Dwyer, 1990). Comprehensive group programs containing educationally relevant topics and strategies (e.g., personal and social skills, concrete information, and information about negative social consequences of drug use, peer pressure, normative education, decision making, goal setting, and interactive learning) have been effective in reducing drug use among adolescents (Celia, Tulsky, Sarafian, Thomas & Thomas, 1992; Dusenbury & Falco, 1995). Small group instruction has also shown to increase negative attitudes toward smoking (Celia et al., 1992).

The female role, along with other specific factors, forms a component in addictions (Najavits, 2002). Teenage girls may be greatly influenced by male counterparts and may place undue emphasis on physical appearance and pleasing others than males (Najavits, 2002). Additionally, females may be unresponsive to confrontational counselling techniques and those geared toward male problem solving (Berg & Reuss, 1998). Treatments such as Solution Focused Brief Therapy may address the experiential component needed to address gender and individual specific concerns faced by females such as relationship, abuse, childcare, sexual, and control issues (Berg & Reuss, 1998). There is a dearth of research defining effective drug prevention methods for females (Blumenthal, 1998). The role of gender in drug use is often excluded from intervention effectiveness studies (Blake, et al., 2001; Blumenthal, 1998; & Najavits, 2002).

Mixed-Methods Problem Statement

Mixed-methods studies use both quantitative and qualitative designs. Abel et al. (2012) used a quantitative design that investigated whether a stress management program would reduce participants' level of stress. In the second phase, using a qualitative design, they explored what participants attributed to their reduced stress levels. In Phase 1 of another study, Cueva (2006) used a qualitative design to explore whether young children could understand complex achievement motivation concepts before designing and implementing an experimental program in Phase 2.

In the following mixed-methods problem statement, E. M. Smith (2004) used both quantitative and qualitative language in the statement of the problem and in identifying the setting of the investigation. Please note how E. M. Smith first provided a lengthy backdrop of the study and then included a concise problem statement in the closing paragraph.

Educators and other interested citizens have long been concerned about the problem of school dropout prevention. In fact, the dropout problem has continued to be one of the major concerns of teachers, counselors, parents, and administrators, even though the percentage of dropouts is smaller than it was in early and middle 20th century society. Graduation rates have risen from 38% in 1940 to 88% in 1998. Despite this improvement, the National Center for Health Statistics reported that about one million students drop out annually, meaning that 25 to 30% of students who begin high school do not finish (Benson, 2001). Each year 400,000 students do not start school at the beginning of the fall semester, and 600,000 more drop out during the remainder of the school year. The dropout rate in large American cities has been estimated at 50% (Walburton, Bugarin, & Nunez, 2001).

Educational interest groups have been equally disturbed by the current increase in school violence, coupled with decreasing levels of academic achievement and performance. In recent years, the literature has been inundated with studies that have attempted to discover the reasons for the large number of students who leave school before graduation. Lara and Pande (2001) pointed out several alarming trends in education. Research indicated that dropping out of school is a social class phenomenon related to work, school failure, inability to get along with teachers, discipline, dislike or fear of school peers, lack of interest, and a sense that schoolwork does not relate to individual needs. Experts in the field of education realized that if schools are going to mount a successful attack on the dropout problem, preventive measures and other programs designed to keep students in school must be developed and implemented. Emotional Intelligence, EI, skill training is a model proposed as a dropout prevention measure that warrants further exploration. Educators need to understand what interventions from programs as EI can help prevent them from dropping out.

The problem under investigation in this study is whether a comprehensive curriculum for a program of EI skills training can significantly impact high school students who have been identified as being at-risk of dropping out of school before graduation. The qualitative phase of the study will collect rich information providing insight into the phenomenon under investigation using individual interviews, focus groups, observations, and action research.

Purpose Statement

The problem statement sets the stage for the purpose statement and lets the reader know how you plan to address the problem. The purpose statement includes information about the direction of your study. The purpose statement is considered the most important statement in a proposal, so it requires clear, specific, informative writing (Creswell, 2014).

The purpose statement is also meant to answer the "what" question (i.e., the question of what you are planning). It sets the foundation for your research questions, hypotheses, methodology, and the remainder of your investigation. Because of its importance, the purpose statement in a dissertation proposal is often included under a heading by itself.

Novice researchers often confuse the purpose statement with the problem statement. What is the difference between the problem and purpose statement? To clarify, the problem statement underscores the problem that needs to be investigated and answers the question of why you are conducting the study. The purpose statement tells the reader how you are going to address the problem.

Qualitative purpose statements identify the phenomenon about to be studied, participants of the study, and the setting. These statements avoid words designating differences and relationships. They use words such as *explore, understand, discover,* and *examine*, along with other action verbs. The verbs used in qualitative purpose statements should not suggest outcomes, differences, or relationships. The language used in qualitative studies differs from that used in quantitative investigations. In addition, quantitative studies investigate variables examining correlations and differences. The purpose statement of a quantitative investigation includes its underlying theory, variables investigated, participants, and research site (Creswell, 2014).

Mixed-methods purpose statements include information pertaining to both quantitative and qualitative phases of a study. Creswell and Plano Clark (2011) identified three mixed-methods designs: convergent, explanatory sequential, and exploratory sequential. A convergent design gathers and analyzes qualitative and quantitative data separately and then merges data sets. An explanatory sequential mixed-methods design obtains data from the quantitative phase of the study, followed by qualitative data to gain a deeper understanding of earlier quantitative findings. An exploratory sequential design gathers qualitative data on a phenomenon and uses these findings to implement a quantitative study.

Example Purpose Statements

Qualitative Purpose Statement

Rodriguez (2014) used a qualitative design to explore the cultural immersion experiences of students. Rodriguez's purpose statement is as follows:

> The purpose of this study is to gain a better understanding of the study abroad experiences of graduate counseling students. The study is informative regarding experiences of students who will be participating in a course including service learning and cultural immersion activities in Costa Rica. The purpose of the study is to gain students' perceptions of experiences contributing to their learning. Information in this study can benefit educators planning for study abroad activities and students interested in participating in similar programs.

Quantitative Purpose Statement

Herrero (2014) investigated relationships among strength-based factors that contribute to college students' academic achievement. Herrero's purpose statement is as follows:

> The purpose of this study is to investigate the relationship among several strength-based factors that contribute to academic success. This research will explore how achievement motivation, hope, and resilience predict academic achievement of first-year college students enrolled in a Hispanic-serving institution. Identifying factors that contribute to academic success is important for helping students cope with the personal and academic stressors of transitioning to college. Furthermore, understanding the impact of nonacademic factors on academic achievement can lead to the development of strategies that can be utilized to help improve the performance and increase the retention of college freshmen.

Mixed-Methods Purpose Statement

Shomaker's (2013) mixed-methods purpose statement identifies the design of the study and the specifics related to the methodology. This purpose statement is as follows:

> The purpose of this study is to examine the effects of a mindfulness training program (MTP) on the establishment of therapeutic alliance among master's level CITs and their clients. A structured mindfulness intervention is expected to have an impact on CIT's level of mindfulness and empathy. Existing research on mindfulness interventions with CITs has predominantly focused on a single research methodology (qualitative). This project will afford the consideration of

combining the benefits of multiple research approaches in an effort to complement previous research. This project uses a mixed-methods convergent parallel design (Creswell & Plano Clark, 2011), whereby quantitative and qualitative data will be collected concurrently, analyzed independently, and compared. Including quantitative and qualitative elements within the study will allow the combined results to have an enriching context and depth. The quantitative portion of the study will include a time-series and pre- and post-data collection method to evaluate the impact of the mindfulness training on therapeutic alliance, mindfulness, and empathy. Therapeutic alliance scores will be collected over 14 weeks in a time-series format while empathy and mindfulness scores were collected pre- and post-training. A qualitative, phenomenological approach (Moustakas, 1994; van Manen (2001) will be used to explore the experiences of CITs as they learn and apply mindfulness practices to their personal and professional lives.

Research Questions

Research questions in a dissertation proposal provide specificity to further clarify what the researcher wants to find. Research questions direct a study by using methods of inquiry and identifying variables under investigation. Qualitative research questions provide avenues for exploration, understanding, and discovery, and they consist of one or two open-ended questions, followed by two or three subquestions. Quantitative research questions correlate variables, predict relationships, and inquire about differences. Mixed-methods designs include both qualitative and quantitative research questions.

Qualitative Research Questions

Rosenbaum (2015) included a grand tour question and three subquestions in the qualitative dissertation proposal. Grand tour questions are broad, thereby allowing interviewees to voice their thoughts without limitations. Grand tour questions also allow interviewees to respond openly without the guidance of the interviewer. Rosenbaum's qualitative research questions are as follows:

> The overarching research question directing this inquiry is "What are the experiences of juvenile offenders who were detained in the juvenile justice system?" The secondary research questions are:
> 1. What is the juvenile's history and background prior to detainment?
> 2. What are the experiences of juvenile offenders during detainment?
> 3. What are the future plans of juvenile offenders upon release from detainment?

Quantitative Research Questions

Arora (2015) proposed several research questions in a quantitative study. These questions are as follows:

> 1. What is the extent of difference between athletes and non-athletes in Achievement Motivation levels?
> 2. What is the extent of difference between athletes and non-athletes in Resiliency levels?
> 3. What is the extent of the relationship between Achievement Motivation and Resiliency levels of student athletes and non-athletes?
> 4. What is the effect of student status as an athlete and non-athlete on the relationship between Resilience and Achievement Motivation?

Mixed-Methods Research Questions

In her mixed-methods proposed study, Shomaker (2013) included four research questions for the quantitative phase of the study and two broad open-ended questions for the qualitative phase. The quantitative research questions included the following:

1. What are the effects of a mindfulness intervention with counselor in training?
2. What are the effects of the mindfulness intervention on therapeutic alliance outcomes as reported by CITs, clients, and instructors?
3. What are the effects of the mindfulness intervention with regard to CITs, mindfulness, and empathy?
4. To what extent is CIT practice related to outcome mindfulness measures?

The qualitative research questions included the following:

1. What are the experiences of CITs as they participate in a mindfulness intervention?
2. How will these experiences manifest in the personal and professional lives of CITs?

Hypotheses

Kerlinger (1979) defined a hypothesis as a conjectural statement of the relation between two or more variables. Creswell (1994) defined a hypothesis as a formal statement that presents the expected relationship between an independent and dependent variable. Hypotheses are more formal than research questions and infer a prediction of what the researcher might expect. A hypothesis is a statement generated from a question using "if" and "then" statements. A well-written hypothesis needs to have clarity and provide the reader with what is expected along with how variables will be measured. Hypotheses include independent and dependent variables. Hypotheses in quantitative studies speculate outcomes based on the researcher's prediction. Both research questions and hypotheses specify what the researcher wants to find as a result of conducting a study. Qualitative designs use research questions, whereas experimental studies often use hypotheses.

Null Hypotheses

A null hypothesis (H_o) states no difference between variables studied. In experimental investigations, the H_o predicts no differences after treatment. For example, if a researcher implements a treatment group program to increase resilience among at-risk students and uses a control group, the H_o would predict no difference in the two groups' level of resilience following treatment. If the H_o is rejected, it is possible for a Type I error. A Type I error can occur, if the H_o is wrongly rejected. Therefore, on the basis of a Type I error, the researcher may theoretically infer that the treatment did not make a difference. When the H_o fails to be rejected and no difference between the two groups is stated, a Type II error is possible, which indicates that differences could have occurred.

Alternate Hypotheses

Alternate hypotheses (H_1) predict a direction expected by the researcher and preferably supported by earlier research findings. For the previous example of the resilience treatment study, the H_1 would state the treatment is predicted to significantly increase levels of resilience when compared with a control group. Researchers using H_1 have confidence in the direction of their prediction and often have the support of previous research findings.

Example Illustrating the Difference Between Hypotheses and Research Questions

Froeschle (2005) included three research hypotheses in her experimental study:

1. There is no significant difference between the mean pretest and mean posttest scores of students in the experimental group and control group in drug use as measured by the American Drug and Alcohol Survey (ADAS).
2. There is no significant difference between the mean pretest and mean posttest scores of students in the experimental group and control group in attitudes toward drug use as measured by the Substance Abuse Subtle Screening Inventory, 2nd Edition (Sassi-A2) Attitude scale.
3. There is no significant difference between the mean pretest and mean posttest scores of students' knowledge of the physical symptoms of drug abuse in the experimental and control groups as measured by the drug knowledge questionnaire.

Comparative research questions for the previous hypotheses are as follows:

1. To what extent will there be a difference in the measured score of American Drug and Alcohol Survey (ADAS) before and after the drug intervention program?
2. To what extent will there be a difference in the measured score of Substance Abuse Subtle Screening Inventory before and after the drug intervention program?
3. To what extent will there be a difference in the knowledge level of the physical symptoms of drug abuse before and after the drug intervention program?

Summary

In this chapter, we covered the introduction section of a dissertation proposal. To assist in writing the literature section of your introduction, Creswell (2014) recommended emphasizing deficiencies found in the literature. This strategy will identify gaps in the literature that will support your topic. By writing a well-crafted problem statement within your introduction, you will be letting the reader know the specific issue that you plan to address. Your problem statement will be setting the stage for your purpose statement and your research questions. The specific problem you plan to address can also be stated at the conclusion of your introduction or under a separate heading. To assist in writing your problem statement, we included examples for qualitative, quantitative, and mixed-methods studies in this chapter.

The purpose statement, according to Creswell (2014), is the most important statement in a dissertation proposal. Your purpose statement will inform readers of your plans to address the problem. Your purpose statement can be included under a separate heading to emphasize the direction of your study. We also included example purpose statements for qualitative, quantitative, and mixed-methods studies in this chapter.

Research questions and hypotheses will provide further specificity and direction to your study. Well-written research questions and hypotheses will indicate how you will be analyzing your data. If you are using a qualitative research design, your research questions will be broad in nature, followed by two or three subquestions. Quantitative investigations use either research questions or hypotheses. Experimental studies use hypotheses stated in either the null or the alternate form. The H_o predicts no difference, whereas the H_1 is directional. We provided example research questions for qualitative, quantitative, and mixed-methods studies in this chapter to assist you in completing this section of your proposal. Example hypotheses are included if you are using a quantitative design in your study. In this chapter, we provided information that introduces you to the method section of the dissertation proposal and prepares you to understand ethical issues related to sampling and data collection, which are covered in Chapter 7. Continue to enjoy learning the process of writing a sound dissertation proposal, completing a dissertation, and graduating.

Checklist

❏ Discuss how a research problem in a qualitative design differs from a research problem in a quantitative design.
❏ For practice, select two concepts from the following listing and develop a one-paragraph problem statement for each.
  • Self-actualization
  • Creativity
  • Resilience
  • Intelligence
  • Leadership
  • Happiness
  • Hope
❏ Select two of the concepts from the previous list and develop a one-paragraph purpose statement for each.
❏ Construct three research questions for Rodriguez's (2014) and Shomaker's (2013) purpose statements included in this chapter.
❏ Complete the introduction section of your dissertation proposal (2–5 pages).
❏ Complete your problem statement (1 paragraph).
❏ Complete the purpose statement (1 paragraph).

❑ Share the completed introduction, problem statement, and purpose statement with your dissertation chair.

❑ Meet with your dissertation chair to draft your research questions.

Additional Resources

Coty-Barker, V. [AshfordScience]. (2013, July 10). *How to formulate a hypothesis* [Video file]. Retrieved from https://www.youtube.com/watch?v=bp2fbzWZDmA

Creswell, J. W. (2014). *Research design: Qualitative, quantitative, and mixed methods approaches* (4th ed.). Thousand Oaks, CA: Sage.

Glen, S. [Stephanie Glen]. (2013, September 4). *What is a null hypothesis (and alternate hypothesis)* [Video file]. Retrieved from https://www.youtube.com/watch?v=tDmCFVQvv2A

Johnson, B., & Christensen, L. (2008). *Educational research: Quantitative, qualitative, and mixed approaches*. Thousand Oaks, CA: Sage.

Luther, B. [blutherWGU]. (2012, September 4). *Research problem and purpose statement* [Video file]. Retrieved from https://www.youtube.com/watch?v=fbwxQBLrkfc

McDaniel, B. [Stomp On Step 1]. (2016, April 19). *Null hypothesis, p-value, statistical significance, type 1 error and type 2 error* [Video file]. Retrieved from https://www.youtube.com/watch?v=YSwmpAmLV2s

Wallace, R. [Ron Wallace]. (2013, May 20). *Research questions hypothesis and variables* [Video file]. Retrieved from https://www.youtube.com/watch?v=_BmjujlZExQ

Chapter 7

Research Methodology and Ethics

By the time you begin writing your dissertation, you probably have completed your research courses, and through these courses, you have learned about a variety of research methods. In this chapter, we discuss the selection of a research method based on the type of inquiry you wish to make. Keep in mind that this chapter highlights research methods for the purpose of designing research for your dissertation. The specifics related to analyzing data, whether quantitative or qualitative, is outside the purview of this text, and students are encouraged to review their research methods texts for a more in-depth review and understanding of research methods. We address important facets related to the design of your study and the research ethics and processes related to your IRB.

The Tail Wagging the Dog: Matching a Research Question to a Methodology

Ask any professor who has chaired dissertations and you will probably hear a conversation that goes something like this:

Student: For my dissertation, I want to make an instrument.
Professor: What do you want to measure?
Student: I don't know.

Or perhaps this one:

Student: I am going to do a _____ for my dissertation. [Fill in the blank. It could be anything, such as multiple regression, structural equation modeling, grounded theory, or phenomenology.]
Professor: OK . . . what's your research question?
Student: I don't know.

I'm sure you see the problem here. You see, this is something you have to know, and unfortunately, the student in each of these scenarios is making a huge, incorrect assumption—that the preference for a research method is the deciding factor of the research that the student chooses to initiate. Such a supposition would be the equivalent of the tail wagging the dog.

Of course, the opposite is true. Your research questions/hypotheses will govern the type of methodology you use. This is not to say that your preference for a methodology will not be a factor in the type of study you undertake. (It certainly will!) However, the methods are selected based on the research question—not vice versa! For example, if you want to evaluate the efficacy of a program or intervention, then you will probably use some type of quantitative method. If you want to understand the clients' experiences during the program or intervention, you might consider qualitative inquiry. To go further, however, as a researcher, you not only need to discern the type of method (e.g., quantitative, qualitative) to best answer your research questions but also need to consider the specific methodological theories and frameworks that underlie a research method. Let's look at our previous example. If you want to evaluate the efficacy of a program or intervention, your study would likely consist of group comparisons—one group who received the treatment or program and another group that did not. Depending on the number of variables being measured, the presence of covariates, and the potential inclusion of random assignment in to the design, you would likely consider some type of univariate or multivariate analysis of variance. A correlational design would not be a likely consideration given the research question. Even if the student insists that this is the type of research strategy preferred, such a strategy does not answer this particular research question. Similar scenarios exist with qualitative research as well. A student who wishes to understand the clients' experiences during the program or intervention is not going to be doing grounded theory but would choose a more appropriate method of qualitative inquiry, such as phenomenology. Once again, the research question is the driving force for the methods used.

With that being said, having an understanding of the types of research strategies and analyses you feel comfortable with is an important consideration. Using a type of analysis outside of your scope of training can be daunting, but it can also provide a wonderful learning experience! Hence, you should talk with your chair about how the dissertation process contributes to areas of personal growth, and there is certainly nothing wrong with choosing a research method that allows you to stretch and develop further tools and areas of expertise. On the other hand, you will be drawn to particular research methods and likely will conceptualize research questions that match your interests. For example, researchers who enjoy qualitative inquiry tend to develop research questions that fit this interest. The same is true for researchers who predominately conduct quantitative research. Keep in mind that some research questions are best answered quantitatively, and some are best answered qualitatively, but the methods selected will be based on the nature of the research questions and vice versa.

Sampling Strategy

Within the dissertation framework, there can be many potential pitfalls, ranging from getting your research approved from the IRB to maintaining discipline in your writing. Most of these things are in your control. However, one area that may be a little outside of your control is obtaining participants for your study. Unless you plan on using a data set collected ex post facto (i.e., a preexisting data set), data collection can be stressful. Let's take a look at sampling strategies in both quantitative and qualitative research.

Matching Sampling Strategy to Quantitative Methods

Recall that the primary goal of quantitative research is to produce findings that are generalizable, and in quantitative research, emphasis is placed on obtaining participants based on random sampling. Random sampling is typically categorized into one of four processes:

- Simple random sampling is when participants from a target population have an equal opportunity of being selected.
- Stratified random sampling refers to a process of random sampling that is proportional; the researcher can set up preestablished guidelines as to what percentage of each group the researcher wants in the study (e.g., 50% male, 50% female; representative percentages of a population according to census).
- Cluster sampling is when preestablished groups are randomly selected (e.g., schools are randomly selected from a district, and the classroom is randomly selected from the school).
- Systematic sampling refers to a process in which a formula is used to select participants (e.g., every 4th house on a block is surveyed).

Although random sampling is important to contributing to generalizable results, the reality is that random sampling is easily compromised in counseling research and is often not even feasible. Hence, counseling researchers often use nonprobability sampling (i.e., convenience sampling). Simply put, counseling researchers often have samples related to who is accessible, rather than random participation. To understand this, you should consider the nature of human subjects research and informed consent.

Who participates in a research study? Consider the numerous times you have been solicited to complete a survey or measure. Did you ignore the solicitation? Did you take time to complete the study? The rise of Internet-based research has resulted in an inundation of opportunities to participate in research, and as a result, people may no longer feel compelled to participate. Furthermore, people who participate in research often have an interest in the study, which could result in a sampling bias. Consider, for example, a study conducted by Perepiczka and Balkin (2010), who studied wellness among counselor education doctoral students.

> Participants were recruited by the first author, who e-mailed faculty members of CACREP-accredited doctoral programs. The faculty members were asked to forward information about the opportunity to participate in the study to their students. One hundred ninety-four students from CACREP-accredited CES doctoral programs representing 25 states completed the online survey within the 4-week time frame. Of the 194 surveys, 21 were unusable because of incomplete or missing data. Thus, a total of 173 surveys were used for analysis. (p. 206)

Here are some unanswered questions based on Perepiczka and Balkin's (2010) description of their methods:

- How many of the CACREP faculty liaisons forwarded the study request to their students?
- How many students received the request for participation?
- Why 21 participants skipped items or chose not to complete the study once they started?
- Why some students chose to participate and others did not?

Hence, the response rate is unknown. In addition, Perepiczka and Balkin identified limitations with the sample, indicating that "recruiting the sample was dependent upon faculty members choosing to collaborate and prospective participants having the time required to participate. These factors could have lowered the number of participants recruited" (p. 213).

These types of limitations are not atypical for counseling research, which often uses nonprobability sampling. Thus, the notion that individuals who qualify for the study had an equal opportunity to participate is simply not the case here. So how can research results in counseling ever be generalizable if the designs typically used lack random sampling? There are two issues to consider with this.

First, we often look at sampling as a dichotomous process—either participants in a study were randomly selected (i.e., probability sampling) or they were not (i.e., nonprobability/convenience sampling). However, an alternative is to view random sampling as a continuum. There is a sense of randomness to Perepiczka and Balkin's (2010) study. All CACREP programs at the time were contacted, and students who chose to participate were in no way selected by the researchers. However, the nature of informed consent (students must agree to participate) and the reliance of CACREP faculty liaisons to provide the announcement to students compromised randomness. Therefore, random sampling may be seen more as a continuum than a dichotomous process because there are aspects of randomness in the study that are not controlled by the researchers.

Second, consider the importance of representativeness over randomness. Once again, consider the nature of informed consent. Doctoral students who choose to participate in the study likely have an interest. Some doctoral students may participate because of a genuine interest in the study. Others may participate for other reasons, such as *research karma*, the belief that by participating in a research study, people will earn karma, which, in turn, will help them obtain an appropriate sample size for their own studies. However, the promotion of research findings that are generalizable is dependent on the extent to which the researcher can argue that the participants were representative of the target population. Consider the following statement from Perepiczka and Balkin (2010):

> An overrepresentation of particular groups (e.g., single, married, female, Caucasian, enrolled in the first 3 years of their CES doctoral program, and in their mid-20s and early 30s) occurred in the sample. However, this occurrence is representative of the accessible and total population of CES doctoral students in CACREP-accredited programs. (p. 213)

The authors defended their sampling method by indicating that despite limitations to random sampling, participants in the study were representative to the target population, which lends credence to the argument of generalizable results.

Matching Sampling Strategy to Qualitative Methods

Qualitative sampling strategies are far more nuanced than quantitative sampling strategies, which either use degrees of randomness (i.e., simple random sampling, stratified random sampling, cluster sampling, and systematic sampling) or do not (i.e., convenience sampling). Qualitative inquiry uses purposeful sampling in which participants for a study are intentionally selected by the researcher. Patton (2015) identified 16 purposeful sampling strategies in qualitative research. Discussing each of the strategies is beyond the scope of this book, but interested readers may refer to Patton's seminal book, *Qualitative Research and Evaluation Methods*, or Suri (2011) for a more succinct summary. It is important to understand that purposeful sampling is not nonprobability sampling and vice versa. For example, a quantitative researcher should not use snowball sampling—a purposeful sampling strategy in which participants are referred to a study from other participants. Instead, the researcher should recruit individuals who meet the criteria of a study to obtain a representative sample. Similarly, in qualitative research, the researcher uses purposeful sampling strategies to obtain narrative data from information-rich sources. In qualitative research, specific individuals are sought out to lend perspective and understanding related to an experience or phenomenon. Although Patton identified convenience sampling as a type of purposeful sampling strategy, such a sampling process should not be considered unless all potential participants could serve as information-rich sources. Counseling researchers should consider the goals of the study and how the sampling method will include participants who can inform the topic of inquiry.

Describing Participant Characteristics

An accurate description of participants is pertinent for counseling research and publication. Participant characteristics provide an understanding of who was included in the study, so the audience can be informed of the representativeness and generalizability (in the case of quantitative research) or the transferability and usefulness (in the case of qualitative research). Studies that lack inclusion of essential demographic characteristics, including sex and ethnicity, are unlikely to be accepted for publication. In addition, researchers should include additional demographic information that serves as key components to the research. Consider variables such as annual income (i.e., socioeconomic status), age, gender identity, and religious affiliation if they are essential to a study. For example, in their study, Perepiczka and Balkin (2010) reported the number of years of experience in a CES program, which was important for understanding doctoral student wellness among the participants and for comparing this study to similar studies with CES doctoral students.

One issue to be conscientious of is the use of artificially categorized variables, which is a common problem in counseling research. Variables such as age, years of experience, or income are naturally continuous variables. Often however, counselors will artificially place them in categories. For example, a researcher conducting a study on career satisfaction might inquire about socioeconomic status related to annual salary with the following categories: $39,999 and below, $40,000 to 99,999, and $100,000 and above. There are two problems with this. First, means and standard deviations cannot be computed from categories. If the participants identified their annual incomes, the researcher could place the values into categories later, but the reverse cannot happen. In addition, the researcher loses information. Consider a participant who makes $90,000 per year. Is this participant really similar to someone who earns $40,000, or is the participant more like someone who earns $100,000? Therefore, the categories are arbitrary and make little sense.

In summary, counseling researchers need to think carefully about the variables needed to accurately describe participants in light of the specific research being undertaken. Researchers should be attentive to how variables are collected and make certain that information is not lost. As a rule, continuous variables can be made discrete, but discrete variables cannot be made continuous.

Discussing Sample Size, Power, and Precision

This is the part of the book where we finally answer the age-old question, "Does size really matter?" Of course, we are referring to sample size. A major error in quantitative research is simply trying to collect as much data as possible without considering the methods used to identify the appropriate sample size necessary for a study. In addition, guidelines for sample size are quite different for quantitative and qualitative research.

Before we get into the specifics related to sample size for quantitative and qualitative research, this is a good time to consider a common misconception about quantitative and qualitative dissertations: Qualitative dissertations take more time to complete than quantitative dissertations. The time required is not really different, but rather, how you spend your time is different. Honestly, data collection might be the most stressful aspect of the dissertation but for different reasons. When you approach a quantitative study, you lose some control in the type and amount of data you collect. This is especially true when you use survey methods because the response rate is difficult to predict and the time required to collect all the necessary data is not in your control. In addition, while you wait for your data to come in, you may be stalled in your writing process.

On the other hand, qualitative data collection is stressful because of the amount of data coming in and the process of transcribing and organizing the data. Unlike quantitative research, you can schedule your observations and interviews and assume responsibility for transcribing and bundling your data. In this case, data collection requires a significant amount of time, but you have control of that time, whereas in quantitative research there might be points where you feel dependent on others completing surveys or measures.

Quantitative Research

For a quantitative dissertation, the best practice is, if possible, to conduct an a priori power analysis. This is a simple procedure (see Balkin & Sheperis, 2011), which can be done with free software such as G*Power, to determine the appropriate sample size of a study given (a) the type of analysis conducted (e.g., analysis of variance, regression), (b) the alpha level for a study, and (c) the estimated effect size for a study. Depending on the analysis, additional information (e.g., the number of predictor variables in a multiple regression, the number of repetitions in repeated measures) may be needed. Unfortunately, G*Power cannot be used for more complicated analyses, such as canonical correlation or structural equation modeling. For situations such as this, researchers may want to rely on published rules of thumb related to sample size, which often vary from five to 20 participants per item or variables, depending on the analysis and other data characteristics, such as reliability or factor structure of the scores on a scale. Researchers are encouraged to evaluate sources that discuss sample size with more complicated analyses (e.g., Pituch & Stevens, 2016).

When conducting an a priori power analysis to determine the necessary sample size, you need to consider the estimated effect size, which is unknown at the time of conducting the power analysis because data were not collected yet. We recommend estimating a moderate effect size, which will enable you to identify the appropriate sample size to establish statistical significance with a moderate effect size based on standards established by Cohen (1988). With an estimated moderate effect size, you can focus on collecting data from a reasonable sample size—one that is not too large so that data collection is not overly burdensome and statistical significance is not found for minor influences and one that is not too small so that risk of a Type II error is more likely. Consider the following example by Balkin, Miller, Ricard, Garcia, and Lancaster (2011):

> A MANOVA was conducted using an alpha level of .05 on RAASI subscales across two groups: adolescents who did not reoffend after court referral and adolescents who reoffended after court referral. Power was adequate for this study. An a priori power analysis given an alpha level of .05, a moderate effect size, and sufficient power calculated at .80 (Cohen, 1988) yielded a minimal sample size of 54 to be necessary; the sample size for this study was 178. (p. 55)

Qualitative Research

Guidelines for sample size in qualitative research are not so objective and specific. Qualitative inquiry is often governed by a concept known as *saturation* in which the researcher identifies that the patterns from data being collected (e.g., interviews, observations) are repetitive and no further data are necessary to identify themes. Hence, the decision to cease data collection is a decision from the researcher, but the researcher must also make the case for the identification of saturation. When proposing a qualitative study, you may wish to consider or estimate how many participants are necessary based on previous research or similar studies. Because of the nature of qualitative inquiry, sample size could be adjusted, but it is nice to go in with an idea or plan that you can communicate to your chair and committee and may be executed upon approval. The decision to cease data collection should be considered under consultation given methods related to trustworthiness, such as researcher triangulation (e.g., consultation with your chair) and peer debriefing. Consider how Koltz and Feit (2012) document saturation in the following example:

> After completion of the first round of interviews, a professional transcriptionist transcribed the audiotapes into transcribed data. . . . After data from the second round of interviews [were] coded, an individual member check interview was conducted. Therefore, a total of 9 interviews were conducted for this research study. Data saturation was achieved when participants no longer described their experiences with the pre-practicum class and were describing thoughts and experiences about the practicum, which was to begin the following semester. (pp. 4–5)

Describing Measures and Questionnaires

The extent to which a study makes a meaningful contribution to the literature relies, in part, on the quality of the measures. Measures that are objective or based on evidence of strong psychometric properties (i.e., validity and reliability) are a foundational element of counseling research. A description of the instruments used in a study typically comes under the subheading of Measures within the method section of a dissertation.

Evidence of Validity

Counseling researchers need to be aware of the modern concepts of measurement validity outlined in the *Standards for Educational and Psychological Testing* (American Educational Research Association, APA, & National Council on Measurement in Education, 2014), which include evidence of (a) test content, (b) response processes, (c) internal structure, (d) relationship to other variables, and (e) consequences of testing. Typically, evidence of test content and responses processes are indicated when you identify the purpose of the measure, describe the scale (e.g., Likert-type, semantic differentials), and provide sample items from the measure as an example of the scale/subscales. You should also provide evidence of internal structure and relationship to other variables by summarizing statistical procedures used to classify the items (e.g., exploratory or confirmatory factor analysis) and research in which the measure was used to predict or establish relationships with other outcomes or measures. A rationale about the selection of the measure with respect to other measures may be relevant to identify consequences of testing.

Reliability of Scores

One of the most common errors counselors will find when reading research is related to the reporting of reliability, in which scales are reported as reliable, often accompanied by a measure of reliability such as Cronbach's alpha. The problem with this type of disclosure is that reliability is a function of scores, not scale! In other words, a measure should never be described as being reliable. Rather, the scores on the scale may be evidence of accuracy of consistency (i.e., reliability). To demonstrate reliability of scores on a measure, researchers should potentially include two points of information: (a) reliability of the scores from the participants in the present study and (b) past research indicative of reliability estimates of the scores.

For example, consider the following format when reporting reliability estimates. Balkin, Perepiczka, Sowell, Cumi, and Gnilka (2016) used the Forgiveness Reconciliation Inventory and reported the following: "Reliability estimates for the scores of the normative sample (and used in this study) were as follows: collaborative exploration (.90), role of reconciliation (.88), remorse/change (.92), and outcome (.93)" (p. 59).

So far, we have emphasized measures that are typical in quantitative research. However, not all research relies on measures with strong psychometric properties. Qualitative inquiry often relies on interviews. Questionnaires may be used to collect important demographic information or obtain data on a specific phenomenon or event (e.g., How many suicidal ideations have you had in the past 24 hours? How many sessions of counseling have you had in the 6 months?). Therefore, scores are not necessarily a component of a measure; data may be more objective, and reliability and validity may not be appropriate features to consider. When using questionnaires, you should make sure that the information gathered in each question will be interpreted and answered in a consistent manner. Pilot testing of questionnaires is important in the research process to identify any glitches within the questionnaire that could lead to ambiguous results.

Describing Procedures to Promote Replication

The results of counseling research, and social science research in general, are often sample specific. What? Wait a minute. Let's review that last statement again. You probably learned that qualitative research is time and context bound (Patton, 2015), but what about quantitative research? You are probably thinking that the overarching goal of quantitative research is to create generalizable results—and that is true—except it does not happen all that often. True replication of findings is an uncommon occurrence, with the majority of studies attempted by the Open Science Collaboration having nonsignificant results that were initially deemed statistically significant, and less than half the studies were replicated in terms of magnitude of effect (Open Science Collaboration, 2015). So what is the point of taking the time to show something as generalizable if the study is not likely to have replicable findings anyway?

The goal of research is to add to the knowledge base of the counseling profession. To do this, the methods used in research need to be explicit enough that other researchers can substantiate the findings. Consider the process of your sampling procedures and participant characteristics; details of your measures; and the process you use to obtain consent, randomize groups and initiate interventions (if applicable), administer measures, and analyze data. Because the majority of counseling researchers use nonprobability sampling, the limitations to generalizability will likely be an ongoing challenge. For example, Lancaster, Balkin, Garcia, and Valarezo (2011) evaluated the effects of a community-based intervention program against a control group for adjudicated adolescents. Within the article, they described the demographic characteristics of the participants with respect to sex, age, ethnicity, and type of initial offense. However, other variables, such as education, were not considered and present as a limitation to the results. In addition, efforts were made to describe the treatment approach and statistical analyses used. However, a serious limitation to replication (and therefore generalizability) was that the intervention was not manualized. Rather, "client need, as evidenced through formal and informal assessment measures given during intake" (Lancaster et al., 2011, p. 490) determined what strategies were implemented. Despite the details provided in the study, replication can still be challenging.

Ethics

So far in this chapter, we have focused on the procedures related to collecting data for your study. Pertinent to these procedures is compliance with the federal law based on the Office of Human Research Protections (OHRP; Public Welfare, 2009) and Section G: Research and Publication in the *ACA Code of Ethics* (ACA, 2014). Before actually collecting data for your dissertation, you will need to have approval from your IRB. All agencies and organizations that receive federal funding and conduct research are required to have an IRB. Although OHRP provides federal guidelines, some latitude exists as to how the guidelines are implemented; therefore, each IRB may have a different culture and may review research protocols in a different way. In addition, if you conduct research with a hospital or clinic, they may have their own independent IRB as well, thereby requiring approval from more than one IRB.

The primary goal of the IRB is to protect human participants. However, determining when participants are at risk, which can include anything from a breach in confidentiality to risk of physical or psychological harm, can be tricky. Essentially, risk may imply items or actions that go beyond what might be asked in a physical or psychological examination or evaluation. But when does this occur? Consider, for example, Balkin, Perepiczka, Whitely, and Kimbrough (2009) who examined the relationships between sexual values and emotional awareness in college freshman. In the study, participants were asked to self-identify in one of the following categories:

1. I have not had intercourse;
2. I have had intercourse, but I am not engaging in intercourse currently;
3. I engage in intercourse but limit my activity to monogamous relationships;
4. I engage in intercourse and do not limit my activity to monogamous relationships. (p. 22)

In Balkin, Perepiczka, Whitely, et al.'s study, the protocol was reviewed by the full IRB, despite the fact that the study was conducted with consenting adults who were all 18 years or older and the items likely did not request information beyond what might be asked in a physical or psychological examination/evaluation. However, the information solicited from participants was deemed sensitive, and the IRB chair made the decision to have the protocol reviewed by the full board. This is a subjective decision and is as much about the culture of the IRB at a given institution as the research study.

Be aware of your institutions' guidelines regarding when you submit your IRB and the dates of the university IRB meetings and deadlines for submitting. Some counseling programs may insist you have IRB approval before proposing your dissertation. Others may want you to propose and then submit your protocol for IRB approval. In the latter circumstance, collecting data may be delayed while you await IRB approval. If possible, we suggest that you seek IRB approval before proposing your dissertation. If a change occurs with your research based on your dissertation committee's recommendations, you may submit an amended protocol, which can usually occur in a fairly accelerated manner.

Federal Guidelines

IRB systems and protocols will vary from institution to institution, but federal guidelines dictate the type of information that must be reviewed and the decisions rendered. You will need to describe your study's methods and procedures, addressing the following topics:

- a description of the research;
- participants;

- risks/benefits;
- confidentiality, anonymity, and data security;
- methods and measures; and
- informed consent.

One important consideration when completing the IRB protocol is to avoid simply copying and pasting paragraphs from your proposal or dissertation. Many students, for example, in describing their study insert Chapters 1 and 3. This is not acceptable. Keep in mind that your IRB is multidisciplinary and consists of faculty from a wide range of disciplines. They are not familiar with your professional jargon and may vary in their understanding of research methods. Providing a lengthy literature review or identifying how you will use SPSS to evaluate model assumptions is not pertinent information for the IRB. The purview of the IRB is to protect human participants, not serve as the research police and evaluate the rigor of your study. Provide the IRB with the information they need to know to evaluate how participants and their information will be kept safe and secure.

When you submit a protocol, one of three decisions will be made. Your protocol will either be exempt from review (i.e., no further review is necessary and you can begin collecting data), expedited (i.e., two reviewers will review your protocol), or scheduled for full review. Determining factors related to whether your protocol is exempt, expedited, or reviewed by the full IRB is determined by the nature of your research (e.g., the risks to participants, sensitivity of your data) and whether your study includes individuals from vulnerable populations (e.g., minors; participants receiving medical care, including counseling; older people; prisoners; women who are pregnant; individuals identified as economically/educationally disadvantaged).

A Description of the Research

Your description should be brief. The IRB does not need to know the entire theoretical framework of your study. However, indicating that your study is grounded in the literature and there is a sound rationale for soliciting participants is important in making the case that your study should be conducted and any benefits from the study outweigh any potential risks. Keep in mind that most social science research is not funded. You are asking the university to assume the risk for your study. Hence, attention to federal guidelines is important and failure to adhere to federal guidelines could result in the university being unable to apply for funded research initiatives.

Participants

A key component to your IRB protocol is indicating the participants you are soliciting for your study. Specifically, are you gathering data from a vulnerable population (e.g., children, individuals who are impaired, prisoners, women who are pregnant)? If your research includes participants from a vulnerable population and is outside the scope of normal educational practices or testing procedures, expect a full review of your protocol. Another concern is the criteria you use for the inclusion or exclusion of participants. Federal guidelines dictate that the opportunity to participate in research should be equitable. Why? Because participation in interventions has the potential to be beneficial, so the decision to include or exclude individuals must be considered thoughtfully. In addition, research contributes to the generalizability of the findings (Public Welfare, 2009). Therefore, equality and diversity among participants is important. As a researcher, you should consider who should be included or excluded. You should not exclude participants simply because including more diversity is an inconvenience to you. For example, consider a researcher who works at a Hispanic-serving institution. If the community has a large Latino population, limiting study participation to only those who read or write English may not be equitable for that community. Providing materials, especially informed consent/assent, in Spanish should be considered. However, if the measures being used have not been normed in Spanish and the validity would be questionable, then such a rationale for exclusion may be sufficient.

Risks/Benefits

Most counseling research is unfunded, which is an important consideration because the university is accepting liability for research that provides no financial benefit. There are always risks in human subjects research. At a minimum, data can be lost (e.g., stolen computer), and confidentiality can be breached. So it is incumbent upon you to make the case that the benefits of your research outweigh the risks. For example, a clear benefit of a study could include that the study adds to the knowledge base of the counseling profession or that the implementation of a program or intervention promotes social change. Risks, however, may be more difficult to define. One of the most frequent errors we have found that social science researchers make is to identify that there were "no risks" to participants in the study. Risks may be minimal, but they are always present. For example, in Lancaster et al.'s (2011) study related to the efficacy of a community-based program for court-referred youth, no names were connected with the data set, but demographic information was collected. Although improbable, it might be possible for a caseworker with access to the raw data from the study to match it to known participants based on demographic characteristics. In other words, data that appear to be anonymous may not really be anonymous. Think carefully about the risks of a study, regardless of how minimal or unlikely they seem. The IRB wants to avoid adverse events (i.e., events in which a participant in a study experiences some type of harm), which could include a breach in confidentiality. Clearly state the benefits and risks for the study so that the IRB can discern whether the university should assume liability for the study and if harm to participants is minimized to the fullest extent.

Confidentiality, Anonymity, and Data Security

Data security is a pertinent issue with respect to the risk of participating in a study. You will need to identify how data security will be maintained. Most researchers use mobile devices, tablets, and laptops, which can be easily stolen or hacked. If you collect hard copies of documents, you should outline where the copies will be stored securely and who will have access to the documents. If data are stored electronically, it may be important to store data so that your data are encrypted and keep your data on separate devices that remain secure.

One way researchers attempt to demonstrate secure data is through maintaining data that are confidential or anonymous. Data that are anonymous refer to data that cannot be linked to identification. When data are confidential, they can be linked to an identity but means are taken to protect that information. Consider the following two scenarios. The first scenario is as follows:

> A counselor is collecting data using a survey platform, such as Qualtrics or SurveyMonkey. Demographic information is collected but not identifying information. However, to prevent multiple submissions from the same individual, an IP address is stored.

In this scenario, you might think that the data are anonymous, but in reality, the IP address could eventually link to an identity. Hence, data are confidential, but not anonymous.

The second scenario is as follows:

> A counselor educator is collecting data from undergraduate at a large public university. Students (ages 18 years or older) sign a consent form and complete the Juhnke–Balkin Life Balance Inventory (JBLI; Davis, Balkin, & Juhnke, 2014). The counselor educator separates the consent form from the JBLI so that the data on the JBLI cannot be linked to an individual.

The counselor educator will not know if the individual who signed the consent form completed the study or be able to match the participant to the data. Thus, data are anonymous.

You will need to be able to discern whether your data are anonymous or confidential. In either case, you will need to demonstrate how data will be kept secure. If data are confidential, be able to explain the possible risks and under what conditions confidentiality could be breached.

Methods and Measures

You will need to explain the process you will use to collect data and what you will do with the data once it is collected. If you are using surveys or established instruments, you should submit a copy of the instruments if possible. Because some instruments are copyrighted, you may not be able to submit a copy of the instrument, but you can provide sample items and briefly describe the psychometric properties to ensure the measure is appropriate and safe. Keep in mind that the IRB is a multidisciplinary board. You do not need to go into detail about the statistical analyses you will conduct; instead, you should provide a broad context of what you will do with the data. For example, you may wish to state that you are conducting a correlational study and will use SPSS to run analyses, as opposed to indicating how you will check model assumptions, run various analyses, and report the results of various statistical tests. Remember to write for a global audience so that they can understand your procedure.

Informed Consent

According to Balkin and Kleist (2017), informed consent includes (a) an explanation and description of the research, including duration and procedures; (b) a description of risks and benefits; (c) the manner in which confidentiality or anonymity will be maintained; (d) processes that involve more than minimal risk and procedures in the event that discomfort or injury occur; (e) contact information for the researcher and IRB; and (f) a statement that participation is voluntary, that the participant can withdraw at any time, and that there will be no loss of benefits or presence of a penalty for refusing to participate or withdrawing from the study. Hence, much of the information in the general protocol is placed in the informed consent for participants to read. The key difference here, however, is the language used to describe the study. The language should not be overly complicated. Key additions from the protocol include listing your contact information and the contact information of an IRB representative with the university. The university will have guidelines for who is listed on the informed consent. Furthermore, the participant must be clearly informed that a lack of participation or withdrawal from the study once started presents no repercussions.

When conducting research with minors or those from a vulnerable population, assent also is required. *Assent* refers to the process of obtaining permission from a participant who may be in the custody of another adult. For example, parents provide consent for their child to participate in a study, but assent may also be required on behalf of the child. Simply because parents want their child to participate in a study does not mean the child does not have a choice. With young children in particular, assent may occur verbally, rather than through a written document. If you must obtain consent and assent, consider obtaining such permissions separately so the assenting individual (e.g., child, adolescent, older person) does not feel coerced to participate. In addition, if a written assent document is used, you must use age-appropriate language and accommodate for variability in reading level. Appendix E provides an example of an informed consent to a parent requesting participation to complete a measure for youth who participate in a community-based program, and Appendix F provides an example of an assent to a minor.

ACA Code of Ethics

The *ACA Code of Ethics* (ACA, 2014) provides ethical guidelines covering research responsibilities, rights of research participants, managing and maintaining boundaries, reporting results, and publications and presentations. A lot of overlap exists between federal guidelines and the *ACA Code of Ethics* because they both address issues such as confidentiality, risk and benefits, participants' rights, consent and assent, and confidentiality and anonymity.

However, the *ACA Code of Ethics* (ACA, 2014) does provide details and additional information specific to counselors' roles and the dissemination of results. Conducting research requires implementing boundaries to reduce bias. Similar to working with clients, researchers should avoid relationships that would be inappropriate.

Although counselors may implement novel approaches, once it is determined that a research study is being undertaken, federal guidelines apply. For example, if your study uses a novel approach or intervention, you must inform the participant. Furthermore, if you plan to disseminate your results, you should acknowledge both favorable and unfavorable findings.

Because the dissertation process is a lengthy one, you will hopefully choose to disseminate your findings in the form of presentations or publications. Because this is your work, you are the lead author/presenter. A common courtesy is to include your dissertation chair (and perhaps your committee members) on the initial publication. As with any publication, you should establish the order of authorship. The *ACA Code of Ethics* (ACA, 2014) establishes that such agreements in terms of acknowledgements and order of authorship are determined in advance. As you seek publication venues, be aware that you must submit to only one journal at a time. Duplicate submissions are unethical because reviewers for journals dedicate a lot of time and energy to providing reviews. If your manuscript is accepted for publication, you are signing a copyright to the publication company of the journal. We will discuss this more in Chapter 11.

Summary

As you embark on your dissertation, you may consider submitting your IRB protocol early in the process of writing your proposal. When you write the IRB protocol, you will be forced to consider the purpose of the study and the research questions or hypotheses that will guide your study. You will also have to identify a basic design and outline a research method to collect and analyze your data, while maintaining ethical conduct, participant safety, and data security. Although many students will write their third chapter and then submit the IRB protocol, you may want to consider using the IRB protocol to inform your third chapter.

Although your research questions/hypotheses will guide your study, your first two chapters provide the theoretical foundation of your research. Moving forward with an investigation without recognition of how the published literature informs your research is ill advised and can easily result in a poorly constructed study. Your study should be derived theoretically, and methods, whether qualitative interviews or quantitative instruments, should be selected based on what has been studied and what is still needed.

As you recruit participants for your study, be sure to consider the risks and benefits of the ensuing research and the extent to which both the participants and their information are kept safe and secure. Many faculty view the IRB as an adversary. However, the IRB has a job—to protect participants in your study. If the study is good and participants are protected, then it can be done, but it may require you to understand the culture of the IRB and obtain training on research ethics so you can properly advocate for your study being approved.

Checklist

❏ Identify your research questions.
❏ Identify what method is best suited to answer your research questions. Be able to support this method through existing literature.
❏ Establish where you will solicit participants for your study.
❏ Evaluate and select a sampling strategy to solicit participants.
❏ For a quantitative study, conduct an a priori analysis to establish a minimum sample size; for a qualitative study, identify the necessary characteristics for your purposeful sampling procedure.
❏ Describe the measures, questionnaires, or interview questions.
❏ In the case of using established measures, make sure you score each instrument correctly and report both the published information on reliability and validity and the reliability estimates for the scores from your participants.
❏ Identify your process for collecting data.
❏ Develop a timeline for submitting your IRB protocol. Remember that it is common to revise a protocol.
❏ Speak with faculty or existing IRB members about the culture of the IRB at your institution. Know what to expect.
❏ Be familiar with federal guidelines and complete an IRB ethics course (e.g., a Collaborative Institutional Training Initiative course).
❏ Be able to concisely provide the following information for your study:

- a description of the research;
- participants;
- risks/benefits;
- confidentiality, anonymity, and data security;
- methods and measures; and
- informed consent.

Additional Resources

Balkin, R. S. (n.d.). *Research methods and statistics*. Retrieved from http://balkinresearchmethods.com/Balkin_Research_Methods/Research_Methods_and_Statistics.html

Collaborative Institutional Training Initiative. (n.d.). *Online courses.* Retrieved from https://www.citiprogram.org/index.cfm?pageID=86

Trochim, W. M. (2006). *Research methods knowledge base* (2nd ed.). Retrieved from http://www.socialresearchmethods.net/kb/

Appendix E

Subject Informed Consent

Introduction and Background Information

Your teenager is invited to participate in a research study. The study is being conducted by Richard S. Balkin, PhD, LPC, NCC at the University of XXX. The researchers will solicit participants from youth involved with the Community Youth program. Approximately 100 subjects will be invited to participate, depending upon availability.

Purpose

The purpose of this study is to evaluate youth on positive and negative factors related to issues adolescents typically face.

Procedures

In this study, your teenager will be asked to complete a survey that will take no longer than 20 minutes. Your teenager can skip any question that causes discomfort and may withdraw from the study at any time. Only the survey is part of the study.

Potential Risks

There are no foreseeable risks other than possible discomfort in answering personal questions.

Benefits

The possible benefits of this study include obtaining further information on risk and protective factors for adolescents. The information collected may not benefit the participant directly. The information learned in this study may be helpful to others.

Compensation

Your teenager will not be compensated for time, inconvenience, or expenses while in this study.

Confidentiality

Total privacy cannot be guaranteed. Your teenager's privacy will be protected to the extent permitted by law. If the results from this study are published, your teenager's name will not be made public. While unlikely, the following may look at the study records:

> The University Institutional Review Board, Human Subjects Protection Program Office; Office for Human Research Protections (OHRP); Office of Civil Rights

The completed survey will be stored in a secure, locked cabinet, which will only be accessible by the primary investigator.

Voluntary Participation

Your teenager's participation in this study is voluntary. Your teenager may choose not to take part at all. If your teenager decides to be in this study, the teenager may stop taking part at any time. If the teenager decides not to be in this study or if the teenager stops taking part at any time, the teenager will not lose any benefits for which the teenager may qualify.

Research Subject's Rights, Questions, Concerns, and Complaints

If you have any concerns or complaints about the study or the study staff, you have three options.

> You may contact the principal investigator at xxx-xxx-xxxx.
>
> If you have any questions about your rights as a study subject, questions, concerns or complaints, you may call the Human Subjects Protection Program Office (HSPPO) (xxx) xxx-xxxx. You may discuss any questions about your rights as a subject, in secret, with a member of the Institutional Review Board (IRB) or the HSPPO staff. The IRB is an independent committee composed of members of the University community, staff of the institutions, as well as lay members of the community not connected with these institutions
>
> If you want to speak to a person outside the University, you may call 1-xxx-xxx-xxxx.

This paper tells you what will happen during the study if you choose to take part. Your signature means that this study has been discussed with you, that your questions have been answered, and that you will take part in the study. This informed consent document is not a contract. You are not giving up any legal rights by signing this informed consent document. You will be given a signed copy of this paper to keep for your records.

_____   _____
　　　Signature of Parent/Guardian　　　　　　　　　*Date*

_____   _____
Signature of Person Explaining the Consent Form　　　*Date*
　　　　(if other than the Investigator)

_____   _____
　　　Signature of Investigator　　　　　　　　　　　*Date*

Appendix F

Subject Assent

You are invited to be in a research study being done by Professor Richard Balkin. When a person is in a research study, they are called a "subject." You are invited because you participate in the Community Youth program.

This means that we would like for you to take a survey. There may be some risks with this study. The questions in the study may make you feel uncomfortable because they are personal.

This information will be completed one time only. The information you provide will be helpful in addressing strengths and problem areas that typical adolescents face.

Your name will not be used to identify you. No one will be able to identify your answers.

I have been told about this study and know why it is being done and what I have to do. If I have any questions, I can ask Professor Balkin or a Community Youth Advisor. If I do not want to be in this study or I want to quit after I am already in this study, I can tell the researcher or Community Youth Advisor, and I will be able to quit at any time without any concern for consequences.

_____   _____   _____
Printed Name of Subject   *Signature of Subject*   *Date*

_____   _____   _____
Printed Name of Parent/Guardian   *Signature of Parent/Guardian*   *Date*

_____   _____   _____
Printed Name of Investigator   *Signature of Investigator*   *Date*

Chapter 8

Collecting and Analyzing Data

Congratulations! You successfully defended your proposal. You established to your dissertation committee that you have thoroughly covered the relevant literature on your topic, provided research questions or hypotheses that require further investigation, and received IRB approval to begin your study. Now it is time to implement the plan you put in writing. In this chapter, we focus on the implementation of your plan for data collection and some key considerations central to analysis. We also focus on common pitfalls you need to avoid in collecting your data (we discuss the pitfalls mentioned in Chapter 7 and highlight a few more) and provide some key components to analyzing your data.

Quantitative Considerations in Collecting and Analyzing Data

When serving on dissertation committees, we commonly hear, "Now that I have successfully proposed, what do I do now?" Now you might be thinking, "Wait, you just do what you said you were going to do in your proposal!" Perhaps the question stems more from anxiety in actually executing the study. The reality is that conducting the study may be much more difficult than simply talking about it. If you have never done data collection for your own study, you are likely going to come face-to-face with the realities of the implementation of an intervention and the difficulties in collecting data. Furthermore, if the dissertation represents the first time you input data and execute the analysis, there might be some apprehension on whether you are doing it correctly. Certainly, it is important for you to work with your chair and the methods expert on your committee. In addition, you might encounter some obstacles or challenges that you did not anticipate when you proposed your dissertation. We highlight some of these issues in both quantitative and qualitative research projects, beginning with issues of fidelity and considerations in analyzing data.

Assessing Fidelity Across Paradigms of Inquiry

In intervention research (e.g., a program or treatment approach in a study), *treatment fidelity* is the accuracy and consistency of the administration of the intervention to the participants. Ray (2015) identified the need to provide evidence of treatment fidelity in single-case research designs, but this concept applies to quasi-experimental and experimental designs as well. Imagine that in either single-case research designs or between-group designs, an intervention may be administered multiple times and perhaps even by a variety of individuals. So how will you ensure that a treatment is administered in a consistent manner? Two commonly used methods are manualization and fidelity checks.

Manualization refers to a process in which the researcher provides specific, written instructions in administering a treatment. A manual is developed to promote replication of the treatment. The manual includes content and instructions for delivery. When implementing a manualized treatment, researchers must not veer away from the specified approach.

Fidelity checks are specific points or time periods in which the researcher collects data to ensure a specified approach is being followed. For fidelity checks, the researcher may develop checklists or conduct observations to evaluate the delivery of the intervention. Self-report, observations, and review of videos are common methods in which fidelity checks are implemented.

Assumptions

Unless research is focused on nonparamtric tests (e.g., chi-square), researchers in counseling more often use parametric statistics in their analyses (Erford et al., 2011). In other words, the most common statistical tools used by counseling researchers assume that the data to be analyzed follow a probability distribution—most often a normal distribution or normal curve. Hence, there are specific rules that the data must fit to use parametric statistical tests. When data do not fit within these rules (i.e., assumptions or model assumptions), then alternative methods, such as nonparametric tests, should be used. The main advantage of using parametric tests is that such tests are more powerful, so there is a stronger likelihood of identifying a significant difference or relationship, should one exist. The use of nonparametric tests often results in the loss of information because common statistics (e.g., means, standard deviations) are replaced with other forms of data (e.g., categorical variables, medians), which produces tests that are less sensitive. Depending on the type of analysis being conducted, specific rules need to be addressed. The following assumptions are not comprehensive but represent assumptions that are routinely evaluated.

Cleaning Data

Maybe you have collected a lot of data: You had approximately 100 participants who completed 40 items, including demographic items and one or two measures. Therefore, you have 4,000 data points in your data set. Before you can begin any type of analysis, you need to take a good look at the data collected. First, make sure the responses fit the parameters of the study. If you collected data using some type of survey platform, then the respondents keyed in the data, and hopefully, you established the correct parameters for the participants to do this correctly. For example, if you asked a question about annual salary, you would need to specify how you want the participant to answer. Otherwise, you could get answers such as "$50,000," "50k," or "fifty thousand." If you input data yourself, you need to make sure that none of the responses were obviously miskeyed. For example, make sure you typed "50" instead of "5." You can easily evaluate this by running descriptive statistics on your items and noticing the minimum and maximum values. Scores that fall below the minimum or maximum were obviously invalid.

With respect to your responses, you need to examine whether you have any irregular responses, such as the respondent marking all extreme answers or obvious outliers. You can often find such responses when evaluating your data for outliers. For example, running boxplots to test normality is an easy way to identify outliers. You also want to have a plan to deal with missing data. In most cases, statistical software will automatically eliminate missing data unless you use some type of missing data imputation. However, sometimes there are patterns to missing data, in which case the data should not be imputed and you need to decide what to do with the measure if participants skipped the same items.

Independence
Independence refers to when the participants in one group do not appear in another group and the selection of participants is not dependent on the selection of other participants. Obviously, if a researcher is comparing groups based on a construct, a participant can be in only one group. Furthermore, recruitment to participate should not depend on the selection of other participants. For example, purposeful sampling, used in qualitative research, is not appropriate for quantitative research because of the assumption of independence. In general, in the method section, you clearly demonstrate that you have met this assumption by examining participant recruitment and the selection of participants into treatment groups, if applicable. Procedures such as random assignment help make the case for independent observations.

Normality/Multivariate Normality
Parametric tests are based on the assumption of a normal distribution. In other words, data collected should follow a normal distribution. Common statistical tests to evaluate the normality assumption include the Shapiro–Wilk test and the Kolmogorov–Smirnov test. Both tests evaluate the distribution of the collected data against a normal distribution. However, such tests are sensitive to large sample sizes, so if your study includes a large sample size, you are more likely to detect nonnormal distributions (e.g., test will result

in $p < .05$). For large sample sizes, it is better to evaluate normality through histograms, boxplots, or quantile-quantile plots, which are commonly produced with statistical software. Although there are some tests with programs that can be used to evaluate multivariate normality, in general, normality is evaluated at a univariate level.

Homogeneity of Variances/Covariances

When making comparisons between groups, the variability between the groups being compared should be similar. For example, a lead counselor for a school district wishes to compare achievement test scores across high schools. One of the high schools in the district is a selective school with an international baccalaureate program. Would it be fair to compare this school with other schools in the district that do not have the opportunity of being selective with their student enrollment? Probably not, and the reason why is due to the assumption of the homogeneity of variances (for univariate analyses) and the homogeneity of covariances (for multivariate analyses). Variability is evaluated by standard deviations or variances, which are estimates or squared estimates, respectively, related to distance from the mean. However, the achievement test scores from the international baccalaureate program would likely have less variability because the majority of students would likely have higher test scores. In the other schools, more variability would be expected because these schools enroll more students at different levels. Therefore, such a comparison is unfair because the populations are quite dissimilar.

Like tests of normality, tests of homogeneity of variances (e.g., Levene's test, Brown–Forsythe test) and homogeneity of covariances (e.g., Box's M test) are sensitive to sample size, so with larger sample sizes, researchers might want to consider using a smaller alpha level (e.g., .01 as opposed to .05) to determine if the assumption is met ($p > \alpha$). If the normality or homogeneity of variances assumptions is not met ($p < \alpha$), you will need to consider changing your analysis to a nonparametric test or conducting a data transformation so that the assumption is met. Minor deviations from normality are usually not problematic, but heterogeneous variances/covariances can be problematic.

Correlations Among Dependent Variables

When conducting a multivariate analysis (e.g., multivariate analysis of variance), there should be some evidence of a relationship among the dependent variables. A small to moderate relationship indicates the variables share commonalities, and as long as they are linked theoretically it makes sense to use a multivariate procedure. Where students get into trouble is when they use variables that have no theoretical connection and therefore are likely to have a negligible correlation. When this occurs, univariate analyses should be selected, rather than multivariate tests. Although Type I error increases because of the number of tests, univariate analyses are more appropriate in this case and likely make a stronger contribution to the literature. The opposite issue should also be considered: When the dependent variables are highly correlated and therefore measure the same phenomenon (known as *multicollinearity*), it is better to either combine the measures into a single variable or drop one of the variables.

Linearity

Linearity is an assumption in multivariate and correlational designs. For multivariate designs, the dependent variables should demonstrate a linear relationship; in correlational designs, a linear relationship should exist between the predictor variable(s) and the criterion variable(s). Scatterplots are used to demonstrate a linear relationship. Hence, this assumption is evaluated through visual analysis and not a statistical test. The linearity assumption is not met when the data points have a noticeable curve or when no linear relationship is apparent; researchers may wish to consider nonlinear analysis when either of these conditions is present (Balkin, Richey Gosnell, Holmgren, & Osborne, 2017) or consider a nonparametric alternative.

Homoscedasticity

This assumption of homoscedasticity in regression refers to the values in a data set being equidistant from the predicted values. In other words, what is predicted and what researchers actually get are different; this is known as error. The amount of error from each of the values should be similar. Homoscedasticity is evaluated by visually analyzing a plot of the standardized predicted values and the standardized residual values (i.e., error). Typically, plots that show a conical pattern in the data (e.g., go from narrow or close to the regression line to wide or far from the regression line) indicate that the assumption is not met. Data transformations can be helpful in addressing this issue.

Multicollinearity

In multivariate and correlational designs, multicollinearity refers to the intercorrelation of the predictor variables in correlational research or the intercorrelation of the dependent variables in multivariate designs. Multicollinearity is problematic because two variables that essentially measure the same thing are included in the model, which results in one of the variables being underestimated. For example, negative self-evaluation and low self-esteem are highly correlated, so you would want to either use only one of these variables or combine the scales for each of these measures. An easy way to detect multicollinearity is to evaluate the Pearson product–moment correlation coefficient (Pearson's r); correlations around .80 or higher are indicative of multicollinearity. More sophisticated statistics, such as the variance inflation factor and tolerance, are also available. In the literature, a variance inflation factor greater than 10 or tolerance less than .10 are indicative of multicollinearity. However, you may come across other thresholds suggested by researchers, such as a variance inflation factor greater than 2.5 or tolerance less than .20.

Homogeneity of Slopes

When using a covariate in a between-group design (e.g., analysis of covariance, multivariate analysis of covariance), the effect of the covariate on the groups should be similar. In other words, if there is an interaction effect (the covariate affects the scores on one group differently from the other groups), which can be found by testing for an interaction and graphing the relationship between the covariate and the groups, then an alternative analysis should be selected (perhaps by separating the groups).

Relationship Between the Covariate and the Dependent Variable

Another rule when using a covariate in your design is that the covariate must be related both theoretically and statistically to the dependent variable(s). In other words, you should link the relationship of the covariate to the dependent variable by citing relevant literature that establishes this linkage. In addition, this relationship can be demonstrated statistically through a Pearson's r.

Overview of Statistical Tests

Now that we have established the essential rules that you should follow for the majority of statistical tests that you might use, we provide an overview of common statistical tests. One way to conceptualize statistical tests and select from among them is to consider the nature of the variables you are evaluating. Recall that variables can be identified along four scales of measurement:

- Nominal: variables are strictly categorical and have no assigned value (e.g., ethnicity, sex, political affiliation, religion).
- Ordinal: variables occur in a specific order but no value is assigned (e.g., very often, often, somewhat often, never).
- Interval: a value is assigned and there is equal distance between each value but no true zero is evident (e.g., a score on a depression inventory—zero would simply indicate infrequent depression but not that there is a total absence of depression).
- Ratio: a value is assigned; there is equal distance between each value; and a true zero is evident (e.g., number of alcoholic beverages consumed in a week, number of suicidal ideations in a day).

The four scales of measurement are further conceptualized into two distinct classifications: discrete (nominal and ordinal) and continuous (interval and ratio). An easy way to discern the difference between discrete and continuous variables is that continuous variables can have mathematical operations applied to them—you can sum the scores and compute descriptive statistics. Discrete variables can be summarized through frequencies and percentages but cannot have mathematical operations applied to them.

Table 8.1 provides an overview of common statistical tests used in counseling research. If you understand the nature of the variables you will be using in your study, you can consult Table 8.1 to identify potential analyses to evaluate the variables in your study.

As you review Table 8.1, you may or may not have familiarity with the common statistical tests listed, depending on how many courses you had in quantitative research. So what do you do if, for example, you believe your study is multivariate in nature but you did not take a class in multivariate statistics? We advise you to avoid using statistical tools that are unfamiliar to you. Some individuals can pick up books and review articles to learn new skills. Others may require courses or in-depth seminars to feel comfortable. So if you are not familiar with a multivariate analysis of variance and are unable to take a class or learn the concepts, use a univariate design. Table 8.1 does not contain a comprehensive list of tests, and the ways to conduct an analysis are not absolute. There is nothing wrong with using *t* tests and analysis of variance, if those are the appropriate tools to answer the research questions. A sophisticated design (e.g., one with random assignment) using a *t* test is probably more generalizable and useful than a correlational design with a sophisticated analysis. So work within your scope of expertise and focus on the design first. The type of analysis will be a function of your

Table 8.1
Common Statistical Tests

Test	Independent/Predictor	Dependent/Criterion
Chi-square	Discrete	Discrete
Independent *t* test	Discrete (2 groups only)	1 continuous
Dependent *t* test	No group	2 continuous measures only
Analysis of variance (ANOVA)	1 discrete variable with 2 or more groups	1 continuous
Repeated measures ANOVA	No group	Continuous—dependent variable with multiple measures
Factorial ANOVA	2 to 3[a] discrete variables with 2 or more groups	1 continuous
Split-plot ANOVA	1 discrete variable with 2 or more groups	Continuous—dependent variable with multiple measures
Multiple analysis of variance (MANOVA)	1 discrete variable with 2 or more groups	Multiple dependent variables
Factorial MANOVA	2 to 3[a] discrete variables with 2 or more groups	Multiple dependent variables
Simple regression	1 continuous	1 continuous
Multiple regression	2 or more continuous	1 continuous
Logistic regression	1 or more continuous	1 dichotomous
Canonical correlation/ structural equation modeling	2 or more continuous	2 or more continuous

[a]We do not recommend running a factorial ANOVA/MANOVA with more than three independent variables.

research questions, the nature of your variables, and your knowledge of how to conduct the analysis.

Qualitative Considerations in Collecting and Analyzing Data

The central focus of qualitative inquiry lies in the collection and analysis of narrative data from interviews, observations, and documents. Unlike quantitative research in which the goal is to establish generalizable findings, the goal of qualitative research is to generate *transferable* knowledge (i.e., information that is coherent, insightful, and useful; Patton, 2015). Transferability, however, is not determined by the researcher but by the reader. Managing your data and demonstrating trustworthiness in your analysis are key concepts in transferability.

Consider How You Will Manage Your Data

You will need to conceptualize how you will collect, organize, and analyze your data. You might be asked to include a conceptual diagram illustrating these processes in your dissertation. The sequence of your data collection processes can play an important role in your study. For example, do you conduct observations first and then interviews or vice versa? In other words, do you want your observations to inform your interview questions or prefer to identify your focus points of your observations from what you learned in the interviews? The same question could be posed as to when you might incorporate a focus group interview: Would you want this before or after individual interviews? What occurs first can inform the nature of your questions posed during interviews. Obviously, there is not a correct answer here, but because the organization of your study can inform the execution of your data collection, and therefore your findings, you want to be able to communicate a sound rationale for the decisions you make. Such a rationale should be grounded in your research questions/hypotheses/purpose and the extant literature that provides further validation for the decisions you made. The following paragraphs provide some issues that you will need to consider as you execute your qualitative study.

Consider the Type of Interviews You Will Conduct

There are different approaches to conducting interviews, and you should carefully consider the best approach given the information you wish to discover. *Standardized open-ended interviews* require that you establish the interview questions a priori and that you ask each participant the same questions in the same order. Standardized open-ended interviews are helpful if a qualitative study is to be replicated. They also establish that the type of information sought from each participant will be similar. However, the interviewer still has flexibility to query a participant should the information provided by a participant be insufficient. Standardized open-ended interviews are useful when there are a number of interviews to be conducted; the interviewer essentially guarantees that the type of information solicited is the same across all participants, thereby reducing researcher bias. *Guided interviews* do not use preestablished questions. Rather, the interviewer asks questions around established topics, but the nature of the questions may be different for each participant. Guided interviews have the advantage of feeling less formal, so participants may be more open in the conversation; however, when questions are asked in different ways, the information garnered will naturally be more diverse, making comparisons of the responses less credible. Despite this disadvantage, a guided interview strategy may work well with focus groups and case studies. *Conversational interviews* do not use an established protocol or outline. Instead, the interview follows an emergent design, which can be appropriate for some type of qualitative methods (e.g., case studies) but may not be appropriate for interviewing a number of participants.

Consider Your Focus Factors in Your Observations

When conducting observations and writing field notes, you will want to identify a priori what you want to focus on during your observations. There are numerous possibilities, such as settings, interactions, rituals, and sequence of events. Obviously, you cannot focus on everything at once. So in a 1-hour observation, maybe you select 4–6 focus factors, and you spend time on each focus factor for 10–15 minutes and then move on to the next. If nothing occurs with a specific focus factor, then move on or select another. The main point here is to establish up front what you plan to focus on during the observation period.

Consider What Documents You Need

Imagine walking into a site, such as a school, hospital, or clinic, with a plan to select participants for your qualitative study. You want to make sure you are selecting participants that can best inform your research topic, but you are unsure how to go about identifying such participants. What type of documents will you need? What kind of information about the site should be reported as part of your study? Without forethought and a specified plan, you might appear unprepared to professionals at the site who agreed to provide you access to participants and data. Consider the types of records and documents you need to execute your study. Some of the data is public domain and can be accessed through marketing materials and websites. However, other data might be confidential and require approval from both the university and site IRBs to access.

Consider How You Will Bundle Your Data

As mentioned in Chapter 7, you have control over when you collect data and how you manage it. Consider, for example, conducting six 1-hour interviews, six member checks, and a 1-hour focus group. In addition to any observations and collected documents, it is not inconceivable to consider you might have over 100 pages of transcriptions, field notes, and documents. Managing this amount of data can be overwhelming. You may want to use qualitative software packages to organize your data. To keep your data organized, consider the following:

- Transcribe your observations and interviews immediately. Your interview or observation is not over after the recording; it is over after your transcribed the interview or observation. This enables you to make sense of your field notes and not be overly tasked with hours of transcription.
- Identify patterns early. As you conduct your interviews and observations and collect your data for each participant, bundle it—keep it together—and see what patterns are already emerging.
- Keep your data secure in more than one location. You should have copies of your data in the event of a computer crash. Be sure data remain encrypted.

Consider How You Will Code Your Data

The goal of coding is to capture the essence of your data by reducing your data to identifiable patterns and themes. Coding is not an exact science, but it is driven by a theory and a systemized process of illustrating the transformation of participants' words into categories, themes, and theories (Saldaña, 2009). Numerous methods of coding are available, but regardless of the method, plan on at least two cycles of coding. First cycle coding usually involves identifying general concepts that occur throughout the narrative data (i.e., observations, interviews, and documents). Second cycle coding reconfigures the first cycle codes by reducing the general concepts into units. Additional cycles may be implemented to generate themes or theories.

Consider How You Will Demonstrate Trustworthiness

Trustworthiness refers to the credibility of your process and findings. Critics of qualitative research argue that the process is inherently biased. However, when qualitative research is done well, bias is reduced. Patton (2015) identified six aspects of trustworthiness: prolonged engagement, persistent engagement, triangulation, peer debriefing, member checks, and audit trail. Prolonged engagement refers to time on task. Did you immerse yourself in this research and spend enough time in the field? Qualitative inquiry may be used to generate theories or describe phenomena in depth. Inadequate time in the field decreases the credibility of the findings. Persistent engagement refers to how you refute your proposed themes. How did you deal with discrepant data? Did you use negative case analysis (evaluate evidence contrary to your themes)? Essentially, you, and potentially other researchers, should pose challenges to your findings to see how they hold up. Triangulation refers to comparisons made based on data, methods, theories, or other researchers. More than one type of triangulation should be used. Peer debriefing refers to the process of sharing your data with other experts in the field to see if they derive the same conclusions. Member checks refer to sharing your transcripts with your participants and identifying if you (a) captured the essence of the interview or observation and (b) allowed the opportunity for expansion or clarification on what was collected and identified. Audit trail is the raw data that you show, sometimes in quotes or tables, to demonstrate your findings. Not all aspects of trustworthiness will be used in a given study, but multiple forms of trustworthiness provide evidence of credibility.

Consider Sequences in Mixed Methods

Earlier we talked about the sequence of collecting data in a qualitative study. This issue is also of particular importance in mixed-methods studies. How does one process inform the other? Usually in mixed-methods research, one method may be weighted more than another, such as a primarily quantitative study supplemented by qualitative inquiry or a primarily qualitative study supplemented by the collection and analysis of quantitative data. Furthermore, consider which process comes first and how that process will inform or be informed by the subsequent method. Ultimately, there should be a rationale of how you execute your study, and this rationale should be apparent in your method section, demonstrated in your results section, and verbalized in your defense.

Summary

In this chapter, we addressed key factors in collecting and analyzing quantitative and qualitative data. Although a typical research article may not go into the details of specific procedures (e.g., evaluating model assumptions, providing details of how data were collected and bundled), a dissertation typically will cover such processes. Perhaps the most important consideration is using procedures that are in your toolbox and avoiding procedures that are outside your scope of understanding. Dissertation defenses can go sour if you attempt to defend findings or processes that you do not fully understand. Therefore, even if your analysis is less sophisticated, stay within your comfort zone, and if you move outside of it, make sure you study and understand the analytical strategies you used in your study.

Checklist

Quantitative

❑ Clean your data and explain your rationale for your decision.
- Manage missing values (e.g., delete the participant, data imputation).
- Keep or eliminate outliers.

❏ Identify the type of variables you are using in your analyses; use Table 8.1 to assist you in selecting a statistical test.

❏ Identify and evaluate the model assumptions consistent with your selected statistical tests.

❏ Report statistical and practical significance of your results (e.g., effect size, confidence intervals).

Qualitative

❏ Have a plan for your data collection and how you will manage the data for transcribing.

❏ Develop a rationale for the sequence of data collection (e.g., Should your observations inform your interviews or vice versa?).

❏ Select an interview strategy.

❏ Select your focus factors for observations.

❏ Identify a method of coding your data consistent with the theoretical paradigm you are using (e.g., grounded theory, phenomenology).

Additional Resources

Balkin, R. S. (n.d.). *Research methods and statistics.* Retrieved from http://balkinresearchmethods.com/Balkin_Research_Methods/Research_Methods_and_Statistics.html

Sterner, W. R. (2011). What is missing in counseling research? Reporting missing data. *Journal of Counseling & Development, 89,* 56–62. doi:10.1002/j.1556-6678.2011.tb00060.x

Trochim, W. M. (2006). *Research methods knowledge base* (2nd ed.). Retrieved from http://www.socialresearchmethods.net/kb/

Chapter 9

Presenting and Discussing the Results

You are done collecting and analyzing your data; now your task is to prepare your results section. In our experience chairing dissertations, Chapter 4 is the easiest to write because it essentially writes itself. You report the results—and only the results. You do not embellish them. You simply report the results as they are. If a finding is important or negligible, you report that finding objectively, indicating the appropriate information, so that the informed reader can make the decision on the relevance or importance. On the other hand, Chapter 5 might just be the hardest to write. By this point, you might have some serious fatigue from writing, and the energy you put forth in discovering literature, designing your study, analyzing your data, and writing your results is not as abundant as when you began the dissertation. Nevertheless, you need to grind it out. In this chapter, we identify some key points in writing your final two chapters.

Writing Your Results

Probably the best way to prepare for writing your results is to read articles in reputable journals that conducted the analyses that you executed for your study. Take particular notice of the order in which findings are presented. Chapter 4 will generally start out with a review of your research questions. This may not necessarily be apparent in a journal article, but it is necessary in a dissertation because readers have not seen the research questions since the beginning of Chapter 3, which might be 20 pages ago! Your research questions provide an outline of how you will present your results. However, before you dive into writing the results of your first research question, you might need to strategize a little bit. For example, if you did a quantitative dissertation, you need to discuss how you cleaned your data. How did you handle missing data or incomplete measures? In addition, if you conducted more than one statistical test, it might be easier to begin the study addressing model assumptions for all the analyses. You also need to decide where you want to report the demographic information about your participants. Often this information goes back in to Chapter 3, where you describe your participants, which is similar to what is done in a journal article, or you may want to report the information about your participants in Chapter 4 before discussing your model assumptions and results. A typical Chapter 4 includes (in this order)

1. an introduction of the chapter and a review of research questions;
2. a presentation of the participants in your study (if not included in Chapter 3), including demographic information of sex, ethnicity, and possibly age as well as other demographic characteristics pertinent to your study;
3. an explanation of the model assumptions in your study (if you conducted a quantitative study); and
4. a presentation of your analyses (e.g., statistical tests, themes, quotes).

Align With APA Guidelines

One way to view APA style is that it is an extension of the scientific tradition. That is, you are to remain objective in your approach to reporting results. Although reporting results in APA style may seem rather nuanced, the purpose is clear: to focus on the findings and allow the reader to be informed and make an appropriate conclusion based on the results presented. In Chapter 5 of your dissertation, you will have the opportunity to explain what the results mean. In Chapter 4, however, you simply present the results.

When you report quantitative results, the format of the results is similar and follows a general pattern. Balkin and Sheperis (2009) outlined this pattern:

> The reporting of statistical results follow this format: a Roman or Greek letter, followed by a number or pair of numbers in parenthesis, followed by a value, and concluded by a comparison to p [e.g., $F(3, 96) = 13.81$, $p < .001$]. While the presented numbers may look complex, they are really a summary statement of the research results. The Roman or Greek letter represents the type of test. In this case an F indicates that an ANOVA was performed. The number(s) in parenthesis identifies degrees of freedom (i.e., an estimate of parameters or variability within a data set). The value after the equal sign is based on a calculation that incorporates changes in the dependent variable and error in measurement. The p-value indicates whether or not the result is statistically significant. (para. 6)

In addition to reporting the results of a statistical test, you should provide an evaluation of practical significance by reporting effect size. In fact, most counseling journals require the reporting of effect size. Effect size is typically reported in standard deviations units (e.g., Cohen's d), variance units (e.g., R^2, ω^2, η^2, λ), or various correlation coefficients (e.g., r, φ), and an interpretation is generally provided indicating a small, moderate, or large effect using guidelines published by Cohen (1988, 1992). For example, let's refer back to Lancaster et al. (2011), discussed in Chapter 7, in which the authors evaluated the effects of a community-based intervention program against a control group for adjudicated adolescents. Notice how the reporting of the results fits the format described earlier: "A statistically significant effect was noted in recidivism rates across the treatment and control groups, $\chi^2(5) = 14.64$, $p = .012$, $\varphi = .25$, indicative of a small to moderate effect size" (Lancaster et al., 2011, p. 490).

Reporting qualitative findings is not as systematic. However, similar to quantitative research, you are required to show your data. This can be done by applying pseudonyms or labels (e.g., Interview 1, Observation 2) to cited materials or quotes demonstrating the identified theme. For example, Lenz, Del Conte, Lancaster, Bailey, and Vanderpool (2014) conducted a mixed-methods study on the effects of a partial hospitalization program for adolescents. In the qualitative portion of the study, they conducted focus groups with adolescent girls, and one of the themes was "renewed well-being" (p. 9). Lenz et al. supported this theme using quotes from the focus group:

> Girls who experienced an uninterrupted stay noted they felt more in control of their emotions, reflected by comments such as, "I'm less up and down," "I'm acting more mature . . . my mood is a little wonky but much better." Girls suggested that the shift occurred around the second to third week into the program when they began to see a difference resulting from the application of skills learned in therapy to various contexts of their lives. "After about 2 week I felt better," "Once I learned to control my behavior things started turning around the end of the second, no the third week I was here." Through therapy they had learned to recognize triggers and traps that escalated their behavior, which in turn had permitted them to modify their responses. "I noticed that my Dad likes to escalate things—I used to escalate with him, but I learned not to respond the same way." Another participant commented that "I changed my responses to them (family members) and that changed how they reacted." (pp. 9–10)

In the above example, Lenz et al. indicated that data came from focus groups, identified relevant themes, and supported the themes through quotes from the focus group interviews.

The incorporation of tables and figures can be helpful when summarizing large amounts of data and providing a single point of reference for readers to refer to when reporting results. A rule of thumb is that you should not report results both in the narrative and in tables/figures. In other words, if you report results narratively, do not use a table or figure. If you report in a table or figure, make sure you reference the table or figure in the narrative section, such as indicating "see Table 1."

Quantitative results, demographic information, descriptive statistics, and demonstration of results from complex statistical analyses (e.g., hierarchical multiple regression) are typically displayed in tables. When using tables to display quantitative results, you should combine tables where appropriate. For example, descriptive statistics can often be combined with correlation coefficients, rather than having two separate tables. As an example, Table 9.1

Table 9.1

Descriptive Statistics and Correlations for the
Forgiveness Reconciliation Inventory

Subscale	1	2	3	4	Clinical		Nonclinical	
					M	*SD*	*M*	*SD*
1. Exploration	—	.23**	.26**	.47**	20.57	6.34	19.85	5.92
2. Role		—	.06	.09	20.15	6.52	16.18	5.60
3. Change			—	.50**	24.26	6.09	20.93	6.33
4. Outcome				—	22.25	7.45	19.52	6.51

**p < .01.

presents a table from Balkin et al. (2016) in which they provided descriptive
statistics and correlation coefficients from scores on four scales of the Forgiveness Reconciliation Inventory. The APA *Publication Manual* also provides
numerous examples of reporting data in tables.

Qualitative results may be summarized using a table or matrix in which
quotes or field notes are organized by participant interview or observation
and placed in a matrix. Table 9.2 provides a matrix for displaying results
across individual interviews, observations, and a focus group. The use of a
table or matrix to display qualitative results may be less common, but it is
still useful in providing a summary resource for the reader and displaying
an abbreviated audit trail to demonstrate trustworthiness.

Writing Your Discussion

And now we get to Chapter 5 of your dissertation! As we mentioned earlier,
many doctoral students view this chapter as the most difficult to write. We
get it. You are tired of this topic and physically fatigued. You want this to
be done, and you have probably been working on it longer than any other
academic project. However, you are in the final haul, and you want to go
out with a bang, not a whimper, right?

What makes the final chapter more difficult than other chapters could
be the nature of the task. In Chapters 1–3, you reflected on what was written about your topic and where the gaps lie. This is an extension of your
doctoral work—writing and reporting on what is known about a topic. In

Table 9.2

Sample Matrix for Qualitative Results

	Interview	Theme 1 Observation	Focus Group
Participant 1			
Participant 2			
Participant 3			
Participant 4			
Participant 5			
Participant 6			

Chapter 4, you simply identified what you found. However, for what could be the first time in your doctoral program, you are being asked to elucidate to your readers what you found and what it means. You have likely been studying this topic for over a year, so you have expertise in this area; you should feel comfortable discussing how to apply what has been learned in your study. To do this, you need to organize Chapter 5, which will generally consist of the following categories:

- discussion,
- implications,
- limitations,
- suggestions for further research, and
- conclusion.

Discussion

We have watched a lot of doctoral students get frustrated writing this section because they are being asked to discuss the meaning behind their findings. In previous writing projects throughout your doctoral program, you probably focused on stating assertions that were grounded in what has been previously published. You still need to do that, but first you are being asked to explicate on your findings based on the data you presented in Chapter 4. However, when discussing your findings, you want to make sure that Chapter 5 does not become a regurgitation of Chapter 4. In the following list, we provide some key points to keep in mind when writing your discussion:

- If you did a quantitative dissertation, refrain from using statistics in your discussion. You already reported the statistics. Rather, focus on the meaning of the statistics. Were your results significant? Was the magnitude of the effects meaningful? Do this without restating values and effect sizes. If you did a qualitative dissertation, refrain from using quotes or field notes because these were already reported in Chapter 4. Focus on the themes you generated and why they are relevant.
- Create a narrative that explains the findings, what they mean, and why they may or may not be important.
- Make sure you do not extend past the results. You can only interpret what you found and project in conditional language why these results occurred.
- Relate your results to previous literature. How were your results similar or different from what was published previously on your topic? When linking your findings back to the literature, you should cite the literature you included in Chapter 2 of your dissertation. In addition, if your findings were similar or different, attempt to explain what happened by citing the conceptual/theoretical texts that are relevant to your topic.

Let's take another look at part of the discussion from Balkin et al. (2016) on the Forgiveness Reconciliation Model and examine how the aforementioned key points were addressed in the discussion. Balkin et al. addressed the finding that the extent to which a perpetrator expressed remorse or changed behavior toward a victim (the client, in this case) increased the likelihood of the victim being willing to reconcile with the offender.

> The relationship between collaborative exploration and the eventual client outcome with respect to interpersonal or intrapersonal forgiveness was partially influenced by the perpetrator's demonstration of remorse and change in behavior. Whether an offender exhibits remorse or changes behavior is external and independent of the client. Regardless of how the client may feel toward the offender, the offender's refusal to express remorse or change behavior may affect the client's decision to pursue or not pursue reconciliation (Aponte, 1998). (pp. 60–61)

Notice that the results were identified without the use of statistical terminology: "The relationship between collaborative exploration and the eventual client outcome with respect to interpersonal or intrapersonal forgiveness was partially influenced" (Balkin et al., 2016, p. 60). The authors also used conditional language to formulate assertions and then reflect back on extant research (i.e., Aponte, 1998): "The offender's refusal to express remorse or change behavior may affect the client's decision to pursue or not pursue reconciliation (Aponte, 1998)" (pp. 60–61). The authors tied the findings to theory but did not reach beyond the findings to make assertions that were unsupported. Instead, the focus was on explaining why the results might have occurred as opposed to asserting something that was more definitive. Remember, rarely can causality be inferred in counseling research. The use of conditional language is important.

Implications

Once you address the question of what does this all mean in your discussion, it is time to turn your attention to the question of who should care about this and why, which is the focus of the implications section. In general, the findings from your study should have some type of impact on the counseling profession. Sometimes implications are specific to counselors; other times the focus may be on training, supervision, and counselor education. Obviously, this is not an either-or situation, and implications can certainly reference both populations. One popular trend in counselor education programs is connecting dissertations to the mission of the university. Most often, this is related to addressing implications to social justice and advocacy. Usually, an implications section will address one of the aforementioned areas (counseling, counselor education and training, or social justice and advocacy), but many articles will address more than one. Balkin, Schlosser, and Levitt (2009) studied the relationship of counselor religious identity and their self-reported attitudes and beliefs related to homophobia, sexism, and multicultural competence and identified implications in all three areas. In the following paragraphs, we highlight the common themes of implications and provide an example from Balkin, Schlosser, and Levitt to demonstrate how to address each theme.

Implications for Counseling

When research is focused on client experiences or client-centered outcomes, you want to turn your attention to how the findings from your research are important to working clients. This is an opportunity to discuss applications of your research to relevant populations. Most important, this section of your discussion is your opportunity to bridge research to practice. When you wrote your research methods and results, you probably demonstrated thoroughness, precision, and sophistication in your design and analysis. Because rigor is essential to elements of generalizability or trustworthiness, the language used may be lost to the average practitioner. Hence, implications to counseling bring the findings back to practitioner language, so your research can be used to move both the knowledge and practice of counseling forward.

Balkin, Schlosser, and Levitt (2009) identified a relationship between counselors' religious identities and the propensity of counselors to engage in attitudes, beliefs, and behaviors related to homophobia, sexism, and multicultural competence. With respect to counseling practice, Balkin, Schlosser, and Levitt indicated the following:

> There is a need for counselors to be aware of the potential for their own religious identity to engender attitudes of sexism and homophobia. Counselors who adhere to more rigid thinking about their faith or reconcile their beliefs in accordance with others of their faith may be more likely to exhibit sexist or homophobic behaviors. Counselors may be more facilitative when they have an awareness of their own beliefs and biases. (pp. 424–425)

Notice that the authors highlighted practical issues in counseling, such as linking more rigid and authoritarian thinking about their faith to exhibiting homophobic and sexist behaviors and the importance of fostering self-awareness among professional counselors.

Implications for Counselor Education and Training

A large amount of research conducted in the counseling profession is related to counselor education and training. The Association for Counselor Education and Supervision publishes *Counselor Education and Supervision,* which focuses specifically on research related to counselor education and training. However, research related to counseling training and practice is common in many counseling journals. Typically, such research includes counselors-in-training or professional counselors as the research participants. When identifying implications to counselor education and training, you establish how the research findings can influence or enhance counselor training.

With respect to counselor training, Balkin, Schlosser, and Levitt (2009) highlighted the following recommendations:

> Counselor educators and supervisors should strive to focus on all aspects of mul-
> ticulturalism, including religion and spirituality (Levitt & Balkin, 2003; Schlosser,
> 2003) in training counseling professionals. Counselors at all levels of expertise and
> training should strive toward self-awareness regarding religion and how their views
> are carried into the counseling relationship. . . . Counselor trainees with highly
> religious orientations may face significant challenges in their development of
> openness to a variety of viewpoints and respect for cultural diversity. Furthermore,
> one might speculate that religious counselors might be more effective with highly
> religious clients because of the rigidity with which some issues may be viewed.
> In this respect, matching highly religious clients with counselors having similar
> orientations may enhance rapport, yet such a partnership may not sufficiently
> challenge clients' perspectives to effect change. (p. 425)

Balkin, Schlosser, and Levitt emphasized the role of counselor educators
and supervisors to promote an increase in self-awareness from counseling
professionals. Furthermore, they addressed concerns related to counselor
trainees with implications for how clients may be affected.

Implications for Social Justice and Advocacy

Counseling research often involves addressing the role of counseling with
disenfranchised populations and diverse clients. A research goal can be to
address issues that have more global ramifications, such as combating racism, sexism, or homophobia. Counseling programs or institutions that have
a particular orientation toward social justice may encourage research that
promotes social change. Many divisions within ACA focus on disenfranchised
or diverse populations and therefore promote and focus on research with
social justice implications. Consider the following divisions or allied organizations and their associated journals:

American Rehabilitation Counseling Association
  Rehabilitation Counseling Bulletin
Association for Adult Development and Aging
  Adultspan Journal
Association for Lesbian, Gay, Bisexual, and
  Transgender Issues in Counseling
  Journal of LGBT Issues in Counseling
Association for Multicultural Counseling and Development
  Journal of Multicultural Counseling and Development

Within the framework of discussing the influence of counselor religious
identity and counselor attitudes, beliefs, and behaviors toward clients related
to homophobia, sexism, and multicultural competence, Balkin, Schlosser,
and Levitt (2009) addressed the role of counselor religion in a broader
context. They stated the following:

> Counselor religion is just as valuable as client religion, and the professional should
> not be challenged to compromise personal belief systems. Rather, as identified
> in this study, counselors need opportunities to explore how their religious values
> may influence their responses to multicultural differences and cultural diversity,
> particularly in the areas of sexism and homophobia. (p. 425)

Hence, the research study not only affected client care and training but also addressed the role of religion for counselors because their faith is not immune to the counseling process.

Limitations

A common section in Chapter 1 of the dissertation addresses assumptions, limitations, and delimitations of the proposed study. So you have probably thought about the limitations of your study. If you addressed limitations previously in Chapter 1, you do not want to simply restate what was already stated. However, some of your previous points were likely salient and can be readdressed.

Limitations in Quantitative Dissertations

You should consider limitations to generalizability. In other words, what would prevent your results from being generalizable to a given population? Consider the design. If you compared groups, were you able to establish group equivalence at the onset of the study? Did you control for extraneous variables? If you did not use random assignment, you are likely not able to account for the influence of all extraneous variables.

Participation in a study is a common limitation. Were the participants in your study representative of the population of interest? Obtaining a representative and diverse sample can be difficult, and many studies have overrepresentation of a particular group as a limitation. Also, you might have to address the adequacy of your sample size. Sometimes the desired sample size is not attained. Balkin, Schlosser, and Levitt (2009) explored the relationship among religious identity, homophobia, sexism, and multicultural competence of professional counselors. They had a 22% response rate in the study, which they addressed as a limitation. Furthermore, the number of participants was less than desirable, so they indicated this limitation by discussing statistical power. For an in-depth example of addressing the adequacy of sample size and statistical power, review Balkin and Sheperis (2011).

The measures you selected for your study should be addressed. If the respondents knew the purpose of your study, you need to acknowledge the presence of response bias. Self-report measures are quite common in counseling research. However, a limitation to self-report measures is the presence of social desirability (i.e., the respondents' tendencies to produce responses that are deemed socially appropriate). For example, when exploring the relationship among religious identity, homophobia, sexism, and multicultural competence of professional counselors, Balkin, Schlosser, and Levitt (2009) thought that counselors would not be likely to admit feelings or beliefs of racism, sexism, or homophobia. They addressed this limitation by stating, "social desirability is a factor in most research on cultural issues, and this study is no exception. The measures used in this study do not correlate with social desirability" (p. 425).

Limitations in Qualitative Dissertations

A good place to start in addressing limitations for qualitative studies is in evaluating trustworthiness (see Chapter 8). Addressing all aspects of trustworthiness is unlikely in any qualitative study. For example, you may have used a single theory or methodology, thereby eliminating theoretical or methodological triangulation. Sometimes member checks are not possible. For example, when Lenz et al. (2014) conducted focus group interviews for adolescents in partial hospitalization, the clients would have been discharged from the hospital, making member checks even more difficult.

Limitations with purposeful sampling are also common. Participants may not always be readily available, and there may be some unintended bias in selection. Researcher bias can also be problematic. Despite the inclusion of details related to trustworthiness, as a qualitative researcher, you are the instrument from which information is filtered.

One common error, however, in addressing limitations to qualitative inquiry is to include a statement about generalizability and purposeful sampling. Qualitative research was never meant to infer generalizability; thus, no mention of generalizability or lack thereof should be mentioned. In addition, you should not be processing limitations related to purposeful sampling because this is an intentional process in qualitative research.

Don't Fall on Your Sword

This brings us to one final word of caution. Whether you are doing a quantitative or qualitative dissertation, you can acknowledge that your study has flaws, but that does not mean the flaws are fatal and that your findings are less important. Limitations are normal and a part of all social science research. You were probably aware of some of the limitations at the onset of your study. Consider how to defend your limitations. For example, if we look back at the Lancaster et al. (2011) study, adjudicated youth in a community-based counseling program were matched with youth from a juvenile database based on age, ethnicity, sex, and status of first offense. The authors did a good job in addressing common variables related to group equivalence, but not all influential variables could be controlled for in the study. The authors acknowledged this limitation but also defended the overall strength of the study:

> Because of the difficulty of controlling for extraneous variables, this study was exploratory. The dearth of extant research with this population probably stems from (a) research with a doubly protected population (i.e., minors and adjudicated), (b) lack of support from external bodies (i.e., juvenile judges), (c) challenges with statistical control, and (d) measurement issues with recidivism. Recidivism in general is not a normally distributed variable and may be difficult to track because of the transient nature of the population. Despite these shortcomings, the focus on counseling outcomes, efficacy, and accountability is important, and this study provides some support for accountability in the practice of counseling. (p. 491)

In other words, Lancaster et al. acknowledged the limitation of controlling for extraneous variables, but they also mentioned that research on adjudicated youth is limited because of the difficulty of collecting data on a protected population and that the findings are still important and meaningful.

Suggestions for Further Research

Having reflected on the findings, implications, and limitations of your study, you need to consider what should come next. In suggestions for further research, you can identify what will be part of your research agenda in the future or how you believe this study should be followed by subsequent studies. Together the limitations and suggestions for further research indicate how future studies can be improved and what should be included in a future study. Suggestions for further research may provide future researchers with an idea of how to expand upon this topic. For emerging researchers, being attentive to this section of a study can be helpful in identifying future research topics. An easy way to conceptualize this section is to review your delimitations in Chapter 1 of your dissertation. If what was not covered in a study is a natural extension of future research, this is a good place to mention it. For example, in processing issues of forgiveness and reconciliation, Balkin et al. (2016) indicated that their study did not address the working alliance between the client and counselor: "Thus, exploring how the various stages affect the therapeutic alliance may be beneficial" (p. 63).

Conclusion

A conclusion is a lot like a long lecture. If you listen to a long lecture, even an engaging one, you likely walk out with limited recollection of what was communicated. For example, if you think about past commencement speeches at graduation, you might remember who spoke, but you probably do not remember what was said. With this in mind, you have submitted to your committee a lengthy document. Although they likely (or hopefully) read the whole thing, you need to consider what you want the reader to walk away with. What were the key points? You do not want your conclusion to be a reconfiguration on all your findings. Rather, you want your conclusion to focus solely on the high points. You can follow these points with a brief explanation of their implications—why these key points are important. Your conclusion is an opportunity to reemphasize the strengths of your study and how it contributes to the counseling profession. Hopefully after writing this section, you feel like you are riding off into the sunset with a sense of accomplishment.

Summary

We covered the elements of Chapters 4 and 5 of the dissertation and emphasized the processes of writing your results and discussing their relevance. Writing your results may appear formulaic. There is a set way to present your findings, and perhaps the best way to master this formula is to read peer-reviewed articles using methods and topics similar to yours. Choose more prestigious journals in your field and notice the organization and style in which results are presented.

Similar to presenting findings, the outline for discussing results is also formulaic. However, you will need to consider the issues related to the meaningfulness and ramifications of your results that are unique to your study. An essential goal of a dissertation is to inform the field through research. You will need to identify the extent to which your study contributes to the counseling profession, the limitations to the contribution, and the direction future researchers should consider.

A dissertation can be an exercise that a student completes to demonstrate research competency to earn a doctorate. Or the dissertation can be your signature—a study that represents your passion and serves as your signature about what you want to influence and to contribute as an academic in the counseling profession. Ultimately, you decide what you want your dissertation to be. Your dissertation will probably not alter the profession in a grand way, but you can pave the way for future research that may influence the next generation of counseling researchers.

Checklist

Chapter 4

❏ Decide how you want to present your results. Results presented narratively should not be in a table, and results presented in a table should not appear in the narrative (but the table should be referenced in the narrative). Report your results either in the narrative or in a table but not both.

❏ For statistical results, make sure you report the following:

- statistical significance,
- practical significance, and
- interpretation of effect size.

For qualitative research, identify how you will present your themes and show relevant data that aligns with each theme; be sure to show a sufficient number of examples for each theme.

Chapter 5

❏ Provide a discussion of your overall findings.
❏ Address implications to counseling, counselor education and training, or social justice and advocacy.
❏ Identify your limitations; this might include an expansion of the limitations you addressed in Chapter 1.
❏ Provide suggestions for further research.
❏ Summarize in one to two paragraphs the overall conclusion of your study; think of this as your elevator speech (i.e., a 1-minute speech that describes your project and its significance).

Additional Resources

We recommend you review research articles from ACA or affiliated divisions to get an idea of how research is presented and discussed (see Table 11.1). Remember to select journals that appear to be a good fit for your research. In addition, you may find the following resources helpful:

Balkin, R. S. (n.d.). *Research methods and statistics.* Retrieved from http://balkinresearchmethods.com/Balkin_Research_Methods/Research_Methods_and_Statistics.html

Balkin, R. S., & Kleist, D. M. (2017). *Counseling research: A practitioner-scholar approach.* Alexandria, VA: American Counseling Association.

Hunt, B., & Trusty, J. (Eds.). (2011). Counseling research and publishing in *JCD* [Special issue]. *Journal of Counseling & Development, 89*(3).

Chapter 10

Preparing for the Defense

This is it! You are almost to the finish line. You have worked extremely hard and tirelessly. This is where the words *scholar practitioner*, with which you are very familiar, now come into play. It is time to speak publically and defend what you have researched and written. Over the years, we have heard students refer to this day as "D-Day," "Defense Day," and "Dissertation Day," but we like to refer to this as "Demonstration of Competence Day." We have found the word *defend* often makes students feel anxious, as if they are under attack. We hope it will ease your mind to know that it is extremely rare for a student to fail a dissertation defense. At your defense meeting, it is important to remember that your chair and committee members want you to succeed. What is most likely the worst-case scenario? You will be required to revise your dissertation.

Our main goal in writing this chapter is to help ease your anxiety as you prepare for your oral defense. We describe what a defense exactly is and explain the oral defense process. We provide you tips to prepare for your oral defense before, during, and after so that this experience is both an exciting and memorable one.

When Should You Schedule Your Defense?

It is important to work closely with your chair to determine if your dissertation is ready to be defended. Keep in mind that your chair probably has served on several committees and chaired other dissertations and therefore will have a good idea if you are ready to defend your dissertation. A defense should only be scheduled when your committee has approved the final dissertation copy. The dissertation submitted to your committee members should have been reviewed several times by your committee and carefully edited. It certainly needs to be free of grammatical errors. You will want to allow at least 2–3 weeks for committee members to return your final project to you.

After your study is approved, you will work with your chair and committee members to set a day and time for your oral defense.

Many online universities schedule a teleconference for the student's defense. In these instances, students are often required to reach out to the chair and committee members and identify several possible dates and times for a teleconference. Arrangements are forwarded to the chair who reserves a university conference call line. To avoid a last-minute glitch, students are encouraged to submit the teleconference reservation form at least 1–2 weeks before the scheduled date being requested.

What Exactly Is a Defense and What Does It Look Like?

So the day is here. What can you expect? A defense is a long-standing academic tradition that allows doctoral candidates the opportunity to share their research and knowledge about their dissertation topic. The defense provides an opportunity for you to demonstrate your competence as a researcher; explain what you did and what you found; and justify the research problem investigated, methodology used, findings obtained, and conclusions made. The whole process usually takes 1–3 hours from start to finish. In the following paragraphs, we provide a scenario of a typical oral defense.

You arrive 30 minutes to an hour early so you can arrange the room and set up your materials. Your chair usually begins the meeting by introducing committee members. If your university allows outside guests, your chair may ask you to introduce any family members or friends. After the introductions, your chair describes the purpose of the defense and the format to be followed. Typically, you can think of the oral defense as divided into two parts: the dissertation and the defense. During the dissertation, you discuss your project for approximately 20–30 minutes. (Please be prepared for committee members' questions during your presentation.) Immediately after you have completed the oral dissertation, the committee members examine the stages of the project. During this time, the committee members ask questions and a discussion takes place for approximately 20–30 minutes.

Once the chair and committee members have finished asking questions, you, along with any visitors, will be asked to leave the room. During this time, your committee will decide if you successfully defended your dissertation. If your dissertation defense is being conducted through a teleconference line, you may be asked to wait for a callback in a reasonable amount of time. During the deliberation, the committee members will decide if you pass with no revisions, pass with minor revisions, pass with major revisions, must continue the oral defense to clarify additional questions, or fail. Please note that some discussions can be brief, whereas can be others lengthy. Do not panic! Lengthy discussions do not mean you failed. We all remember sitting in a deliberation in which faculty members have argued over minor points (e.g., the exact title of the dissertation).

Once the committee has made a decision, the chair will ask you and the visitors to return to the room. The chair will inform you of the decision. If you pass your defense (and we believe you will), expect to hear the words, "Congratulations, Dr. _____," and get ready to celebrate! Before you leave, your committee members will discuss revisions they would like you to make. Your chair will also clarify to you what revisions may need to be made before the committee members sign off.

Before the Defense: How Can I Prepare?

For your defense to be successful, you must be prepared and understand the established rules of your university; the previous example of an oral defense is a typical one that you often see, but do keep in mind that some programs may require a more formal presentation, whereas others may require a more casual approach. We suggest that you schedule a meeting with your chair before your defense and discuss with him or her the following list of questions to help you identify the format of your defense:

- Are there specific days and times designated for a dissertation defense?
- How do I schedule the oral defense—the day, time, room, and so on?
- How many weeks out before the defense should I provide my committee members with a copy of my final draft?
- What forms need to be completed before the defense?
- What forms will I need to file after the defense?
- What forms need to be filed before or after the defense to obtain graduation status?
- Typically, how long are dissertation defense meetings?
- What is the general format of the defense meeting (e.g., Power-Point, audiovisual)?
- Who will ask questions during the defense (the chair, committee members, both, or outside people)?
- Are there specific questions I can expect to be asked?
- Will all committee members ask questions? Will they ask questions randomly or systematically?
- If a disagreement arises between committee members, how will that be handled?
- What materials am I allowed to bring into the defense?
- Who is allowed to attend?
- Are all committee members required to be present? Are people allowed to teleconference in?
- Should I meet with the individual committee members for a final meeting before the defense?
- Am I able to have a colleague sit in and take notes?
- Am I allowed to take notes during the process to keep track of suggested changes?

- Do I need to bring refreshments or food?
- What happens after the meeting?
- Is a unanimous vote of all committee members required to pass the oral defense?
- If changes are required, how soon and to whom do I need to submit the changes? How would you like me to document that all changes were made?
- Who approves the changes (the chair or the chair and committee members)?

In addition to talking with your chair, you should talk with other students about their experiences. You might ask them the following questions:

- What was your experience during the defense?
- How did you prepare for your defense?
- What questions might I be expected to answer?
- Do you have any recommendations of any mistakes or pitfalls to avoid?

Mock Defense

Alternatively, you can prepare for your oral defense by having a mock defense with your colleagues. Many students often do a practice run of their presentations. Your colleagues can ask questions as if they were the faculty members. The following is a list of some common oral defense questions:

- What interested you in this particular topic?
- What surprises did you find in your study?
- What was the most challenging aspect of your study?
- What theory best explains your results?
- Since you wrote your dissertation, what new findings related to your topic have you discovered in the professional journals?
- How generalizable is your study?
- What do you see as the major limitations of your study and how might you correct or avoid this in future studies?
- Your results did not show statistical significance. What could you have done differently? Is there an alternative interpretation of your findings?
- There is a difference between statistical and practical significance. What was the practical significance of your study?
- What implications do your results have for social change? For applied practice?
- How will policy makers be able to use your study?
- How does your study contribute to the counseling literature?
- What do you plan to do next with your results? How will you communicate your results to other scholars in the counseling field?

- Do your findings support or differ from the extent published research on your topic?
- If you had to do it over again, what would you do differently?
- How do you answer the "so what" question in relation to your findings?

The practice presentation will allow you to rehearse your oral defense and make sure that the audio and visual equipment is working and that you have identified the key points, tables, and figures that you may need to refer to during the defense. If your department allows attendance at other dissertation defenses, be sure to take advantage of that policy. Attending other defenses will help relieve some of the mystery of what to expect.

Preparation of Your PowerPoint Presentation

As with any presentation, it is important to be aware of the expected format. If you are required to give a PowerPoint presentation, remember the main point is to present a summary of your dissertation research findings. You are not there to teach your committee by using lengthy PowerPoint slides. For this reason, many dissertation defenses are conducted without a PowerPoint or other props. In case your department does not have a standard format for you to follow and you want to use slides, we have included some tips for you to consider.

- Do not read your slides.
- Elaborate using your notes.
- Use bullet points with phrases and key points on each slide.
- Use no more than five short word bullets or two short sentences on each slide.
- Use the same font on each slide.
- Use the same background on each side.
- Do not overuse color or graphics.

Across different departments, whether working from notes or slides, we have found that students are typically required to address the following:

- title of your dissertation (include your name, department, degree program, and date),
- background information,
- problem statement,
- purpose statement,
- research question(s),
- hypothesis for quantitative study,
- theoretical framework,
- methods/design,
- participants and sample size,
- data collection,

- data analysis and results,
- interpretations,
- limitations of the study,
- implications for professional practice,
- implications for social change (include the implications for social change at the appropriate levels: individual, community, or societal), and
- recommendations.

Helpful Final Preparation Hints

Now that you have identified the date, time, length, and format of your presentation, there are a couple things for you to consider in the days leading up to the defense.

- Make sure your committee has both a hard copy and an electronic copy of your dissertation.
- Continue to read your dissertation carefully and look for any errors. If you notice corrections that need to be made, bring a list of those with you to the defense. Make sure to tab key points or figures that you will be referring to during the defense.
- Review a list of questions you think will be asked and practice your responses aloud.
- Practice strategies for handling questions that are difficult to follow or may not have a right or wrong answer.
- Be prepared to answer why you chose to study certain variables, decided on a particular sample, or used a certain statistical procedure to analyze your data. It is important to note that even though you may have received help from a statistician in your department or outside help, you will be responsible for explaining the statistical procedures used in your study.
- Organize the items you will need for the presentation. Along with organizing all the material you will need, we advise you to decide on how you will professionally present yourself during the defense. This includes deciding on professional attire.
- Finally, be sure to get a good night's rest; use good, healthy, positive thoughts; and enjoy yourself.

During Your Dissertation Defense

You have thoroughly rehearsed your oral presentation and have read your dissertation countless times. Keep in mind that the defense is a positive learning experience in which people come together to hear you publicly speak about your research. You are not expected to be perfect. Repeat after me, "I am not expected to be perfect. But I will be competent." Your goal is not to be perfect during your oral defense but to demonstrate your competence. You will not fail because you take your time to answer a question, stutter, or ask for clarification. Remember you know more about this topic than probably everyone in the room. During the defense, you want to be able to manage your anxiety, be honest about your limitations, and successfully respond to questions.

Managing Anxiety

It is expected that there will be some nervousness and anxiety. Remember to breathe. Try to slow your breathing down and avoid taking fast and shallow breaths. Even if inside you are nervous, try to appear relaxed on the outside. Perhaps visualization or imagery of a successful dissertation defense can be of help before you defend your study. Before your defense, you might find a quiet place, close your eyes, and visualize your favorite place while either taking some deep breathes in and out or sitting quietly and focusing on your breathing to decrease the butterflies in your stomach. Keep in mind that it is perfectly okay to be energetic and show enthusiasm for your project. You have spent a lot of time and money preparing for this moment.

Be mindful of your behavior. Avoid pacing, swaying, shuffling your feet, moistening your lips, clearing your throat, restraining your hands in your pockets, or using exaggerated hand gestures. Try to actively listen and remain calm. Actively listening to your committee will help you focus and decrease your anxiety. By actively listening, you will be able to hear what they are trying to communicate and respond to their questions in a thoughtful manner. As you listen to your committee members and answer questions, maintain eye contact, and it is ok to smile when appropriate.

Being Honest About Limitations

It is important for you to be honest about the limitations of your study and not take feedback personally. If or when a faculty member comments on your work, acknowledge it and remain nondefensive. Keep in mind that acknowledging your committee members' suggestions shows an openness on your part and respect for the committee members' experienced point of view. Often a discussion will take place on how the limitations can be addressed. Breathe and relax! The suggestions or critiques your committee members are voicing can help improve and strengthen your dissertation so it is more likely to be published.

Responding to Questions

We have found that most students seemed to be terrified of the questions that committee members might ask. In addition to reviewing some of the questions frequently asked during a defense and rehearsing your answers, we hope the following strategies to handle the questions will be of help. Keep in mind that you are the expert on your research topic and findings, so you have a wonderful opportunity to present your information as the scholar-practitioner.

When responding to questions, remember to be professional. Think of your committee as audience members at the annual ACA Conference &

Expo. Allow the committee member to ask the full question before you answer. During this time, you want to refrain from joking around or seeming defensive or angry. Your ability to maintain a nondefensive stance is important. Remember the majority of faculty members are on your side, and they want you to succeed. Do not take their questions as personal because it is their job to assess your competence as a researcher.

Take your time! Take a moment to think before responding. After the committee member asks a question, try to paraphrase the question to make sure you are on track before answering. Allow committee members to correct you on any misperception of the question you might have heard. When you answer, try to be precise. Try to answer questions in a succinct manner and avoid jargon. You will want to avoid rambling and lecturing your committee. You may need to refer to the tabs you have marked on your dissertation or PowerPoint. After you answer the question, you may want to follow up by asking, "Does that answer your question?"

What if you do not understand the question? We have been faced with questions that were unclear. Chances are if you do not understand the question, others in the room may feel the same. If you do not understand the question, ask the person to please restate or rephrase what is being asked before attempting to respond. Restating allows the committee member to clarify the question or ask it in different manner.

What if there is no wrong or right answer? If you do not know the answer to a question, it is always best to say, "I'm not sure" or "I do not know." If the response is an opinion, we encourage you to feel free to express your opinion, but do make sure that you preface your response by stating that your answer is an opinion rather than fact supported by the literature.

Here is a final tip when it comes to questioning: Do not compete with the grandstander. Committee members often ask questions because they either want to know if you know the answer or they are genuinely interested in knowing the answer. Nevertheless, the term *grandstanding*, which you may have heard from fellow doctoral students, is when a person speaks in a way intended to attract other members who are watching. Yes, that is right. More often than not, you will have a committee member ask a question that he or she already knows the answer to simply to show other committee members that he or she is academically astute. Although these questions are often lengthy, just answer the question calmly and avoid engaging competitively with the grandstander.

As questions during your defense come to a close, remember to thank everyone in the room who helped you complete this endeavor. This includes your chair, committee members, and family or friends that may be in the room with you.

After Your Dissertation Defense

Revising Your Dissertation

After the final defense meeting, it is not uncommon for students to be required to revise their dissertations. For example, your chair or committee members may ask you to further analyze your data, add to your literature review, or strengthen the implications of your findings. If you distributed hard copies of your dissertation before your defense meeting, you may take back copies that have direct edits to help you make changes. Some universities have a form and style review team at the university writing center, so after passing the oral defense, you may be required to submit your dissertation to the form and style review team where your dissertation goes through a final check (a review for grammar, punctuation, and elements integral to APA style). You and your dissertation chair often have to complete a form in which you explain the revisions that were made, including the page numbers where the revisions were made. If you do not have a form and style review team at your university, you may need the services of a professional editor. As we mentioned in Chapters 1 and 3, a professional editor is familiar with APA form and style. Depending on the amount of work to be reviewed, you can expect to pay anywhere between $500 and $1,500 for professional editing services.

In most cases, your chair and committee members will sign the formal documents during your defense and leave it up to your chair to make sure you make the requested changes. However, if there are major revisions, committee members might not agree to sign formal documents until they are sure that you made all the necessary changes. In these cases, once you have made the requested changes, the chair authorizes you to forward the dissertation to the committee members for their review. We encourage you to work closely with your chair to make sure you understand the changes required. You will want to make the changes as soon as possible while the feedback from your defense is fresh in your mind. Minor revisions can usually be incorporated within a week.

Getting Ready for Graduation

It is important that you are aware of university deadlines for submitting the formal documents that are required for the doctoral degree and of the deadlines for applying for graduation. You may be asking yourself, "Wait, but I thought once I passed my defense I was ready to walk the stage!" You are almost there! However, in addition to your defense paperwork requirements, the graduate student office will have additional papers for you and your committee to sign. Some of this paperwork may be required before your defense (e.g., applying for graduation, verifying all academic requirements were met), whereas others might take place after (e.g., surveys).

In addition to the defense-required documents, some universities will require students to submit their dissertation to ProQuest for publishing before a degree can be validated. ProQuest is a database that produces microfilms of dissertations. Many students are also strongly encouraged, but not required, to complete the Survey of Earned Doctorates. This survey evaluates graduate programs at the federal, state, and university levels.

Acknowledging the Support of Your Committee

Alfred North Whitehead, a mathematician and philosopher, once said, "No one who achieves success does so without acknowledging the help of others. The wise and confident acknowledge this help with gratitude." Completing your dissertation is a tremendous accomplishment. It requires not only your stamina, determination, and emotional resilience but also a great deal of determination between your chair and committee members. Up until this point, much of your time has been involved in writing of a technical nature, but it is now time to reflect on all the people who have encouraged and supported you or were linked to your dissertation. In addition to your personal acknowledgments, in the acknowledgments section of your dissertation, you should list academic contributors, such as your chair and committee members, by their full names and titles. You will also want to list professionals who contributed to your research (e.g., other professors, librarians, statisticians, classmates). In many university settings, it is common practice to provide your chair a hardbound copy of your dissertation with a heartfelt notation on the inside cover. Students often provide their committee members with a spiral-bound copy. Although there is no set protocol in the counseling profession in terms of how to acknowledge your chair and committee members, we believe a hand-written card expressing your gratitude throughout this journey will go a long way. We suggest that any gift you may give your committee members should come after the dissertation defense. We hope that you continue to have a good relationship with your committee members and chair even after graduation and that your mentors will be lifelong friends. In Chapter 11, we discuss additional ways you can include your chair or committee members on professional presentations and articles.

Rewarding Yourself

Congratulations! You have received the highest degree offered in formal education. We hope that you are proud of your accomplishments. This is now the time for celebrating and rejoicing with friends and family. From start to finish, your dissertation was a time for growing academically, professionally, and personally. You had to decide on a topic of interest and demonstrate a gap in the literature. You gained a tremendous amount of knowledge about your topic and most likely confidence as a writer and scholar. You developed relationships with your chair and committee members and made lasting relationships with classmates. You probably had many enlightening conversations but also some hard or disappointing ones as well. If you have ever climbed to the top of a mountain, you know that exhilarating feeling. Andy Rooney once said, "Everyone wants to live on top of the mountain, but all the happiness and growth occurs while you're climbing it." You probably learned to be accepting of yourself, and even when you might have struggled academically, psychologically, or physically, you made it to the top of the mountain.

Over the years, students have shared with us a myriad of emotions as the dissertation comes to an end. Although there is an initial sense of relief and weight taken off their shoulders, for many students there is also a sense of loss. That's why it has been said that completing a dissertation and the doctorate is bittersweet. Students have shared that it is difficult to leave friends whom they have bonded with for over 3 years as well as the university setting. All of a sudden, you find yourself with extra time that might lead to periods of depression. Emotions are aroused because of the transition. You have been juggling your academic and personal life for several years. Perhaps you had to forego many family events or social engagements during this process. Students have shared their guilt of neglecting family and friends while immersed in their studies and writing.

This is a time to reconnect with family and friends. Our hope is that you will take time to engage in the activities that brought you pleasure before. This is a time to reenergize and engage in meaningful rest, relaxation, and self-care. We want to encourage you to tune in to yourself and recognize the self-care needed as you continue in your postdoctoral journey. We hope that taking care of yourself will be a life priority.

Summary

This chapter focused on preparing for the defense. We suggested helpful hints and strategies that you can use before, during, and after the defense. A major purpose of this chapter was to take the mystery out of the dissertation defense. Throughout the chapter, we emphasized the importance of preparation and planning, including working closely with your dissertation chair and committee members. You never want to walk into a dissertation defense without the complete support of the committee members who have provided their suggested revisions weeks before the defense. Therefore, you will need to address all the committee members' suggested changes to their satisfaction before the defense. We are confident that when you follow the suggestions included in this chapter, the dissertation defense will be a success and, in most cases, an enjoyable experience.

In Chapter 11, we present ways you can share your research findings, add to the body of knowledge in counseling, and have an impact on social changes in our society. Now you can look back with pride at the work you have completed and look ahead at how you can use the skills and knowledge gained to make a difference in the lives of the many individuals and groups of people you will be serving.

Checklist

Preparing for the Demonstration of Competence Day (aka Your Defense)

❏ Schedule a meeting with your chair.
❏ Identify the format of your defense.
❏ Prepare your PowerPoint slides and handouts.

❏ Tab your dissertation to readily refer to specific tables, content, and so on.
❏ Attend other dissertation defenses.
❏ Practice a mock defense with your colleagues.
❏ Make sure your audio and visual equipment work.
❏ Practice strategies for handling difficult questions.
❏ Review the commonly asked questions and other questions suggested by your chair.
❏ Practice strategies to manage anxiety on the day of the defense.
❏ Pick out your professional attire.
❏ Revise your dissertation based on defense feedback.
❏ Complete any additional university paperwork needed for graduation.
❏ CELEBRATE with family, friends, and colleagues!

Additional Resources

Anxiety and Depression Association of America. (n.d.). *Tips to manage anxiety and stress.* Retrieved from https://www.adaa.org/tips-manage-anxiety-and-stress

Castleman, M. (n.d.). 37 stress management tips to find the calm in your life. *Reader's Digest.* Retrieved from http://www.rd.com/health/wellness/37-stress-management-tips/

Flynn, S. V., Chasek, C. L., Harper, I. F., Murphy, K. M., & Jorgensen, M. F. (2012). A qualitative inquiry of the counseling dissertation process. *Counselor Education and Supervision, 51,* 242–255. doi:10.1002/j.1556-6978.2012.00018.x

Johnson, R. W., & Conyers, L. M. (2001). Surviving the doctoral dissertation: A solution-focused approach. *Journal of College Counseling, 4,* 77–80. doi:10.1002/j.2161-1882.2001.tb00185.x

Wilson, R. (2016). *Stopping the noise in your head: The new way to overcome anxiety and worry.* Deerfield Beach, FL: Health Communication.

Chapter 11

Disseminating the Project to the Professional Community

If you are reading this chapter, you are likely either someone who is ambitious and keeps their eyes toward the horizon or you have successfully defended your dissertation project. Regardless of which one of these descriptors applies to you, congratulations are in order, but so is the encouragement to disseminate your findings within the professional community. Think of this as your opportunity to pay it back to the members of the counseling community who may use your findings to validate aspects of their research interests or spur along new creative works. It may sound far-fetched, but that is how these things happen—students, just like you, share your project with all of us. Yes, the day you turn in your dissertation defense form with that incredible "PASS" designation and all those beautiful signatures, you may find yourself weary of your topic and not want to talk about your project. That is natural. Give yourself some time to recoup. But do not wait too long because opportunity rarely waits for us and it even more infrequently shows with a cup of coffee, a charged laptop, and perfect timing.

We encourage all our students to disseminate their findings to counselors and related health professionals through at least one of four outlets: (a) dissertation repositories, (b) conference proceedings, (c) peer-reviewed journals, and (d) policy papers that may precipitate social change. In this final chapter, we briefly review each of these outlets and identify some of the important considerations. You certainly do not have to go for each one of these outlets, but we encourage you to shoot for at least one. Regardless which one(s) you choose, you will be contributing to the knowledge base for counselors, counselor educators, and all the other related professionals. We also discuss these venues and how you can prepare for your continued success through the dissemination of your findings.

Inclusion in Dissertation Repositories

Having your dissertation and its abstract included in a dissertation repository is probably the easiest and quickest option for disseminating your project to the many other professionals who could benefit from reading about what you have learned. These large document storage and management platforms include millions of dissertations from scholars all over the world. Moreover, the groups that manage these repositories are great at freely disseminating and circulating your work in perpetuity.

Some of the larger, more highly accessed repositories include ProQuest Dissertations & Theses Global (PQDT Global) and Education Resources Information Center (ERIC). Both platforms have online submission portals that require little more than 10 minutes to complete: Provide a little descriptive information about your project, provide a little information about your document (e.g., number of pages, number of references), upload your document in PDF format, and submit. In addition to these two stalwarts, a number of open-source repositories have cropped up recently that are not as well-established as PQDT Global and ERIC but are making a positive change by sharing knowledge. Two examples include OpenThesis and Open Access Theses and Dissertations. Although some may perceive open-source data warehouses as inferior to more traditional resources, they typically contain millions of documents in their repositories. Just like PDQT Global and ERIC, the process takes just a few minutes to complete and is incredibly streamlined through an online submission portal.

Once your document is included within these databases, it is instantly accessible by scholars through library search engines just about everywhere. For this reason, we strongly urge you to submit to PDQT Global and ERIC at a minimum. When you consider that adding your document to the two additional open-source repositories we mentioned will only take about 15 minutes, the choice seems obvious. They are all free to you and they are far-reaching to many.

Presenting Your Dissertation Findings at Professional Conference Proceedings

The next thing we encourage all our candidates or new graduates to do is present your dissertation findings at one of the myriad professional counseling conferences going on year-round. Counseling conferences range from general to specialized, international to local, and coordinators are always looking for quality submissions. Regardless what level or scope of conference you choose, there are many benefits to presenting at a conference that you should consider. Foremost, and perhaps most practical, you will be afforded the opportunity to share your knowledge and expertise with other professionals who have similar interests. Some of these people may be looking for collaborators, but more important, some of them may be looking to add someone just like you to their faculty or staff. Second, whether presenting a research poster or content session, conference presentations are a great place to receive perspectives and feedback in addition to what your committee members have provided. This information may be helpful in shaping the arc of your project or even support preparation of a scholarly manuscript. Finally, as we mentioned in the previous section, this is just another way to contribute to the knowledge base in counseling and counselor education. It is possible that your presentation will stimulate contemplation, creativity, and action among some of the attendees, which magnifies the practical effect of your project.

So how do you become a conference presenter? Associations typically send out a call for proposals that will ask for (a) a title, (b) a rationale indicating the importance of your work, (c) a synopsis of content, (d) learning objectives, and (e) a summary that can be included in the conference program. It is important when developing your proposal to consider your audience: Are these practitioners, counselor educators, researchers, or a combination of these? Once you have answered this question, you will want to tailor your proposal to speak to the sensibilities of that target audience. For example, practitioners may be more interested in the practical how-to aspects of an intervention, whereas researchers may be more attentive to aspects of design, analysis, and interpretation of results. The content and flow of your presentation will also be indicated by the type of session you are presenting. At counseling conferences, there are typically two broad categories of presentations: content sessions that range from 1 hour to several hours and brief research posters.

When preparing to deliver your content session, you will want to consider some important guidelines, regardless of whether your audience is more practitioners or scholars. First, the presentation is not your formal defense session. The attendees do not need every detail about everything, and there is plenty of room for your personality to flourish within the session. Second, keep your presentation concise and visually appealing. There is something called *death by PowerPoint,* and trust us, your attendees will appreciate you talking and interacting with them rather than reading from a slide show for an hour. In fact, we often encourage our students to use programs such as Prezi, which are novel visual experiences for attendees, and to use a wireless handheld remote to advance their slides so that they can walk around during their sessions instead of being anchored behind a keyboard. Also, make sure that your font type, size, and color are easy to read. Finally, when preparing your presentation, plan for it to run a little short. Chances are that you will have attendees who engage in discussion or want to ask questions about aspects of your project that are of interest to them, so accounting for that is important.

Whereas content sessions provide space for a didactic, more formal presentation, poster presentations are a whole different ball game because they are distinctively brief, yet interactive. Some attendees may just stop by your poster for just a few minutes, collect a handout, and move along to the next poster; others will stick around for a bit and have a more in-depth conversation about your study, your findings, and what is next within your scholarly agenda. Overall, a poster should include some basic elements such as a title, abstract, brief introduction, description of method, reporting of results, and your conclusions. We encourage you to make you poster visually appealing by placing these elements with enough space between them so that they stand out, and we also recommend including some easy-to-interpret visuals, such as tables and graphs. Finally, when preparing to present, we suggest that you put together an elevator speech (i.e., a 1-minute speech that communicates what your project is about and its significance) and practice talking about your project with a friend or colleague. With these tips in mind, you should be well-prepared to disseminate your findings at professional conferences.

Publishing Your Dissertation Findings in a Peer-Reviewed Journal

Submitting a manuscript based on your dissertation to a peer-reviewed counseling journal is a great idea. Many students do not see themselves as the type of person whose study may ever be published, much less cited in someone else's work, but we are here to tell you that it is possible. With that said, the choice to whittle down your dissertation document into a 20- or 25-page manuscript should not be taken lightly and carries with it some additional work beyond your defense during a time when other life priorities may be waiting for you.

We encourage you to share your work with the professional community by submitting your manuscript to a counseling journal, not only for the great feeling of getting an acceptance letter somewhere down the road but also for a number of important professional reasons. Often, the dissertation is an expansive marathon of a writing project, and sometimes students lose perspective about the aspects of their studies that are most relevant to other professionals. Developing a manuscript allows you to deconstruct your dissertation to its most essential self, and the submission of that manuscript marks your entrance into the scholarly community as an individual with unique interests and the skill set to investigate the related phenomena. In addition, although your committee was made up of strong scholars, the peer review gives you access to experts without a vested interest in your success, who are instead consigned to promoting the dissemination of quality scholarship that has the potential to move the field forward. These peer reviews provide an incredible amount of feedback and suggestions that will enhance the impact of your manuscript. Finally, scholarly publications tend to indicate a certain degree of professionalism that carries a great deal of weight when applying for academic and clinical positions. Even if you transition into a teaching position, most universities will require at least a few publications when applying for promotion of rank. So it is important to do, but how do you do it?

At this point, all the serious legwork is done. What is left for you to do are some comparatively simple tasks that require a bit of thoughtfulness and then some substantial editing. Specifically, we think that you will want to (a) consider authorship, (b) identify a target journal, (c) familiarize yourself with author guidelines, (d) transform your dissertation into a manuscript, (e) prepare a cover letter, and (f) settle into the review and revision process. Although the APA *Publication Manual* does a great job of covering each of these domains, we will overview some important considerations here.

Considering Authorship

Obviously, you will be the first author on your manuscript, but credit should also be given for individuals who have made significant contributions to the development of your study, data collection, analysis, reporting, or preparation of your manuscript. The operative term in this process is *substantial contributions*, because providing resources, mentoring, and being supportive during the process does not constitute authorship of your manuscript. In many cases, students elect to include their dissertation chairs in authorship because the chairs have met the requirements for contributing to design, analysis, reporting, and preparation, but any other individuals will be determined by you.

Once you have decided who will be included in your manuscript and what contributions they will make, you may want to consider using an authorship contract. In fact, this is a required activity indicated in the *ACA Code of Ethics* (ACA, 2014): "Students/supervisors establish agreements in advance regarding allocation of tasks, publication credit, and types of acknowledgment that will be received" (Standard G.5.e.). As illustrated in Appendix G, some basic components of any authorship agreement include (a) title of project, (b) identification of author credit and tasks that the cocontributor will be responsible for, (c) a timeline for contributions, and (d) assurances for the voluntary nature of being a part of the manuscript development. With these aspects of involvement accounted for, you will be able to have clear boundaries with others about important activities such as author order, meeting deadlines, type of contributions, and expected target journal.

Identifying a Target Journal

We encourage all our students to publish within counseling journals. There are a considerable number of journal options for you to consider, and each has its own scope of content, frequency of distribution, and author guidelines that suit the identity of the parent organization it represents (see Table 11.1). When selecting a journal to publish in, there are a few important factors to consider.

Matching Your Manuscript to a Journal's Publishing Priorities

You need to match the topic and focus of your manuscript to the subject area that is covered by your target journal. For example, if your study evaluated a school-based preventative stress management program for eighth graders

Table 11.1

Scope of Manuscripts and Author Guidelines for the Journals of the
American Counseling Association and Affiliated Divisions

Journal Name	Association Affiliation	Scope of Manuscripts and Link to Author Guidelines
Adultspan Journal	Association for Adult Development and Aging	*Adultspan* publishes current information about research, theory, and practice in the field of adult development and aging. Leadership is provided on innovative topics focusing on developmental principles and concomitant counseling implications. Link to *Adultspan* Author Guidelines: https://www.counseling.org/docs/default-source/default-document-library/aspan0417authorguidelines.pdf?sfvrsn=0
The Career Development Quarterly (CDQ)	National Career Development Association	*CDQ* fosters career development through the design and use of career interventions and by publishing articles on career counseling, individual and organizational career development, work and leisure, career education, career coaching, and career management. *CDQ* is the preeminent journal for career counseling and career development in the world. Link to *CDQ* Author Guidelines: https://www.counseling.org/docs/default-source/default-document-library/cdq0317authorguidelines.pdf?sfvrsn=0
Counseling and Values (CVJ)	Association for Spiritual, Ethical, and Religious Values in Counseling	*CVJ* is a professional journal concerned with the relationships among counseling, ethics, philosophy, psychology, religion, social values, and spirituality. Its mission is to promote free intellectual inquiry across these domains. Its vision is to attract a diverse readership reflective of a growing diversity in the membership of the Association for Spiritual, Ethical, and Religious Values in Counseling and to effect change leading to the continuing growth and development of a more genuinely civil society. Link to *CVJ* Author Guidelines: https://www.counseling.org/docs/default-source/default-document-library/cvj0417authorguidelines.pdf?sfvrsn=0

(Continued)

Table 11.1 (*Continued*)
Scope of Manuscripts and Author Guidelines for the Journals of the
American Counseling Association and Affiliated Divisions

Journal Name	Association Affiliation	Scope of Manuscripts and Link to Author Guidelines
Counseling Outcome Research and Evaluation (CORE)	Association for Assessment and Research in Counseling	*CORE* provides counselor educators, researchers, and other mental health practitioners with outcome research and program evaluation practices for work with individuals across the lifespan. It presents topics such as treatment efficacy, clinical diagnosis, program evaluation, research design, and outcome measure reviews. Link to *CORE* Author Guidelines: http://www.tandfonline.com/action/authorSubmission?journalCode=uore20&page=instructions
Counselor Education and Supervision (CES)	Association for Counselor Education and Supervision	*CES* is dedicated to publishing manuscripts with original research, theory development, or program applications related to counselor education and supervision. The journal focuses on the preparation and supervision of counselors in agency or school settings; in colleges and universities; or at local, state, or federal levels. Link to *CES* Author Guidelines: https://www.counseling.org/docs/default-source/default-document-library/ces0317authorguidelines.pdf?sfvrsn=0
The Family Journal: Counseling and Therapy for Couples and Families (TFJ)	International Association of Marriage and Family Counselors	*TFJ* advances the theory, research, and practice of counseling with couples and families from a family systems perspective. Research articles include quantitative, qualitative, and evaluation designs. Descriptive articles address current issues, innovative methods, and professional concerns. Other offerings include case studies, interviews, and timely literature reviews. The journal provides groundbreaking, innovative scholarship for counseling researchers, educators, and practitioners. Link to *TFJ* Author Guidelines: https://us.sagepub.com/en-us/nam/the-family-journal/journal200924#submission-guidelines

(Continued)

Table 11.1 (*Continued*)

Scope of Manuscripts and Author Guidelines for the Journals of the
American Counseling Association and Affiliated Divisions

Journal Name	Association Affiliation	Scope of Manuscripts and Link to Author Guidelines
Journal for Social Action in Counseling and Psychology (JSACP)	Counselors for Social Justice	*JSACP* articles reflect on community change and system transformation in which counselors, psychologists, and other human service professionals play a role. The journal aims to highlight engaged scholarship and the very important social change work done by professionals and activists that would not normally find its way into publication. The journal attempts to break down the divide between theory and practice in one of the most critical areas of counseling: social transformation toward social justice and peace. Link to *JSACP* Author Guidelines: http://jsacp.tumblr.com/guidelines
The Journal for Specialists in Group Work (JSGW)	Association for Specialists in Group Work	*JSGW* is directed toward group work practitioners with a focus on group work theory, interventions, training, current issues, and research. This journal also aims to promote the practice of group work, cover the continuum of types of group work, emphasize the processes that make groups effective, integrate theory and practice, and provide specific information about how to lead groups and train group leaders. Link to *JSGW* Author Guidelines: http://www.tandfonline.com/action/authorSubmission?show=instructions&journalCode=usgw20
Journal of Addictions & Offender Counseling (JAOC)	International Association of Addictions and Offender Counselors	*JAOC* focuses on prevention and treatment programs, the attitudes and behaviors of substance abuse professionals, tested techniques, treatment of adolescents and adults, and qualitative and quantitative studies. It also focuses on literature specific to the attitudes and behaviors of addictions and offender counselors. Link to *JAOC* Author Guidelines: https://www.counseling.org/docs/default-source/default-document-library/jaoc0417authorguidelines.pdf?sfvrsn=0

(Continued)

Table 11.1 (*Continued*)
Scope of Manuscripts and Author Guidelines for the Journals of the
American Counseling Association and Affiliated Divisions

Journal Name	Association Affiliation	Scope of Manuscripts and Link to Author Guidelines
Journal of Child and Adolescent Counseling (JCAC)	Association for Child and Adolescent Counseling	*JCAC* seeks to promote the awareness of issues related to the counseling of children and adolescents among counseling practitioners, educators, and students. *JCAC* provides a developmental perspective on the improvement of prevention and intervention mental health services for children from birth through age 18. *JCAC* also encourages the exploration of issues related to counseling caretakers such as parents, teachers, and other primary caregivers who contribute to the mental health of children and adolescents. Link to *JCAC* Author Guidelines: http://www.tandfonline.com/action/authorSubmission?show=instructions&journalCode=ucac20
Journal of College Counseling (JCC)	American College Counseling Association	*JCC* publishes articles that inform the practice of counselors working in higher education settings. Categories of manuscripts include research studies, professional issues, and innovative practice. Link to *JCC* Author Guidelines: https://www.counseling.org/docs/default-source/default-document-library/jcc0417authorguidelines.pdf?sfvrsn=0
Journal of Counseling & Development (JCD)	American Counseling Association	*JCD* publishes practice, theory, and research articles across 20 different specialty areas and work settings. Sections include practice, research, assessment and diagnosis, trends, and practitioner profiles. Link to *JCD* Author Guidelines: https://www.counseling.org/docs/default-source/default-document-library/jcd0417authorguidelines.pdf?sfvrsn=0

(Continued)

Table 11.1 (*Continued*)
Scope of Manuscripts and Author Guidelines for the Journals of the
American Counseling Association and Affiliated Divisions

Journal Name	Association Affiliation	Scope of Manuscripts and Link to Author Guidelines
Journal of Creativity in Mental Health (JCMH)	Association for Creativity in Counseling	*JCMH* publishes practical applications for creative interventions designed to promote positive, growth-fostering relationships. Publication topics include grief and loss, divorce, remarriage, physical health, trauma, gender, and LGBTQ issues. This journal also explores issues from developmental and culturally dynamic contexts. Link to *JCMH* Author Guidelines: http://www.tandfonline.com/action/authorSubmission?show=instructions&journalCode=wcmh20
Journal of Employment Counseling (JEC)	National Employment Counseling Association	*JEC* publishes articles illuminating theory or practice in employment counseling, reporting professional experimentation or research, or exploring current client vocational problems or the professional concerns of counselors. Link to *JEC* Author Guidelines: https://www.counseling.org/docs/default-source/default-document-library/jec0317authorguidelines.pdf?sfvrsn=0
The Journal of Humanistic Counseling (JHC)	Association for Humanistic Counseling	*JHC* focuses on humanistic counseling and development and asserts that humanity is responsible for its own destiny. Research and critical reviews emphasize innovative programs and practices to promote tolerance, nurture diversity, and uphold human rights. Link to *JHC* Author Guidelines: https://www.counseling.org/docs/default-source/default-document-library/jhc0417authorguidelines.pdf?sfvrsn=0

(Continued)

Table 11.1 (*Continued*)
Scope of Manuscripts and Author Guidelines for the Journals of the
American Counseling Association and Affiliated Divisions

Journal Name	Association Affiliation	Scope of Manuscripts and Link to Author Guidelines
Journal of LGBT Issues in Counseling ((JLGBTIC)	Association for Lesbian, Gay, Bisexual and Transgender Issues in Counseling	*JLGBTIC* focuses on empirical research, best practices, and emerging trends and issues focused on counseling the lesbian, gay, bisexual, transgender, queer, questioning, intersex, asexual, ally, pansexual, or other sexual minority communities at all developmental stages of life. Articles represent diverse contexts, including schools, mental health agencies, colleges and universities, substance abuse treatment facilities, the criminal justice system, religious organizations, private practices, and medical centers. Link to *JLGBTIC* Author Guidelines: http://www.tandfonline.com/action/authorSubmission?show=instructions &journalCode=wlco20
Journal of Mental Health Counseling (JMHC)	American Mental Health Counselors Association	*JMHC* provides clinical mental health counselors and researchers with empirically supported best practices, evidence-based approaches, and new developments in clinical mental health counseling. Articles include implications for professional mental health counseling practice and future research. Articles also provide critical analyses of the existing literature and descriptive application of clinical approaches, strategies, and techniques. Link to *JMHC* Author Guidelines: https://amhca.site-ym.com/ ?jmhcguidelines

(Continued)

Table 11.1 (*Continued*)

Scope of Manuscripts and Author Guidelines for the Journals of the
American Counseling Association and Affiliated Divisions

Journal Name	Association Affiliation	Scope of Manuscripts and Link to Author Guidelines
Journal of Military and Government Counseling (JMGC)	Military and Government Counseling Association	*JMGC* promotes reflection and works to encourage, develop, facilitate, and promote professional development for administrators, counselors, and educators working with all members of the Armed Services and their families. The journal aims to highlight engaged scholarship and to conduct and foster professional monographs to enhance individual human development and increase recognition of humanistic values and goals among the members and within the agencies where they practice. Link to *JMGC* Author Guidelines: http://acegonline.org/journal/ jmgc-guidelines-for-authors
Journal of Multicultural Counseling and Development (JMCD)	Association for Multicultural Counseling and Development	*JMCD* is concerned with research, theory, or program applications pertinent to multicultural and ethnic minority interests in all areas of counseling and human development. Link to *JMCD* Author Guidelines: https://www.counseling.org/docs/ default-source/default-document- library/jmcd0417authorguidelines. pdf?sfvrsn=0
Measurement and Evaluation in Counseling and Development (MECD)	Association for Assessment and Research in Counseling	*MECD* articles range from theoretical and other problems of the measurement specialist to those directed to the administrator, the counselor, or the personnel worker in schools and colleges, public and private agencies, business, industry, and government. All articles describe implications for the counseling field and for practitioners in assessment, measurement, and evaluation. Link to *MECD* Author Guidelines: http://www.tandfonline.com/action/ authorSubmission?journalCode=uecd 20&page=instructions

(Continued)

Table 11.1 (*Continued*)
Scope of Manuscripts and Author Guidelines for the Journals of the
American Counseling Association and Affiliated Divisions

Journal Name	Association Affiliation	Scope of Manuscripts and Link to Author Guidelines
Professional School Counseling (PSC)	American School Counselor Association	*PSC* publishes articles on theory, research, and best practices for the profession as well as techniques, materials, and ideas to assist school counselors and related practitioners. This journal focuses on strengthening the bonds among school counselors and maintaining a shared awareness of the roles, problems, and progress of school counseling across various settings and levels. Link to *PSC* Author Guidelines: https://www.schoolcounselor.org/school-counselors-members/publications/journal-author-guidelines
Rehabilitation Counseling Bulletin (RCB)	American Rehabilitation Counseling Association	*RCB* features articles important to rehabilitation counseling practitioners in counseling, education, or research settings. Each issue includes original empirical research, theoretical essays, comprehensive literature reviews, intensive case studies, research critiques, and media reviews. Link to *RCB* Author Guidelines: https://www.sagepub.com/sites/default/files/upm-binaries/53678_RCB_56(2)_ag.pdf

who take standardized tests in school, you may want to consider the *Journal of Child and Adolescent Counseling* or *Professional School Counseling* as a landing spot. Apart from specialty journals, we think it is important to remember that the *Journal of Counseling & Development*, ACA's flagship journal, publishes manuscripts that represent the interests of all professional counselors and therefore is a great venue to submit manuscripts of any nature as long as they have a direct interest for counselors.

Matching Your Manuscript to the Types of Articles a Journal Publishes

Not all journals publish all types of manuscripts, so it is important to make sure that you find a target journal that promotes your chances for success. One way to determine this fit is to review the journal's submission guidelines and categories for submission. Then, you can complete a hand search of a potential journal to evaluate the characteristics of articles published within those categories and decide as to goodness of fit. If a journal has published several types of articles within the category that suites you, that is good news because you have an idea of the trends within the professional literature. If they have not published much in your category, that could be good news too because the moment could be ripe for a great submission.

Reputation of the Journal

You have worked hard to complete your project, so it stands to reason that you would want it published in a respectable source. Some things to consider may be a journal's impact factor, the size of their readership, level of indexing, and acceptance rate. Often, there is a balance between these factors that needs to be considered rather than a dichotomous yes–no decision.

Familiarizing Yourself With Author Guidelines

Once you have selected a journal, it is time to get familiar with the specific guidelines that authors are required to observe before peer review. These guidelines are often found on the journal's website or located on the front or back of the issue. These guidelines describe constraints related to the length of title, word count for the abstract, number of keywords, page limitations, citation and reference style, and permission requirements. It is also important to review the types of work the journal takes into consideration (e.g., theory, best practices, research). You will save yourself considerable time by observing these guidelines while developing your manuscript and before submission.

Transforming Your Dissertation Into a Manuscript

Transforming your lengthy, incredibly thorough dissertation into a brief, easily understood document may seem like a daunting task, but it is more manageable than you may think. As you whittle down a 100+ page dissertation into something that fits the submission requirements of your target journal, there are some things you may want to consider. Foremost, although your dissertation committee may have required you to demonstrate an understanding of your topic since the beginning of time, journal editors will not. With that in mind, challenge yourself to determine not only what narrative is imperative to contextualize your findings but also what references are essential. With that in mind, it is prudent not to include more. On a related note, dissertations typically include lengthy abstracts and a lot of tables/figures, but manuscripts require much less. As such, you should consider not only what is imperative for inclusion but also what can be eliminated or combined to assure a concise presentation. You may want to consider only addressing one or two of your research questions rather than all of them. Also, one mistake many students make when converting their document is the overreporting or overinterpretation beyond what is required by APA reporting standards and most journals, so it is important to meet the standards and move on to your discussion. Furthermore, given the considerable amount of editing that you will be doing, you may want to secure the editorial services available from your writing center or a colleague who has not read your original document and have them attend to not only the content reported but also the format of the document. Counseling dissertations often have a hybrid characteristic that lies somewhere between APA publication standards and what is required by your graduate studies department. This could include margin settings, standard headings, table formats, and so on, so make sure that you have this aspect of the document under control. One common piece of advice when editing the document is "when you think you are done with the document, trim 200 words off of it," and after that, you should be ready to submit.

All these tips revolve around one common theme—reining in your reporting about a topic that you have dedicated the last year or more to bring to life. Some students have mentioned to us that this process feels a little bit like being asked to trivialize aspects of their dissertations. Instead, we encourage you to consider that this is your opportunity to share the most quintessential features and findings associated with your effort. Although publication of your manuscript cannot ever be guaranteed, following these considerations will certainly support your effort.

Preparing a Cover Letter

All the counseling journals listed in Table 11.1 use an online submission platform, which is incredibly convenient but also decreases the importance of a well-developed and highly descriptive cover letter accompanying your manuscript. Still, as editors, associate editors, and review board members for several ACA journals, we contend that a cordial and descriptive cover letter is an important part of any submission. These do not take much time but should include some basic information, including (a) title of your manuscript; (b) a brief, one-sentence synopsis of the content; (c) number of pages, tables, and figures included; (d) testimony that the manuscript has solely been presented to the target journal; (e) assurances that the manuscript was prepared in accordance with the journal submission guidelines and *ACA Code of Ethics* (ACA, 2014); and (f) the names and electronic contact information for all authors, with one identified as the primary contact. With this in hand, you are ready to submit your work and officially enter the professional community as a lead researcher and distinguish yourself among your peers.

Settling Into the Review and Revision Process

Peer review is an interesting thing. A long, humbling, interesting thing that can support the presentation of your project to the professional community in its concise yet impactful way. It is important to know that the initial review of a manuscript submission can take between 60 and 90 days. Then, it is typically reviewed by an associate editor who integrates feedback and provides some of his or her own feedback and recommends a disposition that the editor will consider before sending to you. Possible outcomes include being accepted outright with no revisions, being accepted with some minor revisions to make, being asked to revise and resubmit your manuscript, and being rejected as not meeting the quality or scope of the journal. In our experiences, the most common disposition is a revise and resubmission. It's common. It's actually a great thing because you will be given an incredible amount of recommendations that will help you bring your work closer to publishable form. As you make revisions, you will want to account for them in a document that you send to the editor and review board members upon your resubmission. From there, it is another 60–90 days, which can feel like 600–900 days, so be patient, settle into the process, and work on other products that are possible from your project.

Your Project as a Precipitant of Social Change

All the dissemination venues discussed so far have been associated with making your findings available to communities of professional counselors, counselors educators, and counseling students. We suggest that your project may have implications that are of interest to precipitating social change in your local, state, or national community. Making an impact on this level can consist of submitting brief policy papers or position statements to individuals or groups that are well-situated to advocate for changes in social policy or practice. Within these documents, you will not want to provide a book report of your study, but instead discuss the implications of a certain issue and cite your study as evidence for your position. For example, Bailey Smith (2016) completed a study on individuals residing in Tennessee who had been victims of childhood abuse and found that certain aspects of spirituality and religion were protective factors that promoted resilience from postabuse adversity. The month that she defended her dissertation, the Tennessee legislature passed a bill that permits professional counselors to deny services to clients based on any strongly held belief that is incongruent with that individual's lifestyle (Tenn. SB 1556/HB 1840, 2016). One domain that received considerable attention was religious identity. Specifically, Tennessee Senate Bill 1556/House Bill 1840 (2016) indicates that "no counselor or therapist shall be required to serve a client as to goals, outcomes, or behaviors that conflict with a sincerely held religious belief of the counselor, provided an appropriate referral is made." As such, Bailey Smith suggested that her findings provide empirical evidence that denying certain aspects of someone's religious and spiritual identity would restrict an aspect of himself or herself that would promote resilience and well-being in the face of adversity, particularly in the case of childhood abuse. With such an evidence-supported proposition, a related position would be easily developed and disseminated to stakeholders who can stimulate social change.

Regardless whether you choose to develop a position statement, policy paper, or white paper, identifying the right individual to deliver it to is imperative. Potential outlets include local newspapers, members of Congress, and federal entities (e.g., the National Registry of Evidence-Based Programs and Practices, which guides mental health policy). If you need direction, some common sources of guidance include your dissertation chair, your state counseling association, or ACA's government affairs representative. These layers of influence are important for increasing the imprint of professional counselors on local communities, and they instantly transition your dissertation from a document on a shelf to an artifact of social change.

Summary

In this chapter, we reviewed some important considerations to help you decide how you want to disseminate your dissertation findings. Specifically, we think all students should include their dissertations within the PDQT Global and ERIC repositories. After that, we encourage you to weigh the benefits of presenting at professional conferences, publishing within peer-reviewed journals, and drafting a document that may precipitate social change. As we mentioned, you certainly do not have to do all of these activities, but we encourage you to do at least one. In any case, you will be contributing to the knowledge base for counselors, counselor educators, and all the other related professionals and entering the professional community on the merits of your work.

Checklist

- ❏ Submit a signed, electronic copy of your dissertation to PQDT Global and ERIC.
- ❏ Work with your dissertation chair to identify a local, state, regional, or national conference proceeding where you can present your findings. Obtain the proposal submission criteria and deadlines. Submit a proposal.
- ❏ Work with your chair to identify one of the ACA journals that may be a good fit for publishing your project findings.
- ❏ Modify your dissertation to fit publication guidelines for your target journal and prepare your submission.
- ❏ Celebrate! It's all over, and you are on your way to the next great thing in your life.

Additional Resources

ACA Annual Conference & Expo: www.counseling.org/conference
Association for Assessment and Research in Counseling annual conference: http://aarc-counseling.org/event/conferences

Counseling Outcome Research and Evaluation submission guidelines: http://www.tandfonline.com/action/authorSubmission?journalCode=uore20&page=instructions

ERIC online submission form: http://eric.ed.gov/submit/

Journal of Counseling & Development submission guidelines: http://www.counseling.org/publications/journalguidelines/jcd.pdf

PQDT Global: http://www.proquest.com/products-services/pqdtglobal.html

Example Authorship Agreement

Authorship Agreement

The purpose of this document is to provide you with specific information regarding the nature, expectations, and methods of your involvement in the process of developing the manuscript titled "Effectiveness of School-based Bullying Programs for Decreasing Aggressive Attitudes and Actions."

Author Credit and Personal Contributions

As the lead author of this manuscript, I would like to inform you, as a *second* author, that I expect you to (a) review literature related to bullying in school settings, (b) consolidate candidate files into PDF or HTML formats, (c) contribute to the literature review section, (d) assist with the implications section of this manuscript, and (e) edit and proofread the manuscript. Additional review of other relevant literature and assistance for other sections may be required. You will be informed and involved with a process of manuscript submissions and revisions. We will submit this manuscript to the *Professional School Counseling*. With all these expectations, you will work closely with me and other authors (if any). If you would like to further understand my working and advising style, please request a meeting with me during which I can address your specific questions.

Contribution Timeline

All responsibilities mentioned above are expected to be completed by July 1, 2018. I believe you can potentially contribute to this manuscript. Please understand that your participation in this manuscript is voluntary. If you are willing or able to fulfill these requirements in the timely manner, you will be granted second authorship of this manuscript. However, if you are not willing or unable to fulfill these requirements or decide not to be a part of this manuscript, I understand and will remove you from the authorship. Because this manuscript is in progress, the title of the manuscript is subject to change. In addition, there is no guarantee that the journal will accept our manuscript.

Rationale and Assurances

I have adhered to the *ACA Code of Ethics* (2014) in developing this authorship agreement. Please feel free to discuss any of the items in this document with me at any time and know that if you decide, at any time, to not be a part of this project, that decision will not affect your academic standing or professional development opportunities through the Department of Counseling and Educational Psychology. Please carefully read the entire document and sign in the space provided to indicate that you have read, agree to, and will be consistent with the specifications of this relationship as detailed. Thank you for your consideration on being a part of this manuscript.

_____   _____
Secondary Author Name and Credentials   *Date*

_____   _____
Student Author Name and Credentials   *Date*

References

Abel, H., Abel, A., & Smith, R. L. (2012). The effects of a stress management course on counselors-in-training. *Counselor Education and Supervision, 51,* 64–78. doi:10.1002/j.1556-6978.2012.00005.x

Adler, A. (1931). *What life should mean to you.* New York, NY: Perigee Books.

Albano, A. M., & DiBartolo, P. M. (2007). *Cognitive-behavioral therapy for social phobia in adolescents: Stand up, speak out.* New York, NY: Oxford University Press.

Allen, D. (2001). *Getting things done: The art of stress-free productivity.* New York, NY: Viking Press.

American Counseling Association. (2014). *ACA code of ethics.* Alexandria, VA: Author.

American Educational Research Association, American Psychological Association, & National Council on Measurement in Education. (2014). *Standards for educational and psychological testing.* Washington, DC: American Educational Research Association.

American Psychiatric Association. (2013). *Diagnostic and statistical manual of mental disorders* (5th ed.). Arlington, VA: Author.

American Psychological Association. (2010). *Publication manual of the American Psychological Association* (6th ed.). Washington, DC: Author.

Aponte, H. J. (1998). Love, the spiritual wellspring of forgiveness: An example of spirituality in therapy. *Journal of Family Therapy, 20,* 37–58. doi:10.1111/1467-6427.00067

Arora, S. (2015). *Achievement motivation and resilience among student athletes* (Unpublished doctoral dissertation). Texas A&M University–Corpus Christi, Corpus Christi, TX.

Babic, M. J., Morgan, P. J., Plotnikoff, R. C., Lonsdale, C., White, R. L., & Lubans, D. R. (2014). Physical activity and self-concept in youth: Systematic review and meta-analysis. *Sports Medicine, 44,* 1589–1601. doi:10.1007/s40279-014-0229-z

Bailey Smith, L. A. (2016). *Differential prediction of resilience among individuals with and without a history of abuse* (Doctoral dissertation). Available from ProQuest Dissertations and Theses database. (UMI No. 10296228)

Balkin, R. S., & Kleist, D. M. (2017). *Counseling research: A practitioner-scholar approach.* Alexandria, VA: American Counseling Association.

Balkin, R. S., Miller, J., Ricard, R. J., Garcia, R., & Lancaster, C. (2011). Assessing factors in adolescent adjustment as precursors to recidivism in court-referred youth. *Measurement and Evaluation in Counseling and Development, 44,* 52–59. doi:10.1177/0748175610391611

Balkin, R. S., Perepiczka, M., Sowell, S. M., Cumi, K., & Gnilka, P. G. (2016). The Forgiveness Reconciliation Model: An empirically supported process for humanistic counseling. *The Journal of Humanistic Counseling, 55,* 55–65. doi:10.1002/johc.12024

Balkin, R. S., Perepiczka, M., Whitely, R., & Kimbrough, S. (2009). The relationship of sexual values and emotional awareness to sexual activity in young adulthood. *Adultspan Journal, 8,* 17–28. doi:10.1002/j.2161-0029.2009.tb00054.x

Balkin, R. S., Richey Gosnell, K. M., Holmgren, A., & Osborne, J. W. (2017). Nonlinear analysis in counseling research. *Measurement and Evaluation in Counseling and Development, 50.* doi:10.1177/0748175616664015

Balkin, R. S., Schlosser, L. Z., & Levitt, D. H. (2009). Religious identity and cultural diversity: Exploring the relationships between religious identity, sexism, homophobia, and multicultural competence. *Journal of Counseling & Development, 87,* 420–427. doi:10.1002/j.1556-6678.2009.tb00126.x

Balkin, R. S., & Sheperis, C. J. (2011). Evaluating and reporting statistical power in counseling research. *Journal of Counseling & Development, 89,* 268–272. doi:10.1002/j.1556-6678.2011.tb00088.x

Balkin, R. S., & Sheperis, D. S. (2009). *A primer in evaluating quantitative research for counseling professionals* (ACAPCD-26). Alexandria, VA: American Counseling Association. Retrieved from https://www.counseling.org/docs/default-source/library-archives/profesional-counselor-digest/acapcd-26.pdf?stvrsn=4

Barnes, B. J., Williams, E. A., & Archer, S. A. (2010). Characteristics that matter most: Doctoral students' perceptions of positive and negative advisor attributes. *NACADA Journal, 30,* 34–46. doi:10.12930/0271-9517-30.1.34

Beck, J. S. (2011). *Cognitive behavior therapy: Basics and beyond* (2nd ed.). New York, NY: Guilford Press.

Clark, D. A., & Beck, A. T. (2010). *Cognitive therapy of anxiety disorders: Science and practice.* New York, NY: Guilford Press.

Cohen, J. (1988). *Statistical power analysis for the behavioral sciences* (2nd ed.). New York, NY: Psychological Press.

Cohen, J. (1992). A power primer. *Psychological Bulletin, 112,* 155–159. doi:10.1037/0033-2909.112.1.155

Cohen, J. A., Mannarino, A. P., & Deblinger, E. (2017). *Treating trauma and traumatic grief in children and adolescents* (2nd ed.). New York, NY: Guilford Press.

Conn, V. S. (2010). Anxiety outcomes after physical activity interventions: Meta-analysis findings. *Nursing Research, 59,* 224–231. doi:10.1097/NNR.0b013e3181dbb2f8

Council for Accreditation of Counseling and Related Educational Programs. (2015). *CACREP 2016 Standards.* Alexandria, VA: Author.

Creswell, J. W. (1994). *Research design: Qualitative and quantitative approaches.* Thousand Oaks, CA: Sage.

Creswell, J.W. (2014). *Research design: Qualitative, quantitative, and mixed methods approaches* (4th ed.). Thousand Oaks, CA: Sage.

Creswell, J. W., & Plano Clark, V. L. (2011). *Designing and conducting mixed method research* (2nd ed.). Thousand Oaks, CA: Sage.

Cueva, C. (2006). *An achievement motivation program for young minority students utilizing cognitive-behavioral techniques* (Unpublished doctoral dissertation). Texas A&M University–Corpus Christi, Corpus Christi, TX.

Davis, R. J., Balkin, R. S., & Juhnke, G. A. (2014). Validation of the Juhnke–Balkin Life Balance Inventory. *Measurement and Evaluation in Counseling and Development, 47,* 181–198. doi:10.1177/0748175614531796

DeLee, F. R. (2014). *Group supervision of counselors-in-training implementing the Awareness Wheel* (Unpublished doctoral dissertation). Texas A&M University–Corpus Christi, Corpus Christi, TX.

Dreikurs, R., & Mosak, H. H. (1967). The tasks of life II. The fourth life task. *Individual Psychologist, 4,* 51–56.

Dunn, H. L. (1959). High-level wellness for man and society. *American Journal of Public Health, 49,* 786–792. doi:10.2105/AJPH.49.6.786

Erford, B. T., Miller, E. M., Schein, H., McDonald, A., Ludwig, L., & Leishear, K. (2011). *Journal of Counseling & Development* publication patterns: Author and article characteristics from 1994 to 2009. *Journal of Counseling & Development, 89,* 73–80. doi:10.1002/j.1556-6678.2011.tb00062.x

Fiore, N. A. (2007). *The now habit: A strategic program for overcoming procrastination and enjoying guilt-free play.* New York, NY: Penguin Group.

Froeschle, J. (2005). *The efficacy of a drug prevention/intervention program on adolescent girls* (Unpublished doctoral dissertation). Texas A&M University–Corpus Christi, Corpus Christi, TX.

Heppner, P. P., & Heppner, M. J. (2004). *Writing and publishing your thesis, dissertation & research: A guide for students in the helping professions.* Belmont, CA: Brooks/Cole.

Herrero, D. M. (2014). *The relationship among achievement motivation, hope, and resilience and their effects on academic achievement of first-year college students enrolled in a Hispanic-serving institution* (Unpublished doctoral dissertation). Texas A&M University–Corpus Christi, Corpus Christi, TX.

Hettler, B. (1984). Wellness: Encouraging a lifetime pursuit of excellence. *Health Values, 8,* 13–17.

Joyner, R. L., Rouse, W. A., & Glatthorn, A. A. (2013). *Writing the winning thesis or dissertation: A step-by-step guide* (3rd ed.). Thousand Oaks, CA: Corwin.

Kendall, P. C., Crawley, S. A., Benjamin, C. L., & Mauro, C. F. (2013). *Brief Coping Cat: Therapist manual for the 8-session workbook.* Ardmore, PA: Workbook Publishing.

Kerlinger, F. N. (1979). *Behavioral research: A conceptual approach.* New York, NY: Holt, Reinhart & Winston.

Koltz, R. L., & Feit, S. S. (2012). A phenomenological study: The experience of live supervision during a pre-practicum counseling techniques course. *The Qualitative Report, 17,* 1–24. Retrieved from http://www.nova.edu/ssss/QR/QR17/koltz.pdf

Lancaster, C., Balkin, R. S., Garcia, R., & Valarezo, A. (2011). An evidence-based approach to reducing recidivism in court-referred youth. *Journal of Counseling & Development, 89,* 488–492. doi:10.1002/j.1556-6676.2011.tb02846.x

Lenz, A. S., Del Conte, G., Lancaster, C., Bailey, L., & Vanderpool, E. (2014). Evaluation of a partial hospitalization program for adolescents. *Counseling Outcome Research and Evaluation, 5,* 3–16. doi:10.1177/2150137813518063

Linehan, M. M. (2015). *DBT skills training manual* (2nd ed.). New York, NY: Guilford Press.

Lovitts, B. E. (2001). *Leaving the ivory tower.* Lanham, MD: Rowman & Littlefield.

Machi, L. A., & McEvoy, B. T. (2012). *The literature review: Six steps to success* (2nd ed.). Thousand Oaks, CA: Sage.

Mansager, E., & Gold, L. (2000). Three life tasks or five? *Journal of Individual Psychology, 56,* 155–171.

Morgenstern, J. (2004). *Time management from the inside out: The foolproof system for taking control of your schedule—and your life* (2nd ed.). New York, NY: Holt/Owl Books.

Mosak, H. H., & Dreikurs, R. (2000). The life tasks III: The fifth life task. *Journal of Individual Psychology, 56,* 257–265. (Reprinted from *The Individual Psychologist, 5,* 16–22, 1967.)

Myers, J. E., & Sweeney, T. J. (2005). The indivisible self: An evidence-based model of wellness (reprint). *Journal of Individual Psychology, 61,* 269–279.

Oldridge, N. (2012). Exercise-based cardiac rehabilitation in patients with coronary heart disease: Meta-analysis outcomes revisited. *Future Cardiology, 8,* 729–751. doi:10.2217/fca.12.34

Open Science Collaboration. (2015). Estimating the reproducibility of psychological science. *Science, 349,* aac4716-1–aac4716-8. doi:10.1126/science.aac4716

Patton, M. Q. (2015). *Qualitative research and evaluation methods* (4th ed.). Thousand Oaks, CA: Sage.

Perepiczka, M., & Balkin, R. S. (2010). Relationship between wellness and age, matriculation, and relationship status of counselor education doctoral students. *The Journal of Humanistic Counseling, 49,* 203–216. doi:10.1002/j.2161-1939.2010.tb00098.x

Pituch, K. A., & Stevens, J. P. (2016). *Applied multivariate statistics for the social sciences: Analyses with SAS and IBM's SPSS* (6th ed.). New York, NY: Routledge.

Public Welfare, 45 C.F.R. § 46 (2009).

Ray, D. C. (2015). Single-case research design and analysis: Counseling applications. *Journal of Counseling & Development, 93,* 394–402. doi:10.1002/jcad.12037

Regehr, C., Glancy, D., & Pitts, A. (2013). Interventions to reduce stress in university students: A review and meta-analysis. *Journal of Affective Disorders, 148,* 1–11. doi:10.1016/j.jad.2012.11.026

Richardson, K. M., & Rothstein, H. R. (2008). Effects of occupational stress management intervention programs: A meta-analysis. *Journal of Occupational Health Psychology, 13,* 69–93. doi:10.1037/1076-8998.13.1.69

Rodriguez, K. (2014). *The perceived impact of study abroad activities for graduate counseling students* (Unpublished doctoral dissertation). Texas A&M University–Corpus Christi, Corpus Christi, TX.

Rongen, A., Robroek, S. J. W., van Lenthe, F. J., & Burdorf, A. (2013). Workplace health promotion: A meta-analysis of effectiveness. *American Journal of Preventative Medicine, 44,* 406–415. doi:10.1016/j.amepre.2012.12.007

Roscoe, L. J. (2009). Wellness: A review of theory and measurement for counselors. *Journal of Counseling & Development, 87,* 216–226. doi:10.1002/j.1556-6678.2009.tb00570.x

Rosenbaum, A. L. (2015). *A qualitative investigation of juvenile offenders* (Unpublished doctoral dissertation). Texas A&M University–Corpus Christi, Corpus Christi, TX.

Saldaña, J. (2009). *The coding manual for qualitative researchers.* Thousand Oaks, CA: Sage.

Seligman, M. (2011). *Flourish: A visionary new understanding of happiness and well-being.* New York, NY: Free Press.

Shomaker, S. A. (2013). *The impact of mindfulness training on therapeutic alliances, empathy, and lived experience: A mixed methods study with counselor trainees* (Unpublished doctoral dissertation). Texas A&M University–Corpus Christi, Corpus Christi, TX.

Smith, E. M. (2004). *A mixed paradigm: Study of a transformational learning program for at-risk high school students* (Unpublished doctoral dissertation). Texas A&M University–Corpus Christi, Corpus Christi, TX.

Smith, R. L., Maroney, K., Nelson, K. W., Abel, A. L., & Abel, H. S. (2006). Doctoral programs: Changing high rates of attrition. *The Journal of Humanistic Counseling, 45,* 17–31. doi:10.1002/j.2161-1939.2006.tb00002.x

Suri, H. (2011). Purposeful sampling in qualitative research synthesis. *Qualitative Research Journal, 11,* 63–75. doi:10.3316/QRJ1102063

Tennessee SB 1556/HB 1840. (2016). Amends Title 4, Title 49, and Title 63. *Tennessee Code Annotated*. 109th Gen. Assemb., Reg. Sess. Retrieved from http://wapp.capitol.tn.gov/apps/Billinfo/default. aspx?BillNumber=HB1840&ga=109

White, M. (2007). *Maps of narrative practice*. New York, NY: Norton.

Index

Figures and tables are indicated by f and t following page numbers.

(Continued)